GOD LED AND JOSHUA FOLLOWED:

The Story of the Conquest of Canaan

A Sermon Supplement

Eual D. Blansett, Jr.

PREFACE

PREFACE

The Old Testament Book of Joshua is about God, pure and simple. The book is entitled Joshua because he was God's principal earthly representative who who was in charge of the conquest of Canaan. He was able to mostly carry out God's will in getting the Hebrews into the Promised Land. The word "Lord" is written 57 times in the first seven chapters of Joshua. In the same chapters, "Lord your God" is found 12 times, "God" is found two times, and "Lord, the God of Israel" is found three times. Therefore, God is mentioned, in one form or the other, 74 times in the first seven chapters. If the "God" in "Lord your God" and "Lord, the God of Israel" is counted, then God is mentioned 89 times. It should be obvious that the author of the Book of Joshua wanted the reader to understand clearly that it was God who was the prime mover of everything that happened during the conquest of Canaan.

The author of the Book of Joshua is not known with absolute certainty. However, there are portions of the book that are so detailed that they had to have been written by Joshua or at his direction or by someone who was a close confidant of Joshua. And, there are other segments that were clearly added after Joshua's death. The battles are a clear example of both Joshua as the author of some of the scripture and another person as the author of added scripture. The details of the conquest of Jericho, the Second Battle of Ai, and the Battle of Gibeon could only have been written by someone who was there. On the other hand, the lack of detail of the Battle of the Northern Armies suggests that these passages were penned by someone other than Joshua and probably after his death.

Joshua is about the conquest of Canaan. However, Joshua is not only a record of deeds, it is also a record of deeds. The previous sentence is not a mistake; it is a summary of the Old Testament Book of Joshua. The book not only contains the story of the conquest of Canaan (the record of the deeds of the conquest of Canaan), it also contains the record of the deeds of the lands allotted to the 12 tribes of Israel. Chapters One to Twelve deal with the major events before and after the crossing of the Israelites into Canaan and with the principle battles fought during the conquest of Canaan. Chapters Thirteen to Twenty-One focus on the division of the land between the 12 tribes. Chapters Twenty-Two to Twenty-Four wrap up the book, culminating with the renewal of the covenant with God and the deaths of the principle figures of the conquest.

Joshua would not have been written if it had not been for God's promise to Abraham, Isaac, and Jacob that the Hebrews would eventually possess the Promised Land. Therefore, no study of Joshua should be undertaken without reviewing some of the history of the Hebrews, from Abraham to Moses. And, the review of the history would not be complete without bringing to the reader all of the references to Joshua in Exodus and Deuteronomy after the Hebrews left Egypt and before Joshua was chosen by God to lead the Hebrews across the Jordan River and into Canaan.

One last note to help the reader understand the timelines included in this study. Certain Egyptologists have done their best to ignore the Bible in reconstructing the history of the Hebrews as it relates to Egypt. They consider Moses to be a creature of Myth and not a real person. Christian researchers take a different tack. They believe Moses was a real person and the Exodus really happened. Their research has opened up a whole new view of the past, a past that fits

4

with what is known about Moses, both before and after the Exodus. Therefore, there is a timeline in this study that reflects that research. It is exciting what has been done. This study is primarily about Joshua and is not focused on Moses. However, there are enough facts presented about Moses to give the reader a taste of what Christian researchers have done to revolutionize this area of history.

The El Amarna letters are discussed at the end of this book. They are included because they appear to bear on a period of time in the past when the Habiru or Apiru were actively attacked cities loyal to the pharaoh of Egypt. Some authors believe the Habiru were the invading Hebrew under Joshua. Other authors are not sure. I have included the letters to help the reader decide what he or she thinks about them and their place in the conquest.

TABLE
OF
CONTENTS

TABLE OF CONTENTS

TIMELINE

TIMELINE

a. Discussion

A time line for Joshua is difficult to create for a variety of reasons. One of the authors favorite writers is Immanuel Velikovsky. He was insightful and iconoclastic, questioning so much about Cosmology, Egyptology, and other areas of research. In 1942, he published his second book, "Ages in Chaos." In this book, he discussed the Exodus and its timing. He wrote that the Exodus occurred at the same time as the Hyksos entered Egypt and subjugated that land. He is probably right, but most Egyptologists believe the Hyksos invasion of Egypt occurred about 1780 BC. Instead, Velikovsky associated the Hyksos with the Amalekites who attacked the Israelites in the desert after the Exodus. This would mean the Hyksos invaded Egypt in or about 1446 BC.

The traditional date of 1780 BC is 336 years before the Bible indicates that the Exodus took place. I Kings 6:1 sets the Exodus as 480 years before the date Solomon started building the temple in Jerusalem, which occurred in or about 966 BC. The date of the Exodus, if the Bible gives an exact time frame and not a general time frame, would be 1446 BC. Therefore, the entrance into the Promised Land by Joshua and the Israelites would be in or about 1406 BC.

There is another problem with creating a timeline and it involves the El Amarna letters. If the letters were written during the reigns of Amenhotep III aka Nummuria (about 1390 to 1352 BC) and Akhenaten aka Naphuria (about 1352 to 1336 BC), as most Egyptologists conclude, and the Apiru/Habiru/Hapiru mentioned in the letters refer to the invading Israelites, then 1406 BC is not an accurate date.

Therefore, the **Traditional View Timeline** below reflects the dates which are accepted by Egyptologists. Dates for the events of the Bible as accepted by Christian researchers and authors have been added to this timeline. It should be noted that the names and dates of most of the reigns of the Egyptian pharaohs have not been firmly established and may vary up to 10 years between one Egyptologist and another without considering co-regencies, if they existed between one pharaoh and the next. The events of the 25 years that Joshua commanded the Israelites in Canaan are estimates. All dates in the timeline are BC (Before Christ). BCE (Before the Common Era), adopted by secular historians, is not acceptable.

Ted Wright wrote an article for his blog called "WHO WAS THE PHARAOH OF THE EXODUS?" He argues that "it is very possible" that Amenhotep I was the pharaoh who issued the decree to kill all the Hebrew male children at birth. Amenhotep I had a son known as Thutmose I, who reigned, per Ted Wright, from 1528 to 1508 BC. Hatshepsut was the daughter of Thutmose I. It is possible that the daughter of the pharaoh who rescued Moses from the river was Hatshepsut. Thutmose I also had a son called Thutmose II. Hatshepsut and Thutmose II married. They were siblings by different mothers. When Thutmose II died young, Hatshepsut ruled Egypt along with her nephew (and stepson) Thutmose III. She claimed her right to rule and, as the senior co-regent, she took the lead in decision-making.

Ted Wright continued his analysis by asserting that Amenhotep II, who reigned from 1450 to 1425 BC, was likely the pharaoh of the Exodus. He argues that there are two reasons for his assertion: (1) Amenhotep II ruled from Memphis, which was close to the land of Goshen, and (2) Amenhotep II's power did not pass to his oldest son, but rather to Thutmose IV, a younger son. See **https://crossexamined.org/ancient-israel-myth-or-history-part-3c**

The analysis by Ted Wright is a tempting analysis because of the idea that it was Hapshepsut who rescued Moses. However, the timeline Ted Wright presents does not fit in with the "Traditional View Timeline" or in with what is termed below as the "Alternative Timeline."

The **Alternative Timeline** below reflects the views of certain authors who clearly accept Moses as a real person and the Exodus and the conquest of Canaan as actual events in the history of humankind.

b. Traditional View Timeline

1550 - Hyksos driven from Egypt; **Ahmosis I** was the first king of the 18th Dynasty;

1541 - **Amenhotep I**, the son of Ahmosis I, began his reign; he had no son to succeed him;

1526 - **Moses** was born; he was found in the reeds in the Nile River Delta by a daughter of the pharaoh Amenhotep I and taken into the royal family; the name "Moses" appears to be from the Egyptian word meaning "born";

1520 - **Thutmose I**, a general in the army of Ahmosis I, succeeded Ahmosis I; his name means "born of Thut"; Thur was a minor god in the Egyptian pantheon of gods; his mother was Senseneb, who was not a member of the royal family; he married Ahmose aka Ahmes, believed to be a daughter of Amenhotep I; he extended Egypt's claims south into Nubia; his son **Thutmose II** was born to a secondary wife Mutnofret; his daughter **Hatshepsut** was born to the Great Wife Ahmes; **Moses** was 16 years old;

1492 - **Thutmose II**, began his reign as the fourth pharaoh of the 18th dynasty; Moses would have been 32 years old; Thutmose II married his half-sister **Hatshepsut** and she became his Great Wife; she did not give Thutmose II a son;

1486 - **Moses** killed the Egyptian overseer who was beating the Hebrew slave; Moses fled to Midian; Moses was 40 years old; **Joshua** was born;

1473 - **Thutmose II** died; his successor, **Thutmose III**, was an infant when his father died; **Hatshepsut** became co-regent; she ruled as co-regent until 1453 BC;

1473 - **Thutmose III** began his reign, although he and Hatshepsut shared power for another 20 years; he is considered to be the greatest pharaoh of the 18th dynasty; his wife was Merytre Hatshepsut;

1446 - The **Exodus** of the Hebrews (Israelites) from Egypt; Moses is 80 years old; Joshua led the fight against the Amalekites; the Hebrews fail to honor God by not wanting to enter the Promised Land; the Hebrews are condemned to wander in the wilderness for 40 years;

1425 - **Amenhotep II** began his reign; his wife was Tiaa; El Amarna letter EA37 concerns him;

1407 - The Midianites are destroyed by the Hebrews; Sihon and Og defeated by the Hebrews; the land east of the Jordan River is allotted to the tribes of Reuben and Gad and the half-tribe of Manasseh;

1406 - **Joshua** led the Hebrew Nation into the Promised Land; Joshua is 80 years old; Jericho, Ai, and probably Betel were destroyed; Joshua unwittingly made treaty with Gibeon; Five kings attacked Gibeon and were defeated by Joshua; Joshua renews the covenant at Shechem;

1401/1397 - **Thutmose IV** began his reign; a son **Amenhotep III** was born to him by a minor wife Mutemwiya; Thutmose IV adopted Aten, the sun god, as the god for his family; he secured a treaty with the Mitanni empire (located in modern-day Turkey);

1401 - **Caleb** given Hebron and the surround territories; Caleb and his family help Joshua defeat the cities of southern Canaan;

1396 - **Joshua** defeats the kings of mid-Canaan; Joshua moves the Hebrew camp from Gilgal to Shiloh;

1391/1388 - **Amenhotep III** began his reign; a few years into his reign, he changed his name to **Akhenaten**; he established Aten as the only god of Egypt and outlawing all other worship; he ignored the Egyptian vassals in Canaan; his wife was **Nefertiti**, who probably ruled Egypt to 1332 BC after the death of Akhenaten in or about 1336 BC; his probable son (or grandson) was **Tutankhaten**, better known as the famous King Tut;

1391 - **Joshua** defeated the kings of northern Canaan;

1386 - God reminded **Joshua** that there was more territory to conquer;

1381 - God gave the Hebrews rest; the warriors from the tribes east of the Jordan River were sent home;

1376 - **Joshua** died;

1350 - The time of the judges started after the death of all the elders who were leaders while Joshua lived;

1336 - **Akhenaten** died; **Nefertiti**, his wife took over as pharaoh;

1332 - **Nefertiti** died;

1332 - **Tutankhaten** began his reign; he changed his name to **Tutankhamun** and reversed all of his father's religious reforms; he died in 1324 BC without an heir;

The last pharaoh of the 18th dynasty ruled until 1292 BC.

c. Alternative Timeline

1874 - Hebrews came to Egypt; they had been in Egypt for 350 years when Moses was born; they had been in Egypt for 430 years at the time of the Exodus;

1725 - Amenemhet I began his reign as the first pharaoh of the 12th dynasty; he became pharaoh by assassinating the previous pharaoh Mentuhotep IV, the last of the 11th dynasty; Amenemhet I consolidated all of upper and lower Egypt;, which had been split into at least three dynasties; he did not known about Joseph and Joseph's people the Hebrews; he forced the Hebrews into slavery and forced them to make bricks for the pharaoh's pyramid; his reign was followed by Sesostris I, Amenemhet II, Sesostris II; and, Sesostris III;

Unknown date - Sesostris II began pharaoh; he was also known as Senusret II; he set up slave villages for Hebrews near were pyramids were to be build; the villages stayed occupied until the time of the Exodus; graves of babies were found nearby by Flinders Petrie; graves were even found under the homes;

1547 - **Sesostris III** began his reign as pharaoh; he reigned until 1510 BC, with the last 20 years of his reign as a co-regent with his son Amenemhet III; Sesostris III was also known as Senusret III, Senwosret III, and Khakhare; he was a great warrior who expanded the borders of Egypt into Nubia; he also limited the authority of the local nomarchs or governors and divided Egypt into three regions overseen by viziers, usually members of the royal family; he or his son may have ordered the killing of male Hebrew babies;

1529 - **Amenemhet III** began his sole reign as a pharaoh of the 12th dynasty as a co-regent with his father Sesostris III; he reigned for over 40 years; he was also known as Amenemhat III and Nimaatre; he is considered the greatest pharaoh of the Middle Kingdom; he died without an heir and his daughter Sobeknefru became queen of Egypt; it is believed that **Moses** was adopted by Sobeknefru and **Moses** was being raised to rule Egypt as Amenemhet IV; it was either Amenemhet III or his father Sesostris III who ordered the Hebrew boys to be killed by drowning; Amenemhet III died in or about 1483 BC; Amenemhet III and Moses as Amenemhet IV jointly ruled until 1486 BC, when Moses left Egypt after killing an Egyptian overseer;

1526 - **Moses** was born; he was found in the bullrushes in the Nile River Delta by a Sobeknefru, daughter of pharaoh Amenemhet III, and taken into the royal family; the name

"Moses" appears to be from the Egyptian word meaning "born";

1486 - **Moses** killed the Egyptian overseer who was beating the Hebrew slave; Moses had been a co-regent for nine years with Amenemhet III; Moses fled to Midian to escape death at the hands of Amenemhet III; Moses was then 40 years old; **Joshua** was born this year; it is as if Joshua took the place of Moses, just as he did 80 years later;

1483 - **Amenemhet III** died and his daughter **Sobeknefru** became the last pharaoh of the 12th dynasty; she only reigned four to eight years; her death ushered in the short-lived 13th dynasty, which last only about 30 years;

1457 - Neferhotep I began his reign as pharaoh;

1446 - The **Exodus** of the Hebrews (Israelites) from Egypt; Moses is 80 years old; the pharaoh at the time of the Exodus was Neferhotep I; Neferhotep I's mummy has never been found, as he died in the Red Sea; Neferhotep I's place was taken by his brother because his son was dead;

1446 BC - 1446 - The Hyksos invaded and gradually took over control of all of Egypt and ruled part or all for about 400 years;

1446 - Joshua led the fight against the Amalekites, believed to be of the same people as the Hyksos; the Hebrews failed to honor God by not wanting to enter the Promised Land; the Hebrews are condemned to wander in the wilderness for 40 years;

1407 - The wandering in the wilderness came to an end; the Hebrews/Israelites destroyed the Midianites; Sihon and Og are defeated by the Hebrews; the land east of the Jordan River is allotted to the tribes of Reuben and Gad and the half-tribe of Manasseh;

1406 - **Joshua** led the Hebrew Nation into the Promised Land; Joshua is 80 years old; Jericho, Ai, and probably Betel were destroyed; Joshua unwittingly made treaty with Gibeon; Five kings attacked Gibeon and were defeated by Joshua; Joshua renews the covenant at Shechem;

1401 - **Caleb** given Hebron and the surround territories; Caleb and his family help Joshua defeat the cities of southern Canaan;

1396 - **Joshua** defeats the kings of mid-Canaan; Joshua moves the Hebrew camp from Gilgal to Shiloh;

1391 - **Joshua** defeated the kings of northern Canaan;

1386 - God reminded **Joshua** that there was more territory to conquer;

1381 - God gave the Hebrews rest; the warriors from the tribes east of the Jordan River were sent home;

1376 - **Joshua** died;

1350 - The time of the judges started after the death of all the elders who were leaders while Joshua lived;

INTRODUCTION

INTRODUCTION

PART ONE

Noah

a. Joshua Starts with Noah

The story of Joshua does not start with Joshua 1:1. It starts in the Book of Genesis at the time of Noah. This may surprise a lot of readers, but there should be no doubt in the readers' minds about Noah's involvement once the full history of the Promised Land is reviewed.

b. Trouble in Noah's Family

The historical rendering of the Flood and the survival of Noah, his three sons, their wives, and at least two of every kind of animal on the earth is well known. What happened to Noah and his family **after** the ark landed on Mount Ararat in modern-day Turkey is not always readily recalled by most Christians. Here is the pertinent scripture:

"**18** The sons of Noah who came out of the ark were **Shem, Ham**, and **Japheth. (Ham was the father of Canaan.)**
19 These were the three sons of Noah, and from them came the people who were scattered over the whole earth.
20 Noah, a man of the soil, proceeded [was the first] to plant a vineyard.
21 When he drank some of its wine, he became drunk and lay uncovered inside his tent.
22 Ham, the father of Canaan, saw his father naked and told his two brothers outside.

23 But Shem and Japheth took a garment and laid it across their shoulders; then they walked in backward and covered their father's naked body. Their faces were turned the other way so that they would not see their father naked.

24 When Noah awoke from his wine and <u>found out</u> what his youngest son had done to him,

25 he said, '**Cursed be Canaan! The lowest of slaves will he be to his brothers.**'

26 He also said, '**Praise be to the Lord, the God of Shem! May Canaan be the slave of Shem**.

27 **May God extend Japheth's territory; may Japheth live in the tents of Shem, and may Canaan be the slave of Japheth.**'" **(bold** and <u>underline</u> for emphasis) (Genesis: 9:18-27)

c. Why Curse Canaan?

Strangely enough, Noah did not place a curse on Ham. He placed the curse on Canaan, who was the fourth and probably the youngest of Ham's sons. The curse was that Canaan's descendants would be slaves to the descendants of Shem and Japheth.

Why was Canaan cursed and not Ham and all of Ham's descendants? The answer is hinted at in verses 18 and 22 when Ham was identified as the father of Canaan. The statement appears to be a subtle way of saying that Ham and his son Canaan were peas in the same pod. Or, possibly, that Canaan was even worse than his father. The answer also appears to be in verse 24: "…Noah awoke from his wine and **found out** what his youngest son had done to him…" (emphasis added)

What was it that Ham had done to his father? Certainly, Ham had violated the privacy of his father's tent, saw his father naked, and then he told his two older brothers what he had seen. Ham's behavior was outrageous; but, he was not the one who was eventually cursed. Obviously, there is something very subtle in the words "…Noah…found out…" Surely, because he was drunk, he did not recall what condition he was in when he fell asleep from too much wine. Surely, because he was drunk, he did not recall what garment, if any, he may have used to cover himself when he laid down.

It appears that Noah's knowledge of what had happened to him had more to do with Canaan than it had to do with Ham. It is likely that Ham did not limit his gossiping to his two brothers. He probably told his own family that night or the next morning about what he saw and he may have mixed in a little mirth with the facts. It is highly likely that it was Canaan who spread the story to all of Noah's grandchildren and who made fun of his grandfather while doing so. It would seem that Canaan bore the brunt of the curse because he was the most offensive in relating the story of his grandfather's drunkenness and nakedness and Noah found out about what Canaan had done. There is no way that Shem and Japheth would have told their father what happened. It is not likely that Ham would have mentioned what he saw to his father. It is reasonable to conclude that Noah found out because it eventually got back to him what Canaan had been spreading by word of mouth.

d. Being Cursed Had Consequences

Of course, the real effect of Noah making Canaan the slave of Shem and Japheth was monumental. Being a slave had serious consequences. It meant the slave had absolutely no rights whatsoever and was even at the mercy of the slaveholder for his or her life. In other words, Noah, in cursing Canaan and his descendants, was depriving them of life, liberty, and property without any due process whatsoever. His curse meant that they could never own land lawfully, they could never own personal property rightfully, they could never marry whom they wanted, and they had no control over when, where, or how they died. In short, the descendants of Canaan, even though they eventually settled in the Promised Land or the Land of Canaan, had no lawful right to be there because of Noah's curse, a curse that God would eventually honor.

One commentator has a view point based on a slightly different translation of the first part of Genesis 9:25. He believes that the best interpretation is "Canaan is cursed," rather than "Cursed be Canaan." His position is that Canaan had already show what a sinful person he was and Noah was merely pointing out the natural and probable consequences of his present and future behavior. Canaan would eventually produce groups of people who would follow in his footsteps and be enslaved by their own lifestyles. This, in turn, would make them inferior people spiritually and morally and render them subject to the descendants of Shem and Japheth. There is obviously some truth in this interpretation, but this narrow, naturalistic view is easily incorporated into the wider view of "cursed be Canaan."

While Canaan and his descendants were being cursed, Noah took time to honor both Shem and Japheth. He pointed out fervently that the Lord was the God of Shem and that Canaan may be slaves to Shem. The use of the names Canaan and Shem, by implication, referred to their descendants as well. The use of the word "may" merely meant that the carrying out of the curse would depend upon God's will. In addition, the descendants of Japheth, if God permitted it, would be sheltered in the tents of the descendants of Shem and, if God permitted it, the descendants of Canaan would be slaves to the descendants of Japheth.

The curse of Canaan by Noah set the stage for the two major events of the Old Testament and the New Testament. God would eventually choose a descendant of Shem (Abram/Abraham) to be the patriarch of Israel and it was through Shem, via Israel, that Jesus Christ, the Messiah, the Savior of the World, would offer peace and shelter to the descendants of Japheth and the rest of the people of the earth.

e. The Descendants of Noah

The sons of Noah had descendants who populated different areas of Europe (Japheth), the Near East (Ham), and the Middle East (Shem). See Genesis 10:1-32 to learn about Japheth, Ham, and Shem and their descendants. However, two of Ham's sons should be mentioned briefly. One was

Egypt, Ham's second son. Egypt was the father of the Kasluhites (from whom the Philistines came). The other was Canaan. He was the ancestor of the of the Hittites, Jebusites, Amorites, Girgashites, Hivites, Arkites, Sinites, Arvadites, Zemarites and Hamathites. Canaan's first born was Sidon or Zidon. He was the ancestor of the Sidonians and the Phoenicians. (Genesis 10:6-18)

INTRODUCTION

PART TWO

Abram/Abraham

a. The Descent from Shem to Abram

Abram descended from Shem. See Genesis 11:10-26 for a
full rendering of the descent. Here is a brief synopsis by
generations from Shem to Abram: Shem, Arphaxad,
Shelah, Ever, Peleg, Reu, Serug, Nahor, Terah, and Abram.
Abram's brothers were Nahor and Haran. It appears from
the Biblical narrative that Haran was likely the oldest son.
This conclusion is based on the fact that Haran dies first
and Abram marries Haran's daughter who is just 10 years
younger than Abram.

b. Abram and Sarai

Terah and his family lived in Ur, which is now located in
modern Iraq. Ur was once located on the Persian Gulf, but
is now located inland on the Euphrates River because of
silting at the mouth of the river where it met the Persian
Gulf. Haran had at at least three daughters, but two of them
are of special interest. One daughter named Milkah married
Haran's brother Nahor. The other daughter named Sarai
married Haran's brother Abram. In short, both Abram and
Nahor married their nieces. (Genesis 11:29) Haran had one
son who will mentioned numerous times in the Book of
Genesis. He was called Lot. (Genesis 11: 27b)

c. Abram Left Ur

Terah's son Haran died while the family was still in Ur. After the death of Haran, Terah took Abram, Sarai (Abram's wife and Terah's granddaughter), and Lot (Haran's son and Terah's grandson) to Harran/Haran, which is located today in southeastern Turkey near the border with Syria. (Genesis 11:28-31) The group's original destination was Canaan, but they stopped in Harran and remained there for some inexplicable reason. (Genesis 11:31) Terah later died in Harran at the age of 205 years. (Genesis 11:32)

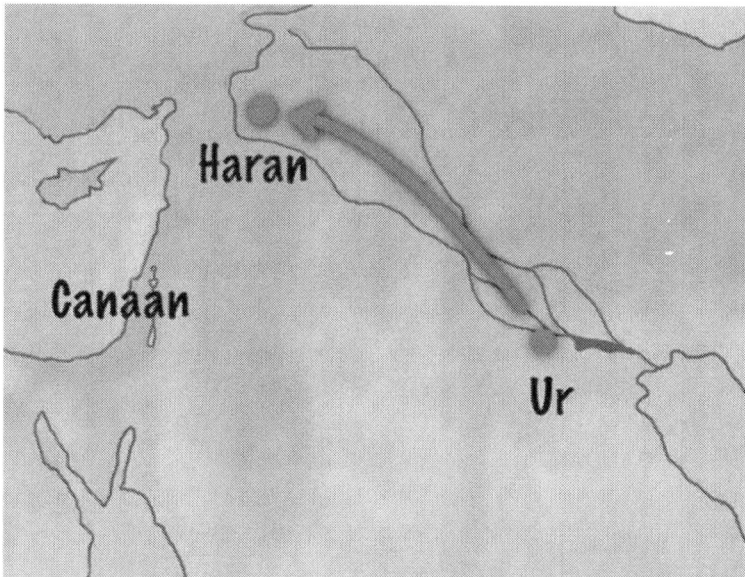

After Terah died in Harran, God told Abram to leave Harran and go to a land that God would show him. God made the following promises to Abram: (1) God will make Abram into a great nation; (2) God will bless Abram; (3) God will make Abram's name great; (4) Abram will be a blessing; (5) God will bless those who bless Abram; (6) God will curse those

God telling Abram to go to Canaan

who curse Abram; and, (7) everyone on earth will be blessed through Abram. (Genesis 12:2-3)

We do not know what Abram thought of the promises God made to him, but, in any case, Abram did as God told him. Abram was probably more convinced about the promise of land than he was of the promise of being made into a great nation. Abram was 75 years old when he left Harran and Sarai had yet to bear any children. Without children, there was not much of a chance that Abram was going to have a next generation, much less a great nation. Abram went to the land of Canaan with his wife Sarai and his nephew Lot. The date that Abram and his entourage entered Canaan has been established by conservative Biblical scholars as **2058 BC**, as best as the date can be determined.

d. God Promised Land to Abram

Abram, Sarai, and Lot stopped at the great tree of Moreh at Shechem, which is in the north central part of Canaan. (Shechem would become important at the time of Joshua.) It was at this point in time that God made yet another more astounding promise to Abram. God appeared to Abram and told him that he would give "this land" to his offspring. This was first time God had specifically mentioned land in any promise, although it was inferred in God's original set of promises. Abram built an altar to the Lord at that spot. It is not clear from the scripture if God was referring to all of Canaan or just the land Abram was occupying at the time. If there was some confusion in Abram's mind, the matter would be broached again later.

Abram then traveled to central Canaan, where he built another altar to God. This altar was between Bethel on the west and Ai on the east. (This site would also become important at the time of Joshua.) Abram then continued south to the Negev, the southern most portion of Canaan. After a brief sojourn in Egypt because of a famine in Canaan, Abram returned to Canaan. (See Genesis 12:4-20.)

e. God Promised Greater Land to Abram

Abram went south to the Negev and then wandered from place to place until he came to the site where he built his altar to God between Bethel and Ai in central Canaan. It was here that Abram and Lot went their separate ways. Lot chose the plain near the River Jordan in the eastern lowland of Canaan and Abram stayed in mountainous region of Canaan. (Genesis 13:1-12)

After Lot left, God appeared again to Abram. God expanded on His promise of land to be given to Abram. He told Abram:

"Look around from where you are, to the north and south, to the east and west. **15** All the land that you see I will give to you and your offspring [seed] forever. **16** I will make your offspring like the dust of the earth, so that if anyone could count the dust, then your offspring could be counted. **17** Go, walk through the length and breadth of the land, for I am giving it to you." (Genesis 13:14b-17)

Interestingly, God's description of the land that God was giving to Abram was more detailed than the description Abram was given at Shechem. However, it only included the land that Abram could see. There was yet no reference to all of Canaan. Even the instruction to walk the length and breath of the land made no reference to the length and breath of any land other than that which Abram could see. In this promise, God also expanded on the number of offspring Abram would have. He was originally going to be the progenitor of a great nation. Now his offspring would be as numerous as the "dust of the earth."

Abram left the land between Bethel and Ai and went to live near the great trees belonging to Mamre, the Amorite, near Hebron. (The site would become important in the conquest of Canaan by Joshua.) Abram built another altar to the Lord at that site. Abram remained near Hebron after rescuing his Nephew Lot.

f. God Promised All of Canaan to Abram

God came to Abram a third time while Abram was in southern Canaan. God promised Abram that he would have a son who would be his heir. God then took Abram outside and showed him the stars. God promised that his offspring would be as numerous as the stars in the heavens. For the first time in scripture, it is mentioned that Abram believed God. He also, for the third time, told Abram that he would possess "this land." (Genesis 15:7.) However, God revealed to Abram for the first time the extent of the land he would be possessing: "On that day the Lord made a covenant with Abram and said, 'To your descendants I give this land, from the Wadi of Egypt to the great river, the Euphrates— the land of the Kenites, Kenizzites, Kadmonites, Hittites, Perizzites, Rephaites, Amorites, Canaanites, Girgashites and Jebusites.'" (Genesis 15: 18-21)

However, God revealed to Abram in a dream that the land would not be possessed by Abram because "the sin of the Amorites has not yet reached its full measure. " (Genesis 15:16b) God let Abram know something of the future. He told Abram that his descendants would be strangers in a country not their own for 400 years. Eventually, they would be enslaved and mistreated in that land. But, God would not allow it to continue unchecked. God would punished the nation that had enslaved Abram's descendants by freeing the slaves and causing them to leave the land with great possessions. Later, the freed slaves would enter Canaan and take possession of it. (Genesis 15:12-16a)

g. The Covenant Was Established

When Sarai still had no son, she allowed Abram to sleep with her slave Hagar. After Hagar bore Abram a son, God came once again to Abram. He again promised to greatly increase Abram's numbers. In other words, he will have descendants. (See Genesis 17:1-2.) God then changed

Abram's name to Abraham and He made all of his promises more binding. He made it into a covenant:

3 "Abram fell facedown, and God said to him, **4** 'As for me, this is my covenant with you: You will be the father of many nations. **5** No longer will you be called Abram; your name will be Abraham, for I have made you a father of many nations. **6** I will make you very fruitful; I will make nations of you, and kings will come from you. **7** I will establish my covenant as an everlasting covenant between me and you and your descendants after you for the generations to come, to be your God and the God of your descendants after you. **8** The whole land of Canaan, where you now reside as a foreigner, I will give as an everlasting possession to you and your descendants after you; and I will be their God.'" (Genesis 17:3-8)

The name Abram means "exalted father." The name Abraham means "father of many." The change was fitting considering God's promises. Even though, at this point in Abraham's life, it appears that the son God promised was Ishmael, God had an even greater miracle to perform for Abraham.

God also changed Sarai's name to Sarah. He also promised her a son so she would become the mother of nations and kings would come from her. God said her son would be called Isaac and he would be born the following year. God promised to establish his everlasting covenant with Isaac for the benefit of all of Isaac's descendants. (See Genesis 17:15-19.)

It is interesting that God changed Sarai's name to Sarah. Sarai means "she who strives." It was likely a name given to a child of a difficult birth. It may have been a genetic condition that manifested itself in Sarai in the worst possible way: the inability to conceive. The name Sarah means "princess." It derives from the Semitic word "sar," which was a word used for a ruler or king. God used Sarah's name as a springboard to announce that Sarah would be the "mother of nations" and "kings of peoples will come from her." (Genesis 17:16)

Sarah with Isaac

God fulfilled His promised to Sarah and Sarah became pregnant. Thereafter, she bore a son and Abraham named the child Isaac. As the Lord had commanded, Abraham circumcised Isaac on the eighth day after his birth. (See Genesis 21:1-7.) God counseled Abraham that he should listen to Sarah and send Ishmael away now that Isaac was born. God said that Abraham's descendants would be through Isaac and not Ishmael. (See Genesis 21:8-12)

h. A Treaty with the Philistines

Abraham made a treaty with Abimelek, a Philistine, who was king of Gerar. The treaty secured for Abraham a well he had dug. The place was called Beersheba, which can mean "well of the seven [lambs]" or "well of the oath." The treaty called for Abraham to swear that he "will not deal falsely with me [Abimelek] or my children or my descendants." (Genesis 21:22-34.) This treaty may have been the reason that the Israelites did not attack the Philistines when they entered the Promised Land. Of course, once the Philistines attacked the Israelites at a later time, the Israelites were not longer bound by Abraham's treaty with Abimelek.

i. The Deaths of Sarah and Abraham

When Sarah died in Kiriath Arba (Hebron), she was buried in a cave in Machpelah near Mamre (close to Hebron] bought by Abraham. In fact, Abraham purchased the field which contained the cave and all the trees within the borders of the field from Ephron, son of Zohar, an Hittite. The field was clearly identified as being "in the land of Canaan." (Genesis 23:1-20.) This was yet another landmark set forth in Genesis. In other words, God not only promised Abraham his descendants would control Canaan, Abraham also spent a good part of his life making his presence known in the land which his descendants would eventually control.

When Abraham died, he was buried beside Sarah by his sons Isaac and Ishmael. (See Genesis 25:7-10.)

INTRODUCTION

PART THREE

Isaac

a. God's Promise to Isaac

After Abraham died, there was another famine in Canaan. Because of the famine, God appeared to Isaac and told him:

2"Do not go down to Egypt; live in the land where I tell you to live. **3** Stay in this land for a while, and I will be with you and will bless you. **For to you and your descendants I will give all these lands and will confirm the oath I swore to your father Abraham. 4** I will make your descendants as numerous as the stars in the sky and will give them all these lands, and through your offspring all nations on earth will be blessed, **5** because Abraham obeyed me and did everything I required of him, keeping my commands, my decrees and my instructions." (emphasis added) (Genesis 26:1-5)

b. God Promised Isaac Descendants

Isaac settled near Beersheba in southern Canaan. The very night he arrived, God came to Isaac. He told Isaac, ""I am the God of your father Abraham. Do not be afraid, for I am with you; I will bless you and will increase the number of your descendants for the sake of my servant Abraham." (Genesis 26:23-25.)

INTRODUCTION

PART FOUR

Jacob

a. Jacob in Canaan

Jacob and Esau were Isaac's sons. It was Jacob who stole Esau's inheritance and became the successor to God's promise that Abraham's seed would someday possess the Land of Canaan. (See Genesis 27:1-46.)

Jacob, whom God called Israel, continued the purchase of land in Canaan. He purchased a plot of ground from the sons of Hamor, the father of Shechem, where he built an altar to God and called it El Elohe Israel, which means "El is the God of Israel" or "mighty is the God of Israel." (See Genesis 33:18-20.)

b. God Renewed His Covenant

It was while Jacob was in Bethel that God renewed the covenant he had made with Abraham and Isaac. He told Jacob:

11"I am God Almighty [that is, El-Shaddai]; be fruitful and increase in number. A nation and a community of nations will come from you, and kings will be among your descendants. 12 The land I gave to Abraham and Isaac I also give to you, and I will give this land to your descendants after you." (emphasis added) (Genesis 35:11-12)

c. Jacob's Family

Jacob had 12 sons in all. Six of the sons were born to
Leah. They were **Reuben** (the oldest of the 12 sons),
Simeon, **Levi**, **Judah**, **Issachar**, and **Zebulun**. Two sons
were born to **Rachel**. They were **Joseph** and **Benjamin**.
Two sons were born to Rachel's servant **Bilhah**. They were
Dan and **Naphtali**. Two sons were born to Leah's servant
Zilpah. They were **Gad** and **Asher**. (Genesis 29:31-30:34
and 46:8-25)

After Jacob and Esau parted ways, Jacob took his family to
Shechem, where he bought land from Hamor. There he built
an altar and called it El Elohe Israel, which may mean
"mighty is the God of Israel." Unfortunately, while living
there, Jacob's daughter Dinah was raped by Shechem, the
son of Hamor. In revenge for the defiling of Dinah, Levi and
Simeon killed every man in the city of Shechem. Levi and
Simeon then plundered the city, taking the women, children,
and all the flocks and herds. Jacob, fearing reprisal from
other people in the area, move his family to Luz (that is,
Bethel or house of God) at God's direction. (Genesis
34:1-35:15) Later, he took his family to Ephrath (that is,
Bethlehem). Unfortunately, en route, Rachel died while
giving birth to Benjamin. (See Genesis 35:16–20.) Isaac
died thereafter in Mamre, near Kiriath Arba (that is, Hebron).
He was buried by both Jacob and Esau. (See 35:27-29.)

d. Joseph Sold into Slavery

It was thereafter that Joseph was sold by his brothers to
some Ishmaelite (Midianite) traders. They, in turn, took
Joseph to Egypt and sold him to Potiphar, who was one of
the pharaoh's trusted officials, as he was captain of the
guard. (See Genesis 37:1-36.) Thereafter, with a few

mishaps beforehand, Joseph became second-in-command in Egypt. (See Genesis 39:1-41:57.) When a famine hit, 10 of Jacob's sons went to Egypt to buy food. Joseph let them buy food, but he kept Simeon in Egypt to guarantee that Benjamin, his full brother, was brought to Egypt in the next trip. The brothers returned to Egypt with Benjamin, while Jacob stayed behind in Canaan. After the brothers had purchased more food, Joseph had a silver cup put in Benjamin's sack of food to make it look as if Benjamin had stolen it from Joseph. When Jacob's son were brought back before Joseph, it was Judah who asked to be made a slave instead of Benjamin. See Genesis 42:1-44:33.) Joseph then revealed himself as their brother and said that God had sent him ahead to preserve Jacob, his brothers, and their family as a "remnant on earth." (See Genesis 45:1-7.) Joseph told his brothers to bring Jacob and the entire family to Egypt. The pharaoh joined in the chorus and, additionally, said that Jacob and his family would be given the best of the land of Egypt. In addition, they should forget about their belongings because they will be given the best clothing and other items that Egypt had to offer. (See Genesis 45:16-20.)

e. Jacob Took His Family to Egypt

Jacob was reluctant at first to go to Egypt. However, God came to Jacob and told him not to "be afraid to go down to Egypt, **for I will make you into a great nation there**." (emphasis added)

Jacob, his sons, and all of their families went to Egypt and settled in the land of Goshen, which was in northeast Egypt. (see Genesis 46:1-47.31.) Conservative Biblical scholars have determined this date to be around **1843 BC**.

47

f. Jacob on His Death Bed

Later, Joseph went to his father as Jacob was on his death bed. Jacob told Joseph about God appearing to him at Luz and making him this promise: "I am going to make you fruitful and increase your numbers. I will make you a community of peoples, and I will give this land as an everlasting possession to your descendants after you." (Genesis 48:1-4)

When Joseph presented his two sons, **Manasseh** and **Ephraim**, to Jacob, he said they would be reckoned as Jacob's children, "just as Reuben and Simeon are mine." Jacob blessed both boys, but he said that Ephraim would be greater than Manasseh, even though Manasseh was the oldest boy. (Genesis 48:5-22)

Jacob then gathered his sons around him and appears to "bless" them according to their birth order. This is the order: **Reuben**, **Simeon**, **Levi**, **Judah**, **Zebulun**, **Issachar**, **Dan**, **Gad**, **Asher**, **Naphtali**, **Joseph**, and **Benjamin**.

The blessing of any significance involved Judah. In the second longest of the blessings, Jacob praised **Judah** and prophesied that he would rule and be rich. Of course, he was right. David was a descendant of the tribe of Judah and it was his line that God ordained would rule Israel forever. It was from this line that Jesus descended.

Jacob then died. (See Genesis 49:1-33.)

After he died, Jacob was taken back to Canaan and buried in the cave where Abraham, Sarah, Issac, Rebekah, and Leah had been buried earlier. Joseph and his brothers then returned to Egypt. (See Genesis 50:1-13)

g. Joseph Died

When Joseph was on his death bed, he gathered his brothers together and said, "I am about to die. But God will surely come to your aid and take you up out of this land to the land he promised on oath to Abraham, Isaac and Jacob." And Joseph made the Israelites swear an oath and said, "God will surely come to your aid, and then you must carry my bones up from this place." Joseph then died in Egypt at the age of 110 years and was buried in Egypt. (See Genesis 50:14-26.)

h. Promises Remembered

God made two promises to Abraham, Isaac, and Jacob. He told them that (1) their people would be as numerous as the stars and that (2) they would be possessors of Canaan.

God fulfilled the first promise while the descendants of Jacob were in Egypt. There were seventy members of Jacob's family when they settled in Egypt. Eventually, Joseph and his brothers died, but the Israelites stayed in Egypt and "became so numerous that the land was filled with them." (See Exodus 1:1-7.) The descendants of Jacob stayed in Egypt for 430 years (See Exodus 12:40-41) and they became figuratively as numerous as the stars.
They occupied the land of Goshen, which was part of the eastern Nile Delta. Goshen was located near the eastern most of the three main divisions of the Nile River after it split about 100 miles south of the Mediterranean Sea. Goshen traditionally has been placed near the ancient city of Rameses. The Hebrews lived in this region because they were shepherds (herders) and shepherds were detestable to the Egyptians. (See Genesis 46:28-34.) Since they were anathema to the Egyptians, it is likely that there was little

intermarriage between the Hebrews, as they were called by the Egyptians, and the locals. For many generations, the Hebrews lived peacefully where they had settled. However, the amicable relationship between the two people changed over time and the second promise would flow out of the first.

In time, a new pharaoh came to power who feared the Israelites because of their numbers. He is not named, but some authors believe he was Ramses II. Others believe he was Ramses VII or Ramses VIII. However, the most likely pharaoh was Amenemhet/Amenemhat I.

Amenemhet/Amenemhat I

Whichever pharaoh he was, his plan was to enslave the Israelites and he soon put that plan into effect. (See Exodus 1:1-14.) He also intended to make sure that the Israelites died out as a people because he feared they would ally themselves with some invading force. He instructed the Israelite midwives to kill all the boys that were born. If the boys survived birth, they were to be thrown into the Nile. (See Exodus: 1:15-22.)

Jochebed placed her son Moses in the river

Thereafter, a child, the son of a Levite man named Amram and a Levite woman named Jochebed was born. The mother hid the child from anyone who would want to kill him and then, when he was three months old, put him in a basket among the reeds of the Nile River. The child was found by the pharaoh's daughter and she named him Moses. (See Exodus 2:1-10.)

Some commentators argue that he was given the name of Moses because the name sounds like the Hebrew for "draw out." Other commentators argue that the name is entirely Egyptian, deriving from the word "mose or mes," which means "son" or "born." This latter derivation seems most consistent with the circumstances. If the princess who rescued Moses was Hatshepsut, the daughter of Thutmose I and the wife of Thutmose II, then the name Moses would be appropriate. Hatshepsut bore no male children and, if Thutmose II did not have any other male children by any other wife, then Moses would have been in line to be pharaoh of Egypt. Other pharaohs with "mose" in their name included Dedumose I, Dedumose II, Ahmose, Kamose, Thutmose I, Thutmose II, Thutmose III, and Thutmose IV.

If the princess who found Moses was Sobeknefru, then the pharaoh who was ruling at the time was Amenemhet III. This pharaoh died without an heir and it was likely that Moses was saved because he would be raised as the son of Amenemhet III and be the next pharaoh.

INTRODUCTION

PART FIVE

Moses

a. Moses Led the Hebrews out of Captivity

It was Moses who grew up in the pharaoh's household, but later led the Hebrews out of Egypt via the Red Sea and into the Sinai Desert. Conservative Biblical scholars believe that the Exodus occurred in or about **1446 BC**. It should be noted that the people of God were called Hebrews by the Pharaoh while they were in Egypt. However, when God spoke to Moses about His people, God referred to them as Israelites. When Moses was to speak with the pharaoh, God instructed him, in that circumstance, to refer to the Israelites as Hebrews. Therefore, the Hebrews of Egypt will hereafter be referred to as Israelites.

After Moses left Egypt to escape punishment for killing an Egyptian overseer, he spent 40 years in Midian, which was located across the Sinai Desert in the area of the Sea of Aqaba. While there, God chose him to bring the Israelites out of Egypt and into the Promised Land. When the Israelites left Egypt, there were "**about six hundred thousand men on foot, besides women and children**" who accompanied Moses. People of other ethnic groups also went with them. In addition, the Israelites drove before them fowl, cattle, and other livestock. (See Exodus 12:37-38.) See also **http://creationwiki.org/Neferhotep_I** for a synopsis of the reign of Neferhotep I, the likely pharaoh at the time of the Exodus.

b. The Journey to the Red Sea

The initial journey out of Egypt took the Israelites from Rameses to Sukkoth. They then went from Sukkoth to Etham, which was on the edge of the desert. (See Exodus 13:20.) The Lord then had the Israelites turn back and encamp near Pi Hahiroth, between Migdol and the sea. This would be in a direction near the mountain called Baal Zephon. (See Exodus 14:1-2.)

Scott Lanser, Executive Director of Associates for Biblical Research, has an interesting view of why God had Moses backtrack to Baal Zephon:

"The study of the history and background of Baal Zephon is utterly fascinating. The worship of Baal was known throughout the Fertile Crescent, the Levant, and down into Egypt. Upon the mountain of Baal Zephon, it was believed that Zephon reigned in power and was lord over the sea. Here, Pharaoh may have sensed that the idol Zephon was going to display his power over the Israelites. God tells us some of Pharaoh's reasoning: 'Pharaoh will think, 'The Israelites are wandering around the land in confusion, hemmed in by the desert.' And I will harden Pharaoh's heart, and he will pursue them' (Exodus 14:3, 4a). Indeed he did, and I believe that Pharaoh considered that Zephon would finally rout the Israelites and that Yahweh would be shown to be inferior in power. (Did Pharaoh *still* think that he and his Egyptian gods had power to subdue the God of Israel unaided by a still more powerful deity?) And it is no surprise that the Lord stopped Israel and turned them around to meet and defeat not only Pharaoh and his army, but also to display his power over Zephon and defeat him at the mountain of his glory and power. Not only this, but Yahweh would lead His people directly through the sea...the

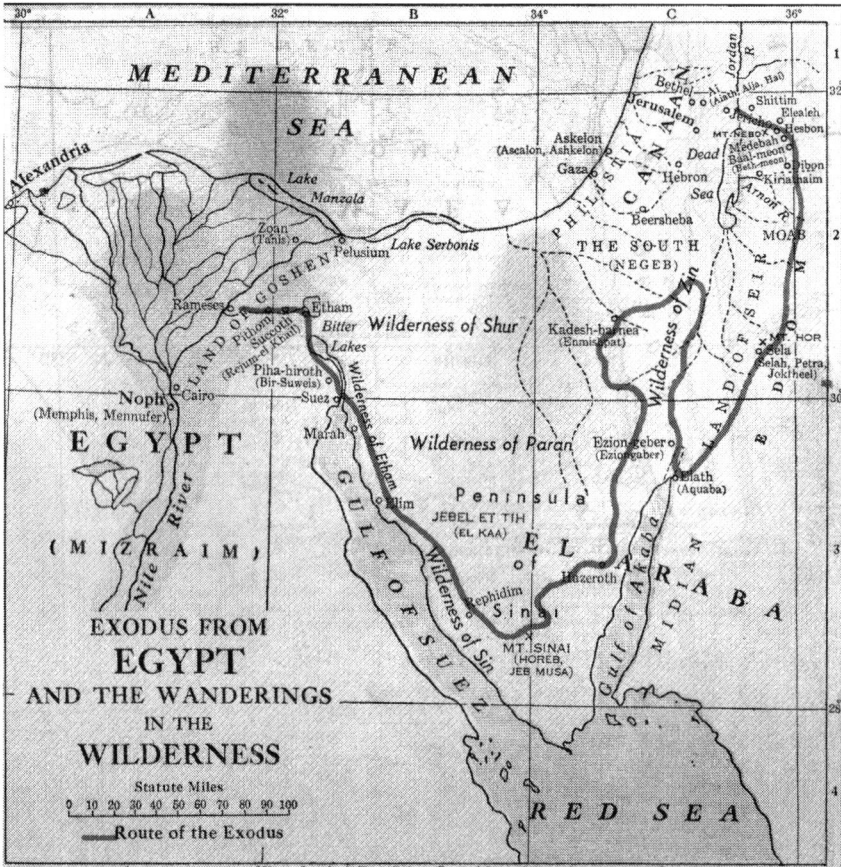

EXODUS FROM EGYPT AND THE WANDERINGS IN THE WILDERNESS

Map labels: MEDITERRANEAN SEA, Alexandria, Lake Manzala, Zoan (Tanis), Pelusium, Lake Serbonis, Rameses, Etham, Pithom, Succoth, Bitter Lakes, Piha-hiroth (Bir-Suweis), Wilderness of Shur, Noph (Memphis, Mennufer), Cairo, Suez, EGYPT, (MIZRAIM), Marah, Wilderness of Etham, Elim, Peninsula, JEBEL ET TIH (EL KAA), Wilderness of Paran, Wilderness of Sin, Rephidim, Sinai, MT. SINAI (HOREB, JEB MUSA), GULF OF SUEZ, EL, Hazeroth, Ezion-geber (Eziongyaber), Elath (Aquaba), Gulf of Akaba, MIDIAN, ARABA, Kadesh-barnea (En-mishpat), Wilderness of Zin, THE SOUTH (NEGEB), Beersheba, Hebron, Gaza, Askelon (Ascalon, Ashkelon), PHILISTIA, Bethel, Jerusalem, Dead Sea, CANAAN, LAND OF SEIR, EDOM, MT. HOR, Sela, Petra, Joktheel, MOAB, Shittin, Elealeh, Hesbon, Medeba, Baal-meon, Beth-meon, Dibon, Kirathaim, MT. NEBO, Arnon R., Jordan R., RED SEA

Statute Miles 0 10 20 30 40 50 60 70 80 90 100
——— Route of the Exodus

sea which the Egyptians believed were under the control of Zephon! And further, that instead of the Israelites being destroyed, showing Zephon's lordship of the sea, it would be the Egyptians who would discover who was both Lord of the mountain, but also Lord over the sea! There were many ways that God could have chosen to eliminate the Egyptian army; it was no accident that He chose to bring this conflict into the sharpest spiritual focus and to a climax of incredible proportions.

"In the end we are left awestruck at the wisdom and power

of our God. We can see clearly that God was showing His people, in the most amazing and startling ways, not only that He was Lord over all other gods and over nature, but was teaching His people Israel what happens to those who worship false gods. And lest we forget His love for the Egyptians, we must remember His words, that ultimately, 'the Egyptians will know that I am the Lord' (Genesis 14:4b). Can we not also conclude, that in the end, God showed His grace to the Egyptians who were in the bondage of following gods who were empty, without power, and unable to save them?

"The Lord said: '...I will gain glory for myself through Pharaoh and all his army, and the Egyptians will know that I am the Lord.' (Genesis 14:4b) God's glory is at stake in all these things. May we praise and glorify our great God, who delivers his people and triumphs over all our enemies!" (See *http://www.biblearchaeology.org/post/2006/07/12/ Confronting-Baal-Zephon-The-Spiritual-Message-of- the-Meeting-of-Israel-and-the-Armies-of-Egypt-at-the- Mountain-Before-the-Sea.aspx#Article*)

While the Israelites were encamped near Pi Hahiroth, the Pharaoh and his army approached to bring the Israelites back into slavery in Egypt. (See Exodus 14:3-10.) God then parted the sea and the Israelites crossed safely. When the Pharaoh and his army attempted to pursue the Israelites, God caused the sea to rush in on the Pharaoh and his army and they were killed. (See Exodus 14:15-31.)

c. The Shrine of el-Arish

Immanuel Velikovsky, in his book entitled "**Ages in Chaos**," quoted from a book written by F. L. Griffith and published in 1890. The book was called, "**The Antiquities of Tell el**

Yahudiyeh and Miscellaneous Work in Lower Egypt during the Years 1887-1888." In the book, Griffith relates the finding of a shrine of black granite in el-Arish that was being used as a cattle trough. The shrine was inscribed with hieroglyphics. Griffith translated the hieroglyphics and published the results in his book. The stone was eventually brought to the Ismailia Museum in Ismailia, Egypt. The museum opened in 1936.

The hieroglyphics tell a story of a time of great upheaval. There was a great wind and the ensuing darkness engulfed the land for nine days and it was so thick no one could see the face of a person standing nearby. The text referred to a King Thom. In the midst of the savageries of nature, "his majesty of Shou" assembled an army of men to take them to a place where they could see light: "We shall see our father Ra-Harakhti in the luminous region of Bakhit." The king then went to battle against an enemy in the desert that were described as "intruders" and "the companions of Apopi," who was the fierce god of darkness. The king and the army with him never returned. Here is a quote from the hieroglyphics:

"Now when the majesty of Ra-Harmachis [Harakhti?] fought with the evil-doers in this pool, the Place of the Whirlpool, the evil-doers prevailed not over his majesty. His majesty leapt into the so-called Place of the Whirlpool."

A few lines later, the king was described as being thrown by the whirlpool high into the air and he departed. He was no longer alive. The place where the king/pharaoh departed was called Pi-Kharoti. In Exodus 14:9, the scripture relates that the pharaoh caught up with Moses and the departing former Hebrew slaves at a place called Pi-ha-hiroth or Pi-Hahiroth (NIV) or Pi-Khiroth (Hebrew Scripture). Velikovsky believed, based on all the similarities, that P-ha-hiroth and Pi-Kharoti are different names for the same location in Egypt and the author of the hieroglyphics was describing what happened at the time of the Exodus.

After the death of the pharaoh, his son "Geb" went out against the invaders, but was burned by a violent blast of heat and his army was destroyed. Geb then retreated to his palace and attempted to negotiate with the invaders. When that did not work, he disappeared and the invaders took over his palace.

Based on additional material in the text and on his own research into the events of the time, Velikovsky believed that the Exodus did not take place at the end of the 18th dynasty, whether in 1446 BC or thereabouts. He believed that the Exodus took place while the Hyksos were invading Egypt, which, based on his calculations, occurred in or about 1650 BC. The Hyksos then became the masters of Egypt for approximately 400 years. Velikovsky postulated that the Amalekites, whom the Hebrews met in the Sinai Desert, were part of the migration of the same people as the Hyksos. He determined that these people came from Saudi Arabia and migrated into the middle east and northeast Africa because of physical upheavels. If Velikovsky is right, then the Exodus took place approximately 200 years before the commonly accepted date by Christian authors.
However, it should also be noted that Velikovsky believed that the dating system used by Egyptologists was flawed. His study taught him that Egyptologists placed the pharaohs too far back in time and the date of 1446 BC, give or take some years, could be still be accurate.
Egyptologists have adopted some of Velikovsky's thinking and have revised their dating systems for Egypt since then.

See **http://www.pibburns.com/smelaris.htm** for a full rendering of the shrine found at el-Arish. It is at the end of a long article.

d. The Pharaoh of the Exodus

If Velikovsky is right about the series of events, but not the date, then the pharaoh who reigned at the time Moses left Egypt for Midian after killing an Egyptian overseer was Amenemhat III. He was the last pharaoh of the 12th dynasty of the Middle Kingdom to build a pyramid. He had a son Amenemhat IV, but his mummy and his tomb, if any, have

Amenemhat III

never been found. In addition, there is no record of the parentage of Amenemhat IV. Some authors believe that Amenemhat IV was Moses.

Amenemhat IV (Moses?)

When Amenemhat III died, his daughter Sobeknefru became pharaoh. It is believed that Sobeknefru was the princess who found Moses in the bullrushes. The revised date of her reign was 1483 to 1479 BC. When Moses returned 40 years later, the pharaoh would have been Neferhotep I. Archeologists have found remains of slave villages that appear to have been abandoned suddenly at the time of his reign. In addition, no mummy for Neferhotep I has never been found, making him a prime candidate for the pharaoh of the Exodus. He was succeeded by his brother rather than his son, who was probably killed as the first born.

For a further discussion on this topic, see **https://pharaohoppressionmosesisraelegyptdynasty.wordpress.com/tag/amenemhat-iii/** and **http://creationwiki.org/Neferhotep_I**

INTRODUCTION

PART SIX

Joshua

a. Lineage

Joshua is identified in 1 Chronicles 7:27 as the son of Nun and a direct descendant of Ephraim, the second son of Joseph. Here are the descendants of Ephraim, from Shuthelah to Joshua: Shuthelah, Bered, Tahath, Eleadah, Tahath, Zabad, Shuthelah, Rephah, Resheph, Telah, Tahan, Ladan, Amminhud, Elishama, Nun, and Joshua. There were 17 generations from Ephraim to Joshua. (See 1 Chronicles 7:20-27.) Today, each generation follows the one before it, on the average, every 20 to 25 years. This would mean that there were 340 to 425 years from Ephraim to Joshua if these generations had been living in the present time. In ancient times, it was about 30 years from one generation to another. (See Genesis 11.) Some authors put the generations at 40 years on the average. In any event, if Biblical scholars are correct in finding that Jacob went to Egypt in or about **1843 BC** and the Exodus was in or about **1446 BC**, then approximately 397 years passed from the sojourn of Jacob in Egypt and the Exodus, give or take a few years. It is believed that Joshua was approximately 40 years old when the Israelites left Egypt to escape slavery.

b. Name

Joshua was given the name of Hosea at birth. The name means "salvation" or "he saves" or "he helps." Because Joshua was born in Egypt, the reference to "he" in the meaning of the name is not definite and it could refer to a god of Egypt, not the God of the Hebrews. It was Moses who changed Hosea's name to Joshua. (See Numbers 13:16). Joshua is the English rendering of the Hebrew Yehoshua, which means "Yahweh is salvation."

c. Joshua and the Amalekites at Rephidim

1. Joshua at Rephidim

Joshua is mentioned for the first time in the Bible when the Israelites battled the Amalekites at Rephidim in the desert of Sinai. (See Exodus 17:8-16.) The Israelites traveled to Rephidim, where they expected to find water. However, none was to be found. God then provided the Israelites with yet another miracle. God instructed Moses to go to Horeb (otherwise known as Mt. Sinai) and strike "the" rock. Moses did exactly as God directed and water flowed to slake the thirst of the quarreling, questioning, and now quaffing Israelites.

The site of Rephidim has not been located with absolute certainty, but Edward Henry Palmer, the author of "Desert of the Exodus," published in 1871, at page 158, believes Rephidim was in the area now called Wadi Feiran. It is located just about 10 miles northwest of the mountain which has been identified as Mount Sinai. Wikipedia gives this description of the wadi: "**Wadi Feiran** is Sinai's largest and widest wadi (valley or dry riverbed). It rises from the mountains around Saint Catherine's Monastery at 2500 meters (8,000 feet) above sea level. It is important because according to Hebrew Scriptures, it was at Rephidim that Moses struck a rock, creating a spring to provide people with drinking water. Wadi Feiran is an 130 kilometers (81 miles) long wadi Egypt's Sinai Peninsula. Its upper reaches, around the Jebel Musa, are known as the Wadi el-Sheikh. It empties into the Red Sea's Gulf of Suez 18 miles (29 kilometers) southeast of Abu Zenima."

Wadi Feiran with Mt. Sinai in the background

While the Israelites were at Rephidim, enjoying the fruits of their relationship with God, they were attacked without provocation by the Amalekites. It was during the telling of this story that the person of Joshua is introduced on the Biblical stage for the first time.

2. The Amalekites

Who were the Amalekites? It appears that they were descendants of Amalek, a grandson of Esau. In other words, the Amalekites were people that came from Jacob's brother Esau. A review of the Biblical text makes it clear that Esau resented the fact that Jacob stole his birthright and he swore to kill Jacob at one point. Even though there appears to have been some movement toward reconciliation with Esau when Jacob returned from living with his father-in-law Laban, Jacob slipped away without the brotherly bond being solidified and there is no mention of Esau again. (See Genesis 32:3-21, 33:1-17.) It seems that the story about the trouble and the lack of any real peace between Jacob and Esau may have been passed down to the generations that followed. The argument for a lasting enmity from the time of Esau is strengthened by the fact that the Amalekites were perpetual enemies of the Israelites and by the fact that God ordered the Israelites to eliminate every Amalekite from the face of the earth. Sometimes feuds just seem to last forever.

3. The Battle with the Amalekites

Israelites (left) battle the Amalekites with Moses on the hill

After the Israelites were attacked by the Amalekites, Moses told Joshua to choose some of the men and engage the Amalekites in combat. Moses said he would stand on the top of a nearby hill "tomorrow" and he would hold the staff of God in his hands. The use of the word tomorrow certainly suggests that the attack by the Amalekites must have been late in the day and the Israelites had enough warning or enough resources to hold off the attackers on that first day. Moses holding the staff of God in his hands surely meant something to both Moses and Joshua and the

Aaron, Moses, and Hur on the hill

significance of it was shown the next day when Joshua brought the full weight of his troops against the Amalekites. Moses, Aaron, and Hur went to the top of a hill the next day and it is likely that Joshua held off on his counterattack until the three were in position. Moses stood so he could be seen and he held up his staff. As long as he did so, the Israelites gained the upper hand in the battle. However, when his arms tired and the staff was lowered, the Amalekites gained the edge. To help Moses, Aaron and Hur put a stone under Moses to allow him to sit. And, to keep the staff raised, Aaron held up one of Moses' hands and Hur held up the other. The staff of God was thereafter held steady until sunset. By that time Joshua and his troops had beaten back the Amalekites.

It should have been clear to anyone in the battle or watching that it was God who controlled the course of the fierce fight, even though it was also evident that the Israelites were not afraid to engage an enemy who was fierce, likely well-armed, and determined. God then ordered that the feat of defeating the Amalekites be memorialized in writing. God also wanted Joshua to know that God would thereafter completely block out the name of Amalek "from under heaven." After the battle, Moses built an altar to God. The meaning of the altar was that God would be at war against the Amalekites "from generation to generation." In other words, God would not give the Amalekites any rest until they were blotted out from the history of humankind. (Exodus 17:8-16)

d. Joshua as Moses' Aide

1. Joshua at Mt. Sinai

While still in the area of Mt. Sinai, God told Moses to go up the mountain to receive tablets of stone on which God had written the law and commandments for the instruction of the Israelites. Moses did as God instructed and he took Joshua with him. When Moses went up on Mt. Sinai, a cloud covered it and the glory of the Lord settled on the mountain. On the seventh day, God called to Moses from within the cloud. Moses then entered the cloud and stayed on the mountain for forty days and nights. (Exodus 24:12-18.)

Mt. Sinai

While Moses was on the mountain, God gave him many tasks to do and laws to obey. In addition, God gave Moses two tablets of the covenant law. The tablets had been inscribed by God himself. (Exodus 31:18) God then instructed Moses to return to the Israelites because they had made a idol in the shape of a calf and, worse, they had bowed down to it and sacrificed to it. God again wanted to destroy them and, again, Moses intervened on their behalf.

Moses then left the immediate presence of God and met up with Joshua, who had been listening to the sounds coming from the people below. Joshua thought they were the sounds of war. However, Moses knew better. He said it was the sound of singing. When Moses re-entered the camp, he saw the golden calf and the people dancing. His anger grew fierce and he threw down the tablets he was holding and broke them. He then took the calf and melted it in a fire. Moses then rallied the Levites, who killed 3,000 of the Israelites. God then finished the punishment by bringing a plague on the Israelites. (Exodus 32:7-35)

Before Moses returned to Mt. Sinai at a later point, he made two stone tablets to take with him. It was God's intention to rewrite on the new tablets what God had inscribed before. Also, God instructed Moses that he was to come alone. This meant that Joshua would stay behind in the camp. Moses was on the mountain for 40 days and nights and there was no repetition in the camp of what happened earlier. (Exodus 34:1-4)

Although the Biblical text is silent on this point, there may have been a good reason why God wanted Moses to come alone: God wanted Joshua left behind to maintain order in the camp while Moses was away. It was obvious that Aaron was incapable of doing it. The combination of Joshua's presence as Moses' aide and the previous anger of God and the punishments He inflicted apparently kept the people in check.

2. Joshua and the Tent of Meeting

As Moses' aide, Joshua had another responsibility. Whenever Moses would go to the "tent of meeting," which was located outside the camp of the Israelites, Moses apparently was accompanied by Joshua. Moses would go to the "tent of meeting" to speak with God. The Biblical text does not make it clear exactly what was expected of Joshua when he went while Moses was in the tent. Joshua may have gone with Moses into the tent, but even that is not clear. The Biblical text does indicate that Joshua, referred to as Moses' "young aide," did not return to the camp with Moses. He stayed behind and "did not leave the tent." (Exodus 33:7-11)

3. Joshua Upset

Joshua is not mentioned again until the Book of Numbers. He is there called "Joshua son of Nun, who had been Moses' aide since youth." (Numbers 11:28) Joshua is re-introduced to the reader in the midst of yet another time of complaining and mumbling by the Israelites in the desert. Even though God provided the Israelites with a daily (except Sundays) supply of manna, there was "rabble" among them that bewailed the fact that there was no meat to eat. They again reminisced about how great life was in Egypt. They recalled the fish they could eat which did not cost them anything. They remembered the field crops (cucumbers, melons, leeks, onions, and garlic) with great fondness. Moses turned to God for an answer. He told Moses, amongst other things, to bring together 70 of the elders at the "tent of meeting." When the elders gathered, God placed on them the same Spirit he had given to Moses. They then began to "prophesy" once and once only. These men would then share some of the burdens the people were placing on Moses. In short, these men would now screen a lot of the complaints that Moses was forced to handle in the past. Moses could now focus on the really important questions as to how to carry out God's plan for the Israelites.

However, the Spirit was not only given to the 70 elders who gathered around the "tent of meeting," it was given to two other elders who were not present. They also "prophesied," but the implication is that their prophesying was not limited to just one time. In any event, it appears that God chose to give the two men who were not present at the tent a special blessing of the Spirit to demonstrate clearly that He was the person in control and He could show that by giving the power of the Spirit to anyone he chose. Unfortunately, their prophesying was upsetting enough that a message about the two men and their activities was sent to Moses, who was still at the "tent of meeting." Joshua was present when the message arrived and he immediately appealed to Moses to stop the two men. Moses explained to Joshua that he wished all of the Israelites were prophets and that God had put the Spirit on all of them. Joshua obviously was concerned about the image of his leader and Moses looked at the matter from another direction. Moses appeared to feel that his job would be a whole lot easier if everyone had the same spirit that he possessed. Of course, he was right. (Numbers 11:4-29.)

e. Joshua as a Spy into Canaan

1. New Name

While the Israelites were in the Desert of Paran, God told Moses to send a leader from each of the 12 tribes into Canaan to explore the land God had given to the Israelites.

The word "leader" has also been translated as prince. The term was obviously meant as a title of respect. Joshua was chosen to represent the tribe of Ephraim. Interestingly, he was then called "Hoshea son of Nun." (Numbers 13:8) However, shortly thereafter in the same chapter, it is noted that "Moses gave Hoshea son of Nun the name Joshua." (Numbers 13:16)

2. Twelve Tribes

The composition of the 12 tribes in the desert had changed from the time of Jacob. The 12 sons listed in Genesis 35:23-26 are in this order: **Reuben**, **Simeon**, **Levi**, **Judah**, **Issachar**, **Zebulun**, **Joseph**, **Benjamin**, **Dan**, **Naphtali**, **Gad**, and **Asher**. The first six were sons of Leah, the next two were sons of Rachel, the next two were sons of Bihah (Rachel's servant), and the last two were sons of Zilpah (Leah's servant). After the Israelites left Egypt, the tribes are listed in this order: **Reuben**, **Simeon**, **Judah**, **Issachar**, **Ephraim**, **Benjamin**, **Zebulun**, **Manasseh**, **Dan**, **Asher, Naphtali**, and **Gad**. The major difference is that both Levi and Joseph were omitted as members of the 12 tribes. Their places were taken by Ephraim and Manasseh, Joseph's sons. (Numbers 13:4-15)

3. Twelve Spies Sent Out

Moses gave the 12 spies, one from each of the named tribes, specific instructions as to what they were do when they went north into Canaan. They were to travel from the Desert of Paran, where they were then located, through the Desert of Zin, into the southern region of Canaan, which was called the Negev, and go as far as the northern hill country.

Moses told the spies to gather information about (1) the land, (2) the people, and (3) the cities.

As to the land, Moses wanted the spies to find out generally what condition the land was in: "see what the land is like." Moses also had specific instructions for them. He offered these suggestions: "Is it good or bad? How is the soil? Is it fertile or poor? Are there trees in it or not? Do your best to bring back some of the fruit of the land." (Numbers 13:17-20)

As to the people, Moses wanted some idea about the kind of people were living in Canaan: "See...whether the people who live there are strong or weak, few or many?" (Numbers 13:18)

As to the cities, Moses needed some idea of their vulnerability to attack: "What kind of towns do they live in? Are they unwalled or fortified?" (Numbers 13:19)

The spies then followed Moses' directions as to where they went and as to what he wanted them to observe. The spies went through the Desert of Zin as far as Rehob, toward Lebo Hamath. They reached the Negev and continued north to Hebron. It was in Hebron that the spies were shocked by the size of the people called Anakites. They were giants compared to the Israelites (and likely giants to people today). The spies even learned the names of three of the giants. They were Ahiman, Sheshai, and Talmai. These names need to be remembered because it was Caleb during the conquest who drove these giants from Hebron when he captured that city. (See Joshua 15:13-14.) The spies traveled as far north as the Valley of Eshkol, which was just south of the Sea of Chinnereth (Galilee). It was in the Valley of Eshkol that the spies cut off a cluster of grapes that had to be carried home on a pole with a spy at each end. (Numbers 13:21-24)

4. Twelve Spies Returned and Reported

Spies returned with bounty from Canaan

After 40 days, the spies returned to the Desert of Paran. (Numbers 13:25) The distance from the Israelite encampment to the Valley of Eshkol is about 220 miles, depending on the route that was taken. The average male can walk about 3.1 miles per hour. Based upon a walking speed of 3.1 miles per hour, the spies could easily have walked the route taken in 20 days. The return trip would also have been manageable. Not only did they give a report to Moses, they gave it to the entire assembly of the Israelites. The spies were effusive in their description of the land of Canaan. They said it flowed with "milk and honey." They even showed everyone the cluster of grapes obtained in the Valley Eshkol. (Numbers 13:26-27)

However, when it came to reporting about the people and the cities, ten of the 12 spies were less enthusiastic. The spies called the people "powerful." They specifically pointed out that they had seen the descendants of Anak "there" (not defined). These were men of great height and extraordinary physical prowess. In short, they were like the giant that David would eventually face in battle about 400 years later. They stressed that the Amalekites lived in the Negev, the Hittites, Jebusites, and the Amorites lived in the hill county, and the Canaanites lived near the Mediterranean Sea and along the Jordan River.

In short, the entire land of Canaan was occupied by people with military strength and the capability to utilize that strength. As if the fact that the people in Canaan were "powerful" wasn't enough, the ten spies were quick to reveal that the cities were "large" and "fortified." Caleb attempted to encourage the people about conquering the Promised Land, but they would have none of it. The ten spies responded by saying that the people they would be attacking were stronger than the Israelites and they especially emphasized that the Nephilim who resided in Canaan were so large that the spies seemed like grasshoppers in the eyes of the Nephilim and in their own eyes. The spies painted a dreadful picture that silenced the Israelites at first. (See Numbers 13:28-33.)

5. Israelites in an Uproar

However, the silence did not last long. At first, the Israelites raised their voices (in mourning it would seem) and wept. Then they began grumbling against Moses and Aaron and soon they were hysterical in fear of being slaughtered in the desert and their wives and children being taken as plunder. And, then the idea, which was not a new one, struck them that they would be better off to choose a new leader and go back to Egypt. It was at this point that Joshua and Caleb tore their clothes and said to the entire assembly of Israelites that they should not rebel against God. They argued that if God is pleased with the Israelites, he would lead them into the "land flowing with milk and honey" and give it to them. Joshua and Caleb asked the Israelites not to be afraid of the people of Canaan because the Israelites would "devour" them. They said the Canaanites were defenseless with God on the side of the Israelites. The speech was impassioned and it drew upon a picture of the God who had preserved and protected the Israelites in their movement through the Sinai Desert. It should have stirred the hearts of the people to believe in the promises that God had made and to believe that God would carry out those promises. (See Numbers 14:1-9)

Despite their pleas and arguements, the Israelites were not moved in the right direction. Instead of being positively aroused by Joshua and Caleb's appeal to their loyalty to God, the Israelites became so angry at Joshua and Caleb that the entire assembly began to speak as one that Joshua and Caleb needed to be stoned for their urging the people to believe in God directly and Moses and Aaron indirectly. (Numbers 14:10)

6. Israelites Commanded to Wander

It was at this very moment that God appeared in His glory before the entire assembly. God threatened to destroy those who opposed Him. When Moses intervened, God said that no one but Caleb and Joshua would ever enter the Promised Land. He then condemned the Israelites to wander in the desert for 40 years until every adult except Joshua and Caleb had died. God even caused the death of the ten spies who convinced the people not to enter the Land of Canaan. (See Numbers 14:10-38.)

7. Some Israelites Disobeyed God

When Moses reported to the Israelites what God had said, they mourned bitterly and many recognized that they had sinned against God. In desperation, those who felt the worse set out the next day to carry out what God had originally told them to do. However, Moses told them they were yet again disobeying God. Moses urged them to stay in the camp because their efforts were doomed for failure because God would not be with them. Moses warned them that they would be facing the Amalekites and the Canaanites and they would be defeated. (Numbers 14:41-43)

The men would not listen to Moses and they set out for the highest point in the hill country north of the Israelite camp. Even though the men were determined to invade Canaan, Moses did nothing to help them and he kept the ark of the covenant in camp. As the men headed for their objective, they were attacked by a combined force of Amalekites and

Canaanites and were beaten badly. The men were forced to retreat all the way to Hormah (an unknown location, but obviously an area that presented no further threat to the Amalekites and Canaanites.) The scripture makes it abundantly clear that they were thrashed in battle because God was not with them. Numbers 14:44-45)

f. Israel Won in Battle with God's Help

In their wanderings, the Israelites eventually came to Edom. This was a land occupied by the descendants of Jacob's brother Esau. Moses sent a message to the king of Edom asking for safe passage across Edom, the king of Edom refused Moses' request. He emphasized his refusal by marching out with a large and powerful army. Moses then led the Israelites from Kadesh to Mount Hor. Moses, Aaron, and Aaron's son Eleazar went up to the top of Mount Hor at God's command. Aaron died on Mount Hor and was buried there. The Israelites mourned Aaron's death for thirty days. (Numbers 20:14-29)

Unable to cross Edom, Moses and the Israelites left Kadesh via "the road to Atharim." It is not certain if Atharim is a community or a place. Whatever it was, its exact location is unknown today. Unfortunately, it was close enough to the territory of Arad for its Canaanite king to become uneasy. Perhaps fearing another attack from the Israelites, he surprised the Israelites and captured some of them. Seeking revenge for the assault, the Israelites vowed to God to totally destroy the cities of Arad if God would deliver them into the hands of the Israelites. God answered their vow with action and gave the cities to the Israelites, who completely destroyed every city and town in the territory called Arad (See map below). The place was thereafter called Hormah, which means "destruction." (Numbers 21:1-3)

Moses then led the Israelites from Mt. Hor on a southern route to go around Edom. The journey took them just north of the Gulf of Aqaba. Once they were around the southern tip of Edom, the Israelites traveled north to go east of Edom, Moab, and Ammon to the plains of Moab. (Numbers 21:4-20)

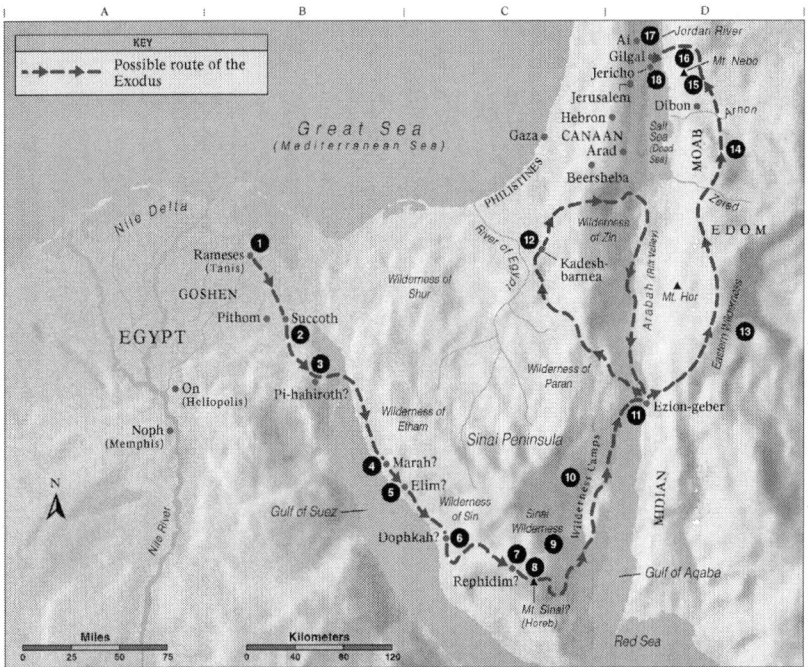

The order of march for the Israelites after they decamped had been established in Numbers 10:14-28. (1) The Israelites would be led by the three tribes of Judah, Issachar, and Zebulun, with Judah in the lead. (2) The tabernacle would then be taken down and carried out by the clans of the tribe of Levi. (3) The third group would then set out, headed by the tribe of Reuben and followed by Simeon and Gad. (4) The "holy things" were then be carried out, with the tabernacle to be set up before they arrived at the next location. (5) The fifth group, which consisted of Ephraim, Manasseh, and Benjamin, in that order, followed. (6) The rear guard then set out. This group was made up of Dan, Asher, and Naphtali, with Dan in the lead.

g. The Wandering Is Almost Over

After 40 years of wandering in the desert of Sinai, the Israelites had moved into a position on the plains of Moab, across the Jordan River from Jericho. It was there that God ordered Moses and Eleazar, the son of Aaron, to take a census of every male who was 20 years or older and **who was able to fight in the Israelite army**. Moses and Eleazar then obeyed God. Here are the results of the census:

1.   In the clans of Judah, there were 76,500.

2.   In the clans of Dan, there were 64,400.

3.   In the clans of Issachar, there were 64,300

4.   In the clans of Zebulun, there were 60,500.

5.   In the clans of Asher, there were 53,400.

6.   In the clans of Manasseh, there were 52,700.

7.   In the clans of Benjamin, there were 45,600.

8.   In the clans of Naphtali, there were 45,400.

9.   In the clans of Reuben, there were 43,730.

10.   In the clans of Gad, there were 40,500.

11.   In the clans of Ephraim, there were 32,500.

12.   in the clans of Simeon, there were 22,200.

There were a total of 601,730 men over the age of 20 years who could serve in the Israelite military. In addition, God decreed that the land of Canaan would be divided among the clans, based upon the percentage of fighting men over the age of 20 years in each tribe. The Levites would be treated differently. They had a special formula that was used to count them. Every Levite male who was one month or older was included in the census. They numbered 23,000. They were not counted with the other clans because they were not going to receive separate land in Canaan. They would be assigned to cities and they would possess adjacent grazing land for their fowl and animals. Not one of the males who were counted by Moses and Aaron in the first census, which was taken right after the flight from Egypt 40 years earlier, were among those counted in this second census, except Caleb and Joshua. (Numbers 26:1-65)

Based on the census taken above and detailed in Numbers 26:52-56, the figures below show how the land in Canaan was to be allotted to each tribe. The percentages were determined by the author of this book based on the number of fighting men in each clan. The numbers below add up to 99.998 per cent.

1.   Judah - 12.713%

2.   Dan - 10.702%

3.   Issachar - 10.686%

4.   Zebulun - 10.054%

5.   Asher - 8.874%

6.   Manasseh - 8.758%

7.   Benjamin - 7.578%

8.   Naphtali - 7.545%

9.   Reuben - 7.267%

10.   Gad - 6.731%

11.   Ephraim - 5.401%

12.   Simeon - 3.689%

Based on a quick glance at the final allotment of land both east and west of the Jordan River after the conquest of the Promised Land, it appears that the tribes of Manasseh, Simeon, and Gad were assigned more land than they should have gotten. It also appears that the tribes of Dan and Zebulun received less land than it should have gotten. It is not clear, without some intense calculations, if the other tribes' shares were equal to the percentage outlined above.

h. Joshua Is Chosen to Lead the Israelites

While the Israelites were in the plain of Moab, Moses was instructed by God to go up a mountain in the Abarim Range to see the land that God had given to the Israelites. After Moses had seen the land, he was told he would die. Moses then beseeched the Lord to appoint someone to take

Moses' place and God honored Moses' request. (Numbers 27:12-17)

God had already decided that the man who would take Moses' position was Joshua, son of Nun. God said that Joshua had "the spirit of leadership." God instructed Moses to lay his hand on Joshua as Joshua stood before Eleazar the priest and the entire Israelite community. Moses was to give Joshua "some" of Moses' authority so the Israelites would start learning to obey him. Joshua was also to consult with Eleazar, who would determine what Joshua should do by "inquiring" of the Urim before God. God concluded his instructions by saying that once the Israelite community saw that Moses had transferred some of his authority to Joshua and that Joshua would be making decisions based upon his consolation with God through Eleazar, the entire community of Israelites "will go out" and "will go in" at Joshua's command. Moses then did exactly as God commanded him to do. (Numbers 27:18-23)

i. The Midianites Are Destroyed

While the Israelites were camped opposite Jericho on the east side of the Jordan River, the king of Moab sought to have Israel cursed, but Balaam refused to disobey God. However, the Israelites would be plagued from another source. Moabite women and then a Midianite woman seduced men into engaging in sexual immorality. God then ordered Moses to take vengeance on the Midianites. (Numbers 25:1-18 and Numbers 31:1-2))

Moses ordered 1,000 men from each tribe to gather and then go to battle against the Midianites. The troops appeared to have been led by Phinehas, a son of Eleazar. He took with him articles from the sanctuary and "the"

83

trumpets for signaling. In this way, the troops would know that God was with them. (See Numbers 10:9.) In addition, the trumpets could be used so God's troops would know when to charge, when to retreat, when to move to the left or the right, and when to reinforce a unit under heavy assault. The 12,000 soldiers then fought against the Midianites and killed very man. This included the five kings of Midian and Balaam, the man who advised the Midianite women to entice the Israelites. The troops burned all of the towns and the camps of the Midianites and brought the spoils of war back to Moses, Eleazar, and the rest of the Israelite community. It was then that Moses ordered all the Midianite boys and all the non-virgins to be killed and his order was carried out. The remainder of the spoils was divided between the soldiers and the Israelite community. (Numbers 31:3-54)

It is interesting that Joshua, with his experience as a military commander, was not chosen to lead the expedition. However, it is easy to understand why he was not selected. He had just been given "some" of the authority of Moses and he was on the verge of leading the Israelites into Canaan. There was no reason to risk his being killed in a foray against the Midianites.

It should not be forgotten that Moses' wife and his father-in-law, called Jethro, were Midianites. Jethro was even with Moses just after the Exodus. At Exodus 18:27, Jethro left Moses and returned to his own land. It appears that a Midianite by the name of Hobab stayed with Moses. He is identified later in Numbers 10:29 as "Hobab son of Reuel, the Midianite, Moses' father-in-law." According to scholars, it is likely that Reuel was another name used by Jethro. The identity of Hobab is not as certain as theologians would like to have it. In any event, whether Hobab was a brother-in-law to Moses or some other relation, it seems clear that he was a Midianite and he was with Moses at the time the Israelites were leaving the area of Sinai. Hobab wanted to go back to his "own land," but Moses encouraged him to stay with the Israelites, to be "our eyes," and to share in whatever "good things the Lord gives us." The passages seemed to imply that Hobab had been of some help in the past and Moses expected him to be of assistance in the future. It is not mentioned in the scripture what Hobab's response was. If Hobab did go back to Midian, then Hobab and his family may have perished in the fighting between the Israelites and the Midianites. (Numbers 10:29-32)

j. Defeat of Sihon and Og

Moses requested of Sihon, the king of the land of Heshbon, to allow the Israelites to pass through his country to get to the Jordan River north of the Dead Sea. The Israelites would even be willing to buy food and water from the king's people and they would pay in silver. However, Sihon refused the Israelites passage through his country. God then made Sihon's spirit stubborn and his heart obstinate. As a result, the king of Heshbon, went out with his army to oppose the Israelites in battle at a site called Jahaz. (See map below.)

Unfortunately for Sihon and his army, they were decisively beaten. The Israelites then captured every town in Heshbon, killing everyone in them. However, all of the livestock was taken and carried off by the warriors. (Deuteronomy 2:24-36) Jahaz was located in the hill country east of the northern part of the Dead Sea (Sea of Arabah) and SSE of the main city of Heshbon. (See the map on the next page.)

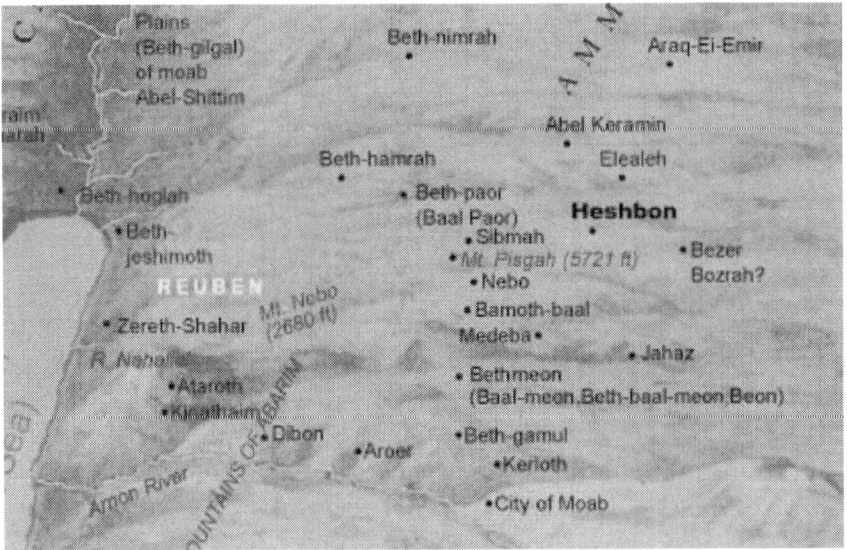

After the Israelite army decimated the army and the people of the land of Heshbon, they continued north toward the land of Bashan. Scripture does not indicate that there were any exchanges between Moses and Og, the king of Bashan. Instead, Og and his entire army confronted the Israelites at Edrei. (See map below.) God told the Israelites not to fear Og, the last of the Rephaites (giants) or his army. God would deliver them into the hands of the Israelites, just as He had done with the people of Heshbon. And, God was true to His word. The entire army of Bashan was destroyed. There were no survivors. The Israelites then attacked all sixty cities in the kingdom and they did to the cities and the people in the cities as they had done to Heshbon. The livestock and items of value were carried off as plunder. (Deuteronomy 3:1-11)

It is of interest and Edrei is no where near the Jordan River. It is located east of the southern end of the Sea of Chinnereth/Kinnereth (Sea of Galilee). (See **Edrei** in the lower right of the map on the next page.) It appears that the

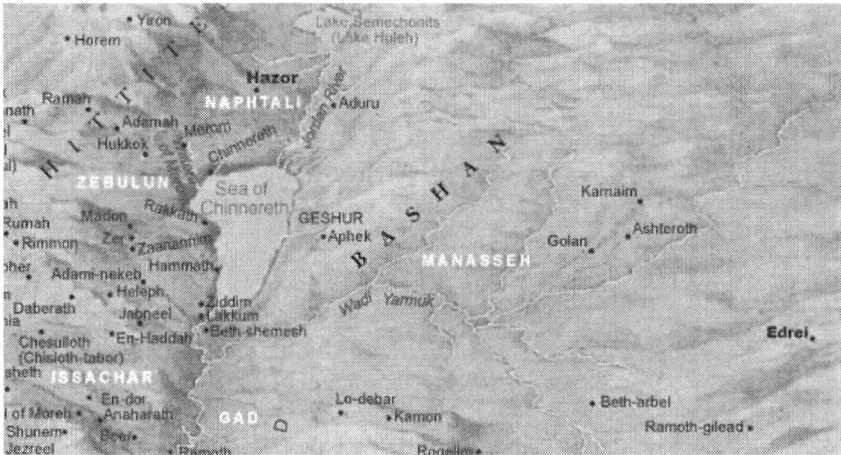

Israelites were not interested in just crossing the Jordan River, they were interested in conquest. Of course, there was a good reason for attacking and destroying the military capability of Bashan. The ultimate plan was the conquest of all of Canaan. This meant that Bashan would be to the east of the Jordan River as the Israelites moved north after crossing the Jordan River. Since the people of Bashan were ethnically related to the people west of the Jordan River, there is a good likelihood they would have responded to any plea from their kinsmen west of the Jordan River. Therefore, it was a good idea to knock Bashan out of the equation from the start. In addition, this area proved to have land that was suited to livestock grazing.

k. Land East of the Jordan Distributed

While the Israelites were still east of the Jordan River, leaders of the tribes of Gad and Reuben approached Moses, Eleazar, and the entire Israelite community with a proposition. Because these tribes had large herds and flocks, they ask to be given the land east of the Jordan River as their inheritance. They argued that the lands of Jazer and Gilead would be suitable for their livestock. They asked

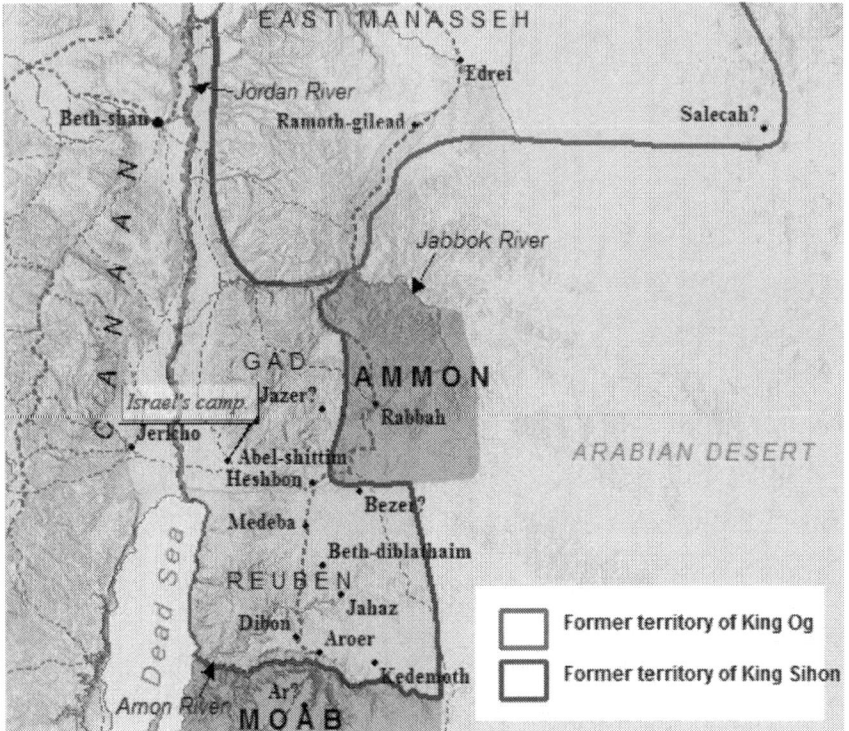

not to be forced to cross the Jordan River into Canaan. Moses immediately foresaw a problem with the plan proposed by the Gadites and the Reubenites. First, if the Gadites and the Reubenites were allowed to stay on the east side of the Jordan River, then there would be no incentive for the warriors of those two tribes to cross the river to fight along side the other ten tribes. Second, the mere fact that the Gadites and the Reubenites wanted to abandon the other ten tribes would have the effect of discouraging the other ten tribes from even wanting to go into Canaan. Moses pointed out that this would have the same impact that the spies had on the Israelite community 40 years before, which resulted in only Caleb and Joshua being left from the original Exodus community. To emphasize his point, Moses called the Gadites and the Reubenites "a brood of sinners." (Numbers 32:1-15)

The Gadites and Reubenites, sensing their proposal had not been received in a positive light, came up with an idea that met both their desires and the needs of the entire community. These were the terms of their proposal: (1) we will build pens for our livestock and fortified cities for our women and children; (2) we will arm ourselves for battle; (3) we will be at the forefront of the battle until the land of Canaan is secured; (4) we will not return home until all the other tribes receive their inheritance; and, (5) we will not ask for any inheritance west of the Jordan River. (Numbers 32:16-19)

Moses accepted the offer of the Gadites and Reubenites. He then gave orders to Eleazar and Joshua that reflected the substance of the agreement. (Numbers 32:20-30) Moses repeated thereafter the promise that the Gadites and the Reubenites made about fighting west of the Jordan River before they returned to their inheritance on the east side. (Deuteronomy 3:12-20)

Later, the tribe of Manasseh also received part of its inheritance in the land east of the Jordan River. (Numbers 34:13-15 and Deuteronomy 3:13-15)

I. God Gave Joshua Added Authority

After God told Moses the boundaries of the land he had promised to the Israelites, Moses told the Israelites that the land west of the Jordan River would be assigned by lots to the inheriting tribes (all but Reuben and Gad). God also told Moses that Eleazar and Joshua would be the ones who would assign the land to each of the tribes. God then told

Moses to appoint one person from each of the ten tribes (with Manasseh to be counted as a half tribe) who would receive land west of the Jordan River. These leaders would be responsible for allotting specific plots to specific persons within each tribe. Caleb was chosen to represent the tribe of Judah. (Numbers 34:1-29)

m. Told Moses to Commission Joshua

Moses was told by God that Moses should go to the top of Pisgah and look in each direction of the compass. Moses would then see the land that the Israelites would possess but he would not touch with his own feet. God then told Moses to commission Joshua, encourage him, and strengthen him, as Joshua would be the one to lead the Israelites across the Jordan River and be the force that would cause the Israelites to inherit the land that Moses would see. (Deuteronomy 3:27-29)

Earlier, Moses commanded Joshua to remember that the Israelites had defeated in battle Sihon, the king of the Amorites, and Og, the king of Bashan. The Lord had delivered both of these kings and their armies into the hands of the Israelites and were destroyed by them. Their fortified cities were destroyed and all the people in them were killed. Moses told Joshua that what God had done to these kings he would do with the kingdoms across the Jordan River. He told Joshua not to be afraid of anyone in the land of Canaan as God himself would fight for Joshua. (Deuteronomy 3:21-22)

n. Moses Encouraged Joshua

After Moses gave the Israelites the law as given to him by God, he assembled them one last time. He told the people that he was 120 years old and he would not be crossing the Jordan River with them. However, God would be there with them and God will destroy all the nations that oppose them, just as he did to Sihon and Og. They would then take possession of the land. Once God had delivered the people into the hands of the Israelites, they must do to the Canaanites as Moses had commanded and Joshua will lead the Israelites as God ordained. Then Moses delivered an impassioned plea: "Be strong and courageous. Do not be afraid or terrified because of them, for the Lord your God goes with you; he will never leave you nor forsake you." (Deuteronomy 31:1-6)

Moses then had Joshua stand before the entire assembly of Israelites. He said, "Be strong and courageous, for you must go with this people into the land that the Lord swore to their ancestors to give them, and you must divide it among them as their inheritance. The Lord himself goes before you and will be with you; he will never leave you nor forsake you. Do not be afraid; do not be discouraged." (Deuteronomy 31:7-8)

Thereafter, God had Moses bring Joshua to the "tent of meeting" so God could personally commission Joshua. God then appeared in a pillar of cloud and, after telling Moses about the spiritual dangers that lie ahead for the Israelites that will cause them to forsake God, He gave this command to Joshua, *"Be strong and courageous, for you will bring the Israelites into the land I promised them on oath, and I myself will be with you."* (emphasis added) (Deuteronomy 31:14-23)

Moses, with Joshua present by his side, then read to the Israelites a song that God had given to Moses. When Moses was finished, he told those assembled, *"Take to heart all the words I have solemnly declared to you this day, so that you may command your children to obey carefully all the words of this law. They are not just idle words for you—they are your life. By them you will live long in the land you are crossing the Jordan to possess.*" (emphasis added) (Deuteronomy 32:44-47)

o. Who Were the Canaanites?

At Genesis 10:15-17, it was pointed out that Canaan was the father of the Hittites, Jebusites, Amorites, Gergashites, and the Hivites. Therefore, it appears that the word Canaanites is a general term that refers to all of the descendants of Canaan, including those not specifically mentioned. Interestingly, the Perizzites are not mentioned as descendants of Canaan. However, they are mentioned in Genesis 15:20 as people who inhabited a portion of the land God gave to Abraham and his descendants. According to Easton's Bible Dictionary, the Perizzites were villagers or dwellers in the open country who lived in the fertile regions south and southwest of Carmel. The people given this name may not be a specific ethnic group, clan, or separate people. The name may have been given to any group of people who lived in the countryside, as opposed to the city. According to the Eerdmans Dictionary of the Bible, the name may be related to a Hebrew term meaning "rural person." Another suggestion is that these were people who occupied portions of the Promised Land even before the Canaanites (descendants of Canaan) arrived.

p. How Big Was Canaan?

Every Christian knows that the Land of Canaan was conquered by the Israelites, who were led by Joshua while powered and empowered by God. That area looms big in

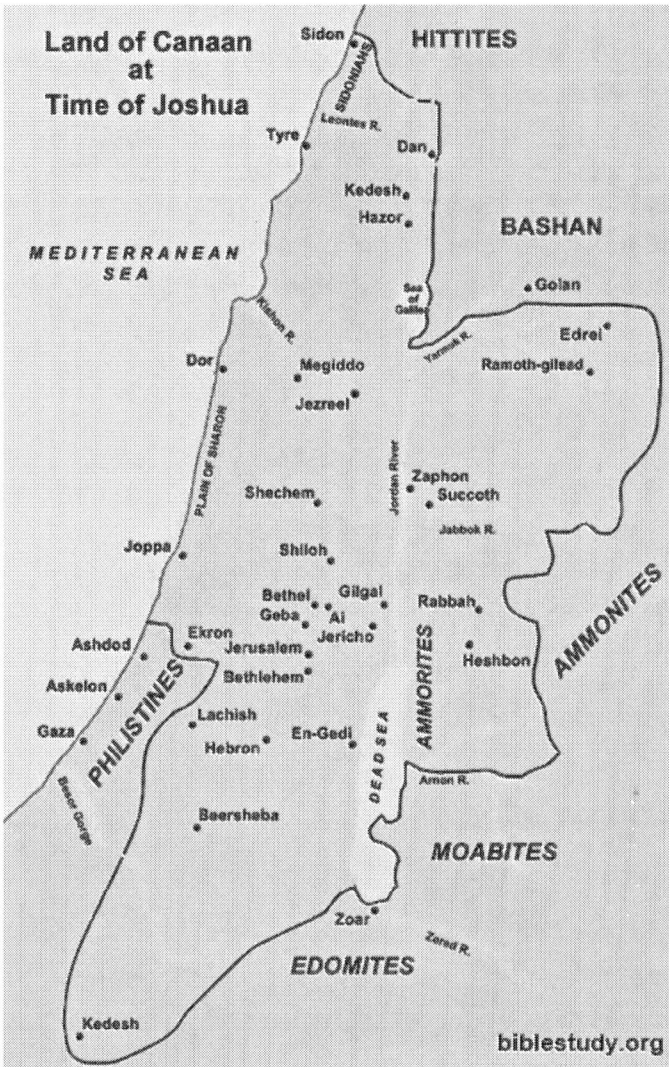

Land of Canaan at Time of Joshua

Sidon — HITTITES

SIDONIANS
Leontes R.
Tyre
Dan
Kedesh
Hazor
BASHAN

MEDITERRANEAN SEA

Kishon R.
Sea of Galilee
Golan
Edrei
Dor
Megiddo
Ramoth-gilead
Jezreel
Yarmuk R.

PLAIN OF SHARON

Shechem
Jordan River
Zaphon
Succoth
Jabbok R.

Joppa
Shiloh

Bethel Gilgal
Geba Ai
Ekron
Rabbah
AMMONITES
Ashdod
Jerusalem Jericho
Askelon
Bethlehem
Heshbon
PHILISTINES
AMMORITES
Gaza
Lachish
Hebron En-Gedi
DEAD SEA

Besor Gorge
Beersheba
Arnon R.

MOABITES

Zoar
Zered R.

EDOMITES

Kedesh

biblestudy.org

the eyes of every Christian because it was eventually ruled by David and from the line of David was born our Savior and Lord, Jesus Christ. If asked, most Christians would have no idea how big the Land of Canaan was at the time of its conquest by Joshua and the Israelites. Most Christians would be shocked to find out how small it was.

93

The Land of Canaan, from Mount Herman to the Negev
(north to south) and from the Jordan River to the the
Mediterranean Sea (east to west), was only 6,600 square
miles in size. For comparison, it is about the combined size
and shape of the California counties of Sutter, Sacramento,
San Joaquin, Stanislaus, and Merced Counties, which have
a combined area of 6,423 square miles.

There are four California counties that are bigger than the area of the Land of Canaan that Joshua conquered. They are San Bernardino (20,057 square miles), Inyo (10,181 square miles), Kern (8,132 square miles), and Riverside (7,206 square miles). The total square mileage of California is 163,707, which is 23.6 times the square mileage of the Promised Land. All of these statistics are not meant to diminish what Joshua and the Israelites accomplished. They are meant to give the reader a geographical perspective that goes beyond the religious perspective that Christians have.

Of course, Joshua and the Israelites, despite the effort they did make, were not able to fulfill the goal that God had for them. It took the reigns of David and Solomon to finally conquer all the lands that God had promised to Abraham, Isaac, and Jacob. David expanded his kingdom to 12,000 square miles and Solomon pushed it to its greatest extent at 60,000 square miles. Unfortunately, as the Bible tells us, that expansion did not last long. Solomon's son caused the division of the land into Israel (the northern tribes) and Judah (the southern tribes) and everything was lost by 586 BC, when the southern kingdom was dragged into exile.

See this website for an interesting article on the geography of the Promised Land: **http://www.gospelgazette.com/ library/pdf%20books/biblegeographyyouthseries.pdf**

q. God's Preparation for the Invasion

1. Have Courage

God encouraged the Israelites in this way: "When you go to war against your enemies and see horses and chariots and an army greater than yours, do not be afraid of them, because the Lord your God, who brought you up out of Egypt, will be with you. When you are about to go into battle, the priest shall come forward and address the army. He shall say: 'Hear, Israel: Today you are going into battle against your enemies. Do not be fainthearted or afraid; do not panic or be terrified by them. For the Lord your God is the one who goes with you to fight for you against your enemies to give you victory.'" (Deuteronomy 20:1-4)

2. How to Treat the Canaanites

(a) Destroy the People and Idols

God made it perfectly clear to the Israelites that they were to completely destroy all the people in Canaan and their entire culture. The Israelites were to leave absolutely nothing in Canaan that would lead them astray spiritually once the territory was conquered. God left no question as to what should happen during the conquest of Canaan. He told Moses early and he told Moses late. It is all recorded in the Book of Deuteronomy.

God gave Moses specific instructions regarding the invasion of the Canaan. God said: "**When the Lord your God brings you into the land you are entering to possess and drives out before you many nations—the Hittites, Girgashites, Amorites, Canaanites, Perizzites, Hivites and Jebusites, seven nations larger and stronger than you— and when the Lord your God has delivered them over to you and you have defeated them, then <u>you must destroy them totally</u>. Make no treaty with them, and show them no mercy. Do not intermarry with them. Do not give your daughters to their sons or take their daughters for your sons, for they will turn your children away from**

96

following me to serve other gods, and the Lord's anger will burn against you and will quickly destroy you. This is what you are to do to them: Break down their altars, smash their sacred stones, cut down their Asherah poles and burn their idols in the fire. For you are a people holy to the Lord your God. The Lord your God has chosen you out of all the peoples on the face of the earth to be his people, his treasured possession." (emphasis added) (Deuteronomy 7:1-6)

(b) Destroy Any Evidence of Worship

God was so concerned about the spiritual condition of the Canaanites and the physical evidence of a decadent spiritual life that God ordered that everything about that witnessed to that decadence should be destroyed completely. He commanded: "*These are the decrees and laws you must be careful to follow in the land that the Lord, the God of your ancestors, has given you to possess—as long as you live in the land. Destroy completely all the places on the high mountains, on the hills and under every spreading tree, where the nations you are dispossessing worship their gods. Break down their altars, smash their sacred stones and burn their Asherah poles in the fire; cut down the idols of their gods and wipe out their names from those places.*" (emphasis added) (Deuteronomy 12:1-3)

(c) Warnings and Commands by God

God again warned the Israelites about being caught up in the spiritual weakness of the people who then lived on the land. Here is what God said to the Israelites: "*The Lord your God will cut off before you the nations you are* *about to invade and dispossess. But when you have driven them out and settled in their land, and <u>after they have been destroyed before you</u>, be careful not to be ensnared by inquiring about their gods, saying, 'How do these nations serve their gods? We will do the same.' You must not worship the Lord your God in their way, because in worshiping their gods, they do all kinds of detestable things the Lord hates. They even burn their sons and daughters in the fire as sacrifices to their gods."* (emphasis added) (Deuteronomy 12:29-31)

God repeated his commands yet again: "***<u>However, in the cities of the nations the Lord your God is giving you as an inheritance, do not leave alive anything that breathes</u>. Completely destroy [totally devote to the Lord] them—the Hittites, Amorites, Canaanites, Perizzites, Hivites and Jebusites—as the Lord your God has commanded you. Otherwise, they will teach you to follow all the detestable things they do in worshiping their gods, and you will sin against the Lord your God***." (emphasis added) (Deuteronomy 20:16-18)

God repeated much of His commandments:
On the plains of Moab by the Jordan across from Jericho the Lord said to Moses, "Speak to the Israelites and say to them: '**<u>When you cross the Jordan into Canaan, drive out all the inhabitants of the land before you</u>. Destroy all their carved images and their cast idols, and demolish all their high places. Take possession of the land and settle in it, for I have given you the land to possess. Distribute the land by lot, according to your clans. To a larger group give a larger inheritance, and to a smaller group a smaller one. Whatever falls to them by lot will be**

theirs. Distribute it according to your ancestral tribes." (emphasis added) (Numbers 33:50-54)

(d) People outside of Canaan

God gave the Israelites further instructions as to how to treat the people they would encounter outside the Promised Land: "*When you march up to attack a city, make its people an offer of peace. If they accept and open their gates, all the people in it shall be subject to forced labor and shall work for you. If they refuse to make peace and they engage you in battle, lay siege to that city. When the Lord your God delivers it into your hand, put to the sword all the men in it. As for the women, the children, the livestock and everything else in the city, you may take these as plunder for yourselves. And you may use the plunder the Lord your God gives you from your enemies. This is how you are to treat all the cities that are at a distance from you and do not belong to the nations nearby*." (emphasis added) (Deuteronomy 20:10-15)

r. Moses Died

After Moses pronounced a blessing on each of the 12 tribes (see Deuteronomy 33), Moses climbed Mount Nebo to the top of Pisgah, which is 5721 feet above sea level. God showed him the land that he promised "on oath" to Abraham, Isaac, and Jacob. God said he would give it to Moses' descendants. Moses then died at the age of 120 years, even though he was still strong and did not have weak eyes. It was now time for Joshua to step forward and attempt to guide his people as Moses had done for 40 years. Joshua was filled with the "spirit of wisdom" because Moses had laid his hands on him. (Deuteronomy 34:1-9a)

The people now listened to Joshua as their leader. (Deuteronomy 34:9b)

JOSHUA

CHAPTER ONE

a. Leadership Change

The Israelites were now primed and ready to enter the Promised Land. Moses and every adult male who crossed through the Red Sea 40 years earlier were dead, except for Joshua and Caleb. This was not the same people who had escaped from Egypt and who wandered through the deserts of Sinai and Zin as a punishment for their distrust of God. These people no longer had the mentality of slaves. They no longer grumbled to Moses about how life was so much greater in Egypt than it was in the deserts, wandering from place to place. They were no longer a people who had lived in a land with a multitude of gods. They had lived under one true God and he had brought them through every circumstance they encountered when they trusted in him. In short, they were a people steeled, physically and mentally, for the job that lay ahead of them.

They only negative that could possibly impact their success in capturing the Promised Land was the death of the man whom God had chosen to lead them from the time of the Exodus right up to where they were now camped in the plains of Moab. Moses had died on Mount Nebo and was buried "in Moab, in the valley opposite Beth Peor." (Deuteronomy 34:1-6) Moses was given the title "servant of the Lord" because of his status before God. He was the man whom God had personally called to lead his people out of Egypt. He was the great interceder for a people God wanted to destroy on numerous occasions. Through Moses, God had performed miracles for the Israelites. He was the man to whom God had given the Law. He was the man who lead his people to the doorstep of the promised

Canaan Land. He was revered by this new generation of Israelites and they had followed him without question. He was now gone and who would or could replace an irreplaceable leader of such stature?

The short answer is "no one." The postscript to Deuteronomy made that point abundantly clear. The author wrote: "Since then, no prophet has risen in Israel like Moses, whom the Lord knew face to face, who did all those signs and wonders the Lord sent him to do in Egypt—to Pharaoh and to all his officials and to his whole land. For no one has ever shown the mighty power or performed the awesome deeds that Moses did in the sight of all Israel." (Deuteronomy 34:10-12) However, someone had to be called by God to lead the Israelites into the land God promised to the descendants of Abraham, Isaac, and Jacob and that man was Joshua. The same author who summarized Moses' meaning to God and to God's people also gave us a glimpse of the man who would provide leadership for the Israelites for the next 25 years. He wrote: "Now Joshua son of Nun was filled with the spirit (or Spirit) of wisdom because Moses had laid his hands on him. So the Israelites listened to him and did what the Lord had commanded Moses." (Deuteronomy 34:9)

b. The Preparation Began

The Israelites grieved over the death of Moses for 30 days while they were on the plains of Moab. The length and depth ("weeping and mourning") of the grieving showed the enormous respect God's people had for their fallen leader. (Deuteronomy 34:8) These people had grown up under Moses and they would revere him for the rest of their lives. However, at the end of the weeping and mourning for their leader of the past, the Israelites now had to prepare to follow a leader of their future, a man whom God had chosen and whom Moses had taken under his wing.

Joshua was first introduced in scripture as a military leader in the battle against the Amalekites. Soon thereafter, Joshua became a trusted aide to Moses. He was one of the 12 spies chosen to go into Canaan to gather intelligence for Moses. He and Caleb were the only two of the 12 spies to honor God by championing for an invasion of the land God promised them. He went up Mt. Sinai with Moses and stood watch while Moses climbed further up the mountain and had a personal encounter with God. Joshua was with Moses whenever Moses went to the "tent of meeting" to speak with God or to conduct God's business. And, it was Moses who personally brought Joshua before the entire assembly of Israelites and told them that Joshua would lead them into the land promised to them by God and Joshua would divide the land amongst them as their inheritance. Joshua had the intelligence, the training, the experience, the will, and the right relationship with God to lead God's people. However, at the apex of his credentials was this supreme fact: God had personally selected Joshua from all the men amongst the Israelites to carry out His will. All Joshua needed at this point was to follow God's command to be "strong and courageous." (Deuteronomy 31:23)

Following Moses' death, God again spoke to Joshua, who was identified both as the son of Nun and as Moses' aide. In this way, there was no mistake as to whom God had chosen to lead His people. (Joshua 1:1) In addition, God made it imminently clear that Joshua was the leader chosen by God. He commanded Joshua to get ready to cross the Jordan River into the land he had given to the Israelites. (Joshua 1:2) God understood that the task awaiting His people was a formidable one and God needed a fearless leader to bring the conquest to a successful conclusion.

Joshua could not falter at any step. God told Joshua: "Be strong and courageous, because you will lead these people to inherit the land I swore to their ancestors to give them." (Joshua 1:6) To make sure Joshua understood completely what state of mind was necessary to carry out God's will, God told Joshua two more times to "be strong and courageous." (Joshua 1:7, 9a) God even expressed the state of mind in the negative: "Do not be afraid; do not be discouraged." (Joshua 1:9b)

God then told Joshua what he needed to do to be strong and courageous. **First**, Joshua had to understand to his fullest that God would be with Joshua as He had been with Moses and it did not matter where Joshua was or what he as doing. (Joshua 1:5, 9b) **Second**, God would give to Joshua every piece of land where Joshua set his foot. (Joshua 1:3) **Third**, no one would be able to stand against Joshua in any situation because of God. (Joshua 1:5a) **Fourth**, Joshua had to know in the deepest recesses of his heart that God would never leave or forsake him. (Joshua 1:5) **Fifth**, Joshua had to be careful to obey every bit of the law that God had given to Moses. Joshua could not, under any circumstance, depart from the road that the law mapped out. The law had always to be on Joshua's lips, he must mediate on it constantly, and he had no option but to obey the law in everything he did. In other words, the law must be the master of what he thought, said, and did. If Joshua obeyed the law in every aspect of his life, then Joshua would be prosperous and successful. (Joshua 1: 7-9)

Once God made sure that Joshua knew that the ultimate success of the upcoming invasion depended upon God and Joshua's obedience to God and to the law, Joshua gathered his officers together and gave them instructions consistent with God's command to cross the Jordan River. Joshua told them to go through the camp and tell the people to get provisions ready, as in three days they would be crossing the Jordan River to take possession of the land God had given to them. (Joshua 1:10-11) One can only imagine the emotions those words must have stirred in each and every Israelite. In soldiers, those words likely brought up visions of hand-to-hand combat with enemy forces and images of the enemy's strength, training, battle experience, leadership, and tactics. The soldiers were battle-hardened, having defeated the Midianites and the Amorite kings Sihon and Og. Each warrior had a job to do and each probably thought about their place in the upcoming battles. The spearmen, the archers, the swordsmen, and the horsemen knew their roles and they knew how they would fit into the strategy and tactics of Joshua and the military officers, from the commanders of thousands, hundreds, and tens. Those not thrust into the heat of the battle would stay behind to guard the women, children, and older men against a sudden attack from any quarter. Despite the confidence of the warriors, no doubt there was a certain amount of apprehension amongst the women, children, and older men as they were to forced to leave an area that had been subdued and was at peace to go into a land that was occupied by a people who would resist the Israelites at every step.

c. Council of War Held

While the camp prepared to cross the Jordan River in three days, Joshua held a council of war. The first order of business was to remind the tribes of Reuben and Gad and the half-tribe of Manasseh about the agreement that they had made with Moses. He told them that their women, children, and livestock could stay on the east side of the

Jordan River. However, all of their "fighting men," ready for battle, were to go ahead of the rest of the Israelites as they crossed the Jordan River into Canaan and they would keep fighting until the land was in possession of the other tribes and half-tribe. (Joshua 1:12-15) Even though they were not mentioned, it should be obvious that the older men and the younger men not a part of the "fighting men" would remain on the east side of the Jordan River. It would be ridiculous to leave the women, children, and livestock defenseless.

The representatives of the tribes of Reuben and Gad and the half-tribe of Manasseh had absolutely no disagreement with what Joshua ordered. They agreed to do whatever Joshua commanded and to go wherever Joshua commanded them to go. They pledged the same obedience to Joshua as they did to Moses. They even went further with their pledge. They said that whoever disobeys any command given by Joshua, no matter what it is, that person would be put to death. If Joshua had any doubts about the loyalty of these tribes and half-tribe to the rest of the Israelites, this council certainly put his mind at ease. They not only were willing to fight for the other tribes, they were willing to be at the forefront of any battle. They ask only two things in return. One depended upon God and the other depended upon Joshua. They asked this of God: "Only may the Lord your God be with you as he was with Moses." They asked this of Joshua: "Only be strong and courageous!" (Joshua 1:12-18)

The repeated admonition to Joshua to be strong and courageous can be seen in at least two ways. **One**, Joshua had not yet had the opportunity to show the qualities of leadership that Moses had portrayed in his 40 years of leading the Israelites. Therefore, his subordinates were concerned as to how Joshua would stand up to the stress of leading the Israelites into Canaan. If this was the concern of the officers, then it would have been natural. These officers had witnessed Moses in action on many occasions and his leadership qualities were second to none and his decision-making was decisive. They had possessed confidence that whatever Moses chose to do that it would turn out to be the right thing to do. Unlike their fathers before them, they had unquestionable loyalty to the great man of God. They wanted nothing more than to trust Joshua also, but Joshua needed to earn that trust, both outwardly and inwardly. **Two**, the repeated admonition to Joshua may just have been an idiomatic expression used by Israelites whenever a new person assumed an unfamiliar role of leadership, wherever that role was in the chain of command. In the circumstance where Joshua found himself, the repeated admonition may have been a combination of both ideas. Inferiors in the chain of command may outwardly give the appearance of trusting a commander, but, when the situation becomes a matter of life and death, the trust must also be felt in the innermost being of the soldier in the field. Without the outward and inward trust, then the battlefield could soon turn into chaos, retreat, and, ultimately, defeat. Joshua still had much to prove.

CHAPTER TWO

a. Reconnoitering

Like Moses before him, Joshua wanted information about the land on the immediate west side of the Jordan River. Therefore, Joshua chose spies to "look over the land... especially Jericho." (Joshua 2:1) However, instead of sending out 12 men, like Moses did, Joshua only sent out two men. Why two men? The quick answer is that Joshua only sent out two men because of history. Moses sent out 12 men and only two men had a report that encouraged the invasion of Canaan from the south 40 years earlier. Joshua did not want to repeat what happened to Moses. He did not want any dissension created on the eve of the entry into Canaan from the east.

Also, to Joshua, two men would have been symbolic of Caleb and himself, the only two spies who gave a favorable recommendation to invade. There may have been another reason. Joshua could have just sent one spy, but he chose two. One spy could enter more stealthily and might attract less attention than two men. Why did Joshua then choose two? Because Joshua wanted four eyes on the area near Jericho instead of just two eyes. One spy may see something significant that the other spy might miss. Also, if one spy was captured, then the other spy might have a chance of escaping and returning to Joshua with at least some information.

The Biblical narrative indicates that the two spies were sent out "secretly" from Shittim. (Joshua 2:1) The narrative does not make it completely clear as to what "secretly" meant, especially in light of what occurred shortly thereafter when the two men were immediately identified by the king's men

109

as spies. It is altogether possible that Joshua sent out the two men without telling anyone else in the command structure. Joshua had good reasons for sending the spies without discussing it with others. **One**, he did not want any dissent from what he planned to do. **Two**, he did not want any discussion as to how many spies should be sent across the Jordan River into Canaan. **Three**, he did not want any criticism of what he had done in case the spies did not return at all or returned with scanty and useless information. **Four**, he did not want anyone in the camp to know what he was doing for fear there were spies within his own camp who would betray his plan.

If the term "secretly" meant the people of Jericho would not know the spies were Israelites sent from Shittim, then the plan did not work at all. After the spies left Shittim by some unknown means and by some undisclosed route, they entered the gates of Jericho and went straight to the home of a prostitute by the name of Rahab. (Joshua 2:1) The scripture also relates that the king of Jericho knew immediately that the two men were spies and where they went. (Joshua 2:2)

It should be obvious that the king was not a stupid man. He and everyone around him knew about the Israelites who were camped just on the other side of the Jordan River and he and everyone else knew that the only thing between the invading Israelites and the end of everything they held near and dear was the swollen Jordan River. There is no doubt that the king had his own spies everywhere to detect anyone coming from the Israelite camp. Even if the spies used some mis-direction to throw off any suspicion while they approached Jericho, it became obvious to the king's men who the Israelites were once they entered the city. What gave the spies away? It could have been the clothes they were wearing. It could have been their facial features. It could have been the fashion of their hair or beards. It could have been the language they spoke or it could have been their accent if they attempted to speak the language of the people of Jericho. Maybe the answers they gave to questions asked of them at the city gate tipped off the king's men. Or, it may have been when the spies asked for directions to the home of the nearest prostitute. Sometimes it is subtle things that give away a spy.

A movie about World War II called "Charlotte Gray" had a scene where a British spy cut his meat with a knife held in his right hand while holding down the meat with a fork held in his left hand. When he was through cutting off a piece of the meat, he laid down the knife and moved the fork from his left hand to his right hand. Unfortunately, the British spy was eating in a restaurant in German-occupied France. The innocuous social custom of the British caught the eye of a German SS officer sitting nearby. In France and Germany and in other places on the mainland of Europe, a person would cut with the knife in the right hand and then eat the piece of meat with the fork held in the left hand. This scene showed how even the most attentive spy can be tripped up by one small detail. In the next scene, the British spy's body was being dumped somewhere on the outskirts of town.

b. Why Send Spies?

At this point, the question that jumps immediately to mind is this: why did Joshua send out spies at all? The question has to be asked because (1) scripture does not indicate that God told Joshua to do it and (2) God had already told Joshua that he and the rest of the Israelites would be crossing the Jordan River in three days. It would almost seem as if sending out the spies was totally unnecessary

111

and unwarranted and it might even suggest that Joshua did not have the full faith in God he should have had at this time. However, there is one answer that makes the decision a good one. No commander-in-chief ever wants to lead his troops into unchartered territory. Joshua did not know at this point what God had in store for Jericho. Joshua needed intelligence about the people of Jericho to prepare for any eventuality, including a surprise attack from the king of Jericho while the Israelites were crossing into Canaan. Even though Joshua would follow God's commands completely, he would still want answers when subordinates pressed him for the reasons for his decisions. The spies could possibly supply him with the information he needed.

Joshua did send out the spies and result was significant to the history of Israel. What followed thereafter in the narrative was the introduction of one of the major female characters in the Bible. The female was the prostitute Rahab. It was Rahab who survived the destruction of Jericho because of her developing faith in the God of the Israelites and that faith also saved the lives of the spies and her family. She later married Salmon and became the mother of Boaz. It was Boaz who married Ruth and Obed was their child. Obed was a direct ancestor of Jesse and Jesse was the father of the giant killer who later became King David. (Matthew 1:5-6) Now, the reader knows how important Rahab was and why God may have prompted Joshua to send out the spies, even though the command is not related in the Biblical text.

c. Rahab Is Clever

As mentioned earlier, the king of Jericho was immediately told that the Israelite spies had gone to the home of Rahab, a prostitute, and had not left. Interestingly, the king sent a message to Rahab instead of dispatching a troop of men to break down her door, invade her home, and drag out the spies. The message sent to her was in such polite language that the only thing missing was the word "please." The note asked her to bring out the men who came into her home because they were spies. (Joshua 2:3) It appears that the answer to two questions may be the same. Question one: "Why did the spies go to the place owned by a prostitute?" Question two: "Why did the king send a polite note to a prostitute?" The answer to both questions is probably this: "Because Rahab knew too much!" In any society that is degenerate in nature, prostitutes are used by men on a regular basis, whether the men are married or not and whether the men are poor, middle class, or wealthy. It is to such women that men tell things that they do not tell their wives. The more the prostitute is sought after, the wealthier the clientele. The wealthier the clientele, the greater the chance such a client is going to be close to the king or have the king's ear. Such people then brag about how close to the king they are, how much the king depends upon them, and how much the king has told them. All of this goes into the ears of the most sought-after of the prostitutes. No doubt, all of this was known to Joshua and his officers and the spies had direct orders to seek out Rahab to find out as much as she knew. And, the fact that she was willing to risk hiding the spies seems to indicate that she may have told them all that she knew and she did not want them taken to the king and tortured to find out what the spies had learned.

Rahab answered the king's request with subterfuge, or, as some would call it, a bald-faced lie. Whether she sent a return message to the king or spoke directly to the king's messenger, the scripture does not detail. However, her message was clear. Despite the fact that the two spies were hiding on her roof under stalks of flax, she told the king that the two men had left at dusk, just before the closing of the city gate. Of course, Rahab knew the men guarding the gate would have left their posts and would not be available to determine the truth of Rahab's statement. At the beginning of spring, dusk would be between 6 pm and 6:30 pm. The tenor of Rahab's answer to the king would suggest that it was already dark when the king sent his message to Rahab.

Despite the hour, the king's men set out immediately to catch up with the spies. They took the road that led directly to where the Jordan River could be crossed, believing the spies would take the most direct route back to the Israelite camp. The gate was then shut behind them. (Joshua 2:4-7) This last detail is interesting. The shutting of the gate would accomplish three things: (1) preventing the spies, if they were still in Jericho, from getting out; (2) preventing the spies, if they had left Jericho, from getting back in and escaping apprehension; and, (3) preventing any enemy from using the open gate as a means to attack the city under cover of darkness. Likely, the king's men were concerned mostly about reasons one and two.

Now it was time for Rahab to trade favor for favor. She had saved the lives of the two spies and now she wanted guarantees in return. However, she prefaced her request with what she knew about the Israelites and their God. The list reflected a knowledge of the history of the Israelites from the time God dried up the water of the Red Sea to the time the Israelites completely defeated Sihon and Og, the two kings of the Amorites. She knew that God had given "this land" to the Israelites and, because of that, everyone was in anguish over it. She expressed the feeling as "great fear," "melting in fear," "hearts melted in fear," and "courage failed." She said everything was true because "the Lord your God is God in heaven above and on the earth below." She then got to her main point. She wanted the two spies, who were in no position to argue, to swear by the Lord that they would show the same concern for her and her family as she had shown for them. She wanted a "sure sign" that they would spare the lives of her mother and father, her sisters and brothers, and all of their family members and "save us from death." (Joshua 2:8-13)

Knowing that she had saved them from death and, possibly even torture before the death, the two spies readily agreed to her terms. Of course, they spelled it out even more clearly when they included further terms. They wanted Rahab not to tell anyone what they were doing then and, by implication, what they would be doing once they left Jericho. But, the spies were not through. They did not want the blood of Rahab or any of her relatives on her hands. Therefore, they said that their oath would not be binding unless Rahab did two things at the time Jericho was attacked by the Israelites. She had to bring every person she wanted to save into her house and she had to tie a scarlet cord in the window of her home. Rahab agreed to their terms. She told the spies, once they were out of Jericho, to hide themselves in the hills for three days and, once their pursuers had returned to Jericho, then go on their way. Rahab then lowered the two spies down by a rope in a window in the outer wall of Jericho. Scripture seems to suggest that Rahab tied a scarlet cord in her window right after the spies departed. However, it is also reasonable that she waited until after the Israelites crossed over the Jordan River in Canaan. (Joshua 2:13-22)

Why a scarlet cord in the window? People might say that a scarlet cord could be seen easily at a distance, but there may have been another reason. It is interesting that the word "blood" was brought up twice in the same conversation as when the scarlet cord was mentioned. In Exodus 12:1-13, God told the Israelites to take a lamb, slaughter it at twilight on the 14th day of the month, and then take some of the blood and put it on the sides and tops of the door frames of the houses where they were to eat the lambs. That same night, the Lord will pass over Egypt and strike down the first born of all people and animals. He will pass over all the houses were the blood has been applied. The Israelites did as God commanded and God then carried out his wrath on the Pharaoh and all the Egyptians and no Israelite was killed. (Exodus 12:29-30) There seems to be a parallel that is being drawn here. Blood is red and scarlet is a bold shade of red. Those who apply the red material (blood or scarlet cord) will be spared by God. Later, Rahab and her family will be saved. But, that is getting ahead of the story.

The spies escape Jericho

116

After they escaped Jericho, the spies did as Rahab instructed them to do. They hid out in the hills for three days. The king's men returned to Jericho without finding the two spies. When it was safe, the two spies went down from the hills, returned to the Jordan River, forded it somehow, and then reported to Joshua everything that had happened to them. They would have returned to Joshua just as the Israelites were preparing to cross the Jordan River. It will be discovered later that the report included their promise to Rahab that she and her family would be spared once Jericho was taken by the Israelites. Joshua was pleased with the account given to him. His summary echoed what Rahab had told the two spies: "The Lord has surely given the whole land into our hands; all the people are melting in fear because of us." (Joshua 2:22-24)

CHAPTER THREE

a. The Journey Begins

Chapter Three of the Book of Joshua basically picks up where Chapter One left off with one minor exception. When Chapter Three is placed into the chronology of events, it appears that Joshua 3:1 occurred before Joshua 1:10-11. In Joshua 3:1, it is recorded that "Early in the morning Joshua and all the Israelites set out from Shittim and went to the Jordan, where they camped [for three days] before crossing over." In Joshua 1:10-11, it is written that Joshua commanded "the officers of the people" to go throughout the camp and order the people to "Get your provisions ready. Three days from now you will cross the Jordan here to go in and take possession of the land the Lord your God is giving you for your own."

Shittim, which means "acacia" or "the acacias," was also called Abel-Shittim (see Numbers 33:49). Shittim was located about five miles east of the Jordan River in the plain of Moab. Shittim was where the Israelites were camped out while awaiting word as to when they would be moving to the area right next to the Jordan River. Once the Israelites left Shittim, they traveled directly west to the Jordan River at a point about five miles north of the Dead Sea.

The stalks of flax on the roof of Rahab's home in Jericho is an interestingly sidelight. One would think that every home in Jericho would be filled with edible plants, rather than plants used to make linen. After all, there was an army of over 600,000 men sitting just across the Jordan River ready to invade and conquer any people in their path and Jericho was in their path. Even though the seeds of the flax plant have commercial value today, it was not so in ancient times, when the flax plant was used only for clothing. It is also strange that a prostitute would have stalks of flax on her roof. Perhaps it was a sideline or maybe it belonged to some member of her family. The stalks of flax gives no indication as to the time of the year as the flax goes through an extended curing process that can take, depending on the circumstances, up to a year before it is usable for clothing. The time of year, however, can be determined by one natural phenomena that was occurring at this time: the Jordan River was at flood stage.

The Jordan River at flood stage

When the Jordan River was at flood stage, it could be up to a mile wide and as deep as 12 feet. The river would have been fed by runoff from months of rain and from the melting snows on Mount Hermon. However, that is not the worst of the problems facing anyone who would want to cross the

119

Jordan River at flood stage. There was an even more serious impediment. This impediment is captured in the name of the river itself. "Jordan" means "descender" and that is what the river does as it flows out of the Sea of Galilee down to the Dead Sea (or Sea of Arabah). The Sea of Galilee is 682 feet below sea level, but the Dead Sea is even lower. It is about 1,400 feet below sea level. This means that the Jordan River drops 620 feet in 70 miles or about one foot every 600 feet. The steep descend means that the Jordan River at flood stage is not only high, it is also swift. Anyone attempting to ford the river while it is at flood stage is in danger of being swept to his or her death into the Dead Sea. Because of the swiftness of the water, most of the bed of the Jordan River is made up of rocks and pebbles instead of layers of mud. Interestingly, where the Israelites planned to cross the Jordan River was about 1,350 feet below sea level and just north of the Dead Sea. God had chosen this moment to have the Israelites ford the Jordan River. Why? Because the Lord wanted to show His people yet another miracle. God parted the Red Sea so the Israelites could escape from Egypt. God would now provide this new generation with yet another miracle so they could see for themselves that it was their God who controlled not only the waters of the Jordan River, but He controlled their destinies as well. As long as they obeyed him by doing what seemed impossible, then they would obey him in doing what was possible.

b. The Crossing Plan

The Israelites had already gotten provisions together for their entry into the land God promised to them. (Joshua 1:10-11) Now, after three days of anticipation and preparation, the officers when through the camp and gave orders to the people. When they saw the ark of the covenant being carried by the priests from the tribe of Levi, they were to file behind the ark and follow it. However, the people were to keep a distance of about "two thousand cubits" (about 3,000 feet) between themselves and the ark. (Joshua 3:2-4). Normally, the tribe of Judah would move out first, followed by the tribe of Issachar and then the tribe of Zebulun. The ark would not be carried out until after the sixth tribe was in motion. Why was the ark to take the lead in the march to the River Jordan? For one, it was what God wanted. But, it was more than that. The ark of the covenant was a symbol of the presence of God. It contained the two stone tables on which God had written the Ten Commandments. It also contained a jar of manna and Aaron's rod. (See Hebrews 9:4) It was sacred and holy to the Israelites. If the tribe of Judah went forward, then any miracle would be attributed to them and that is not what God wanted. God wanted the people of Israel to understand that He was the one who was going to bring about a miracle and it was no one or nothing else.

The day before the people were to cross the river, Joshua told them to consecrate themselves "for tomorrow the Lord will do amazing things among you." (Joshua 3:5) And, the next day, Joshua, believing what God had told him and without knowing what was going to happen, commanded the priests to take up the ark of the covenant and move to a position in front of the other people. (Joshua 3:6)

After the ark was in position, the Lord spoke to Joshua. He said he would begin to exalt Joshua "in the eyes" of the Israelites so God's people would know that He was with Joshua just as He was with Moses. (Joshua 3:7) Joshua was going to be elevated once more in the estimation of the Israelites, a process that began 40 years earlier. God then opened up His playbook for Joshua so His chosen leader could see what was ahead. Certainly what God showed to

Joshua took a lot of faith on Joshua's part to believe what he was hearing was actually going to come about. And, if it failed to happen and the ark of the covenant was swept away and into the Dead Sea, then the blame would fall directly on Joshua's shoulders. Joshua would then not be raised in the eyes of the Israelites, he would likely be stoned to death.

God told Joshua to tell the priests who would be carrying the ark of the covenant that they were not to stop at the edge of the rushing Jordan River, they were to continue and then stand in the river. (Joshua 3:8) Joshua had great faith in God (as did the priests who were carrying the ark). Joshua was an adult when God parted the Red Sea. However, there was one very significant difference between the situation then and the circumstances now. Then, the Israelites were in great danger from the pursuing Egyptians. Then needed help immediately. In addition, no one had to step into the Red Sea before it was parted. And, even if they did, no one would have been swept away by a rapid and unforgiving flow of water. As God spoke to Joshua, no enemy was pursuing them. They were in no danger. Everyone seemed to have enough to eat as they were still being fed a daily ration of manna and it was cozy there in the plains of Moab. Even though God's revealed plan would take an enormous amount of faith to carry out, Joshua believed God would do it. There is no evidence of any negative emotion or action from Joshua. Soon thereafter, Joshua called the Israelites together to hear what God had told him.

Joshua gave the Israelites the plan God had for them after they entered Canaan and the plan God had for them to get there. God would give the Israelites proof that day that He was among them and, by that proof, they would know with absolute certainty that He will drive out all the people who then inhabited Canaan. These people included the Canaanites, the Hittites, the Hivites, the Perizzites, the Girgashites, the Amorites, and the Jebusites. Joshua even told the Israelites what the proof would be. The priests will carry the ark of the covenant before them. The priests will then enter the Jordan River. When they do, "the Lord of all the earth" will cause the swiftly flowing water to be cut off and stood up in a heap. (Joshua 3:7-11, 13) Joshua also added one other command to his revelation. He told each tribe to choose one man each. (Joshua 3:12) Interestingly, Joshua did not tell the people at this time the purpose of choosing the 12 men. It will be revealed later.

There is no doubt that Joshua's words caused an immediate stir amongst the Israelites, from shouts of "hallelujah" to raised eyebrows of skepticism to snorts of derision and every other possible human reaction. Most, if not all, of the Israelites who were camped just east of the Jordan River had been wondering just how they were going to cross a swiftly flowing aka dangerous aka deadly river that would sweep anyone off his or her feet once they stepped into the water from the bank. Some probably thought that maybe God would provide some sort of reliable transportation across the water. Some may have envisioned that God would somehow miraculously take them over the water from one side to the other. And, some may have had such great faith and vision and a knowledge of the past that they believed God would somehow part the Jordan River to allow them to pass through the waters untouched. Those with little faith and less imagination were probably happy that they would be one of the last tribes to have to deal with whatever disaster befell the other tribes. Others probably wondered why God did not wait until a time when the river was narrower and shallower so it could be forded.

c. The Crossing

Whatever was going through the minds of the Israelites, they did not have time to ponder it for very long. After the people had gathered everything that belonged to them, the order was given for everyone, except the tribes of Reuben and Gad and the half-tribe of Manasseh to start moving. The ark of the covenant took the lead position. No doubt there was some apprehension on the part of the priests carrying the ark as they walked toward the river. No matter how much faith they had in God, there had to have been at least some small doubt as to whether or not what they were doing was a good idea. The river was at flood stage and it was moving swiftly. Although it would not be flowing as turbulently as in other spots on the Jordan River, where the speed has been calculated as high as 40 miles per hour at flood stage, water moving as low as seven miles per hour can knock a person off his or her feet in only six inches of water.

There is no indication as to how many Levites carried the ark. Nowhere in the Bible does it spell out how many priests were assigned to carry the ark when it was moved from spot to spot. Based on the instructions given by God when the ark was constructed, it would appear that a minimum of four priests would carry the ark at any one time. The instructions are found at Exodus 25:12-15: "You shall cast four rings of gold for it, and put them in its four corners; two rings shall be on one side, and two rings on the other side. And you shall make poles of acacia wood, and overlay them with gold. You shall put the poles into the rings on the sides of the ark, that the ark may be carried by them. The poles shall be in the rings of the ark; they shall not be taken from it." However, at II Samuel 15:29, only two people are mentioned as having carried the ark. The caveat to the conclusion that the ark of the covenant could be carried by two men is that each of the two men who were mentioned as carrying the ark had a son with him at the time, per II Samuel 15:27. Also, since the ark contained two stone tablets, a jar of manna, and the budded staff of Aaron, it is likely that four men, at a minimum, would be required to carry it comfortably. And, it is likely the ark was too wide to allow only two men to carry it. On another point, the priests who carried the ark may have been descendants of Kothah, one of the three sons of Levi. The relevant scripture can be found at Numbers 4:15: "And when Aaron and his sons have finished covering the sanctuary and all the furnishings of the sanctuary, when the camp is set to go, then the sons of Kohath shall come to carry them; but they shall not touch any holy thing, lest they die. These are the things in the tabernacle of meeting which the sons of Kohath are to carry."

It would appear that four men normally carried the ark and it was probably the case as the ark was taken toward the Jordan River. Anything out of the norm might suggest a lack of confidence in God and might cause turmoil among those lining up behind the ark. In any event, once the feet of the priests in the front touched the water's edge, the water upstream stopped flowing and it began backing up at a town called "Adam in the vicinity of Zarethan." (Joshua 3:14-16) The town of Adam was located on a gorge of the Jordan River, where the river narrows between two high banks. It was about 20 miles north of where the Israelites were crossing the Jordan River. The name probably survives in the location called Tell ed-Damiyeh. With the flow of water cut off, the priests carried the ark into the middle of the river bed and then they stopped. The ground beneath their feet was dry. The priests stayed in the middle of the river bed while the Israelites crossed over to the west side of the river bed. It is in the description of the people crossing over that the word "nation" is used for the first time to describe the Israelites. (Joshua 3:16-17) This appears not to be a casual use of the word. The author of Joshua was clearly making a statement that the Israelites were now "home" and they constituted a united people in the land that God had given to them. The word will be used again in Joshua three more times, at 4:1, 5:8, and 10:13.

As they had promised to Moses and to Joshua, 40,000 soldiers from the tribes of Reuben and Gad and the half-tribe of Manasseh crossed over ahead of the rest of the Israelites. They were armed and prepared for any battle. (Joshua 4:10-13)

CHAPTER FOUR

a. A Memorial to God

After every Israelite, except for the priests holding up the ark of the covenant in the middle of the river bed, were across the bed of the Jordan River, God commanded Joshua to choose 12 men, one from each tribe. Joshua was to tell each of the men to go to the middle of the Jordan River and pick out a stone where the priests were standing. The men were told to pick up the stone and carry it with them. They were to keep the stone in their possession and then put it down in the place where the Israelites were going to spend the night. Without further explanation, it appears that the 12 men mentioned here are the same 12 men Joshua chose earlier. (See Joshua 3:12.)

Joshua called together the 12 men he had chosen and gave them instructions consistent with the commands God had given to Joshua. He told them to go before the ark in the middle of the river bed and select 12 stones, one for each of the 12 tribes. Joshua then explained why the stones were being taken. They were to be an everlasting memorial to the fact that God, represented by the ark of the covenant, stopped the waters of the Jordan River. In addition, the stones were "to be a memorial to the people of Israel forever." When children asked about the stones in the future, the men would know how to answer them. (Joshua 4:4-7)

At this point, the scripture narrative moved a little ahead of the story of the crossing. It will picked up later. When the men brought back the 12 stones, they carried them to their camp. Joshua then set up the stones at a place that was later called Gilgal. (See Joshua 5:9) The stones were set up as a memorial to the miracle that had occurred that day. Joshua told the Israelites that when their children ask about the memorial, they should "tell them that the flow of the Jordan was cut off before the ark of the covenant of the Lord. When it crossed the Jordan, the waters of the Jordan were cut off. These stones are to be a memorial to the people of Israel forever." (Joshua 4:6-7) Of course, Joshua did not mean that the memorial was *dedicated* to the people of Israel. He meant that the memorial was to be a *remembrance* to the people of Israel. In other words, it was to be a reminder of what happened that day.

Later, Joshua expanded on what he said earlier. He said to tell the descendants of the people who crossed that day that "Israel crossed the Jordan on dry ground." (Joshua 4:21-22) Joshua expanded on that thought by giving God all the credit for what happened. He said (bold added for emphasis): "For the **Lord your God** dried up the Jordan before you until you had crossed over. The **Lord your God** did to the Jordan what he had done to the Red Sea when he dried it up before us until we crossed over. **He** did this so that all the peoples of the earth might know that the hand of the **Lord** is powerful and so that you might always fear the **Lord your God**." (Joshua 4:23-24) Joshua made it very clear to the Israelites that it was God who planned and orchestrated the crossing of the Jordan River in such a spectacular manner that no one on earth could take the credit for such an event. He showed how powerful He was by what He accomplished. And, the stones were still there as of the time when the Book of Joshua was written. (Joshua 4:8-9)

b. Joshua Is Exalted By God

God exalted Joshua in front of the Israelites and they stood in awe of Joshua for the rest of his life, just as they had been in awe of Moses. (Joshua 4:14) Now, the scripture narrative jumped back to pick up the end of the story about the river bed crossing. God then told Joshua to command the priests carrying the ark to come out of the river bed. (Joshua 4:15) Even though the narrative about Joshua setting up the stones appears to have occurred before the priests were commanded to leave the river bed, it seems logical in the chronology of events that the stones were set up by Joshua after the priests and the ark had rejoined the Israelite community. The rendering of events listed in Joshua 4:18 seems to be the correct order. In that verse it indicates that once all the people had crossed to the west side of where the Jordan River had flowed earlier and once the stones had been gathered from the middle of the river bed, the priests carried the ark of the covenant to the plains of Jericho to join the rest of the Israelites. As soon as their feet left the river bed, the waters of the Jordan River came rushing down at flood stage as it had been before.

Although it is not absolutely set in stone, it appears that the Israelites crossed over into the Plain of Jericho on the tenth day of the first month. (See Joshua 4:19.) If so, then the crossing would have taken place exactly 40 years from when God instructed Moses and Aaron to tell the Israelites in Egypt to take one lamb for each family and set it aside to prepare them for slaughter. The lambs would then be slaughtered at twilight on the fourteenth day of the first month. The meat was then to be roasted over a fire and eaten in its entirety. In addition, the people eating the meat must be dressed as if they were going on a trip. Their cloaks should be tucked into their belts, with sandals on their feet and staffs in their hands. God called it "the Lord's Passover." (Exodus 12:1-11) Four days later, the Israelites celebrated their first Passover meal in the land of Canaan.

CHAPTER FIVE

a. The Rest Before The Storm

The Israelites were now gathered at Gilgal. Interestingly, the place was not then named Gilgal, which sounds like the Hebrew for "roll" (to remove or to take away). It was not named until after the events described below occurred. (See Joshua 5:9) Additionally, no one today knows where Gilgal was then located. Some maps have it southeast of Jericho, some have it northeast of Jericho, and some display both locations. In any event, it appears to be off the plains of Jericho and slightly into the hill country. In addition, it was a community that has been mentioned in excess of twenty times in scripture after the time of Joshua, especially in relation to Elijah and and Elisha. See **https:// www.bible-history.com/geography/ancient-israel/ot/ gilgal.html**.

Since it was on the eve of Passover, the Lord told Joshua to make flint knives and circumcise all of the Israelites "again." (Joshua 5:2) Now, it should be obvious that the word "again" did not mean circumcise men who had already been circumcised. It meant that the Israelite men who were alive at the time of the Exodus had been circumcised. When God instituted the Passover while the Israelites were still in Egypt, He told Moses and Aaron that no man could participate in the first Passover unless he was circumcised. (Exodus 12:43-49) The scripture then relates that all "the Israelites did just what the Lord had commanded Moses and Aaron." (Exodus 12:50) The scripture in Joshua echoes what was written in Exodus. It relates that all of the men who came out of Egypt had been circumcised.

However, all of the men of military age who had left Egypt at the time of the Exodus had died during the 40 years in the wilderness. The sons born to these men had never been circumcised and these were the men whom Joshua was commanded by God to circumcise. (Joshua 5:4-8)

Joshua followed the command of God. He made flint knives and circumcised the Israelites at Gibeath Haaraloth. (Joshua 5:3) Flint knives were the perfect tool at the time for circumcision. No bronze knife could come close to having the edge of a flint knife. The sharper the edge of the knife, the faster and more efficient the job in removing the foreskins, and the less pain to the male being circumcised. The phrase Gibeath Haaraloth means "the hill of foreskins."

Once all the men were circumcised, God removed "the reproach of Egypt from you [the Israelites]." (Joshua 5:9) This phrase appears to refer to two separate incidents where God threatened to destroy the Israelites because of their rebellion in the desert. Each time, Moses brought up the Egyptians as a people who would deride God for not living up to His promises. He said the people of Egypt will say that God was not able to take them into the land He had promised and, because he hated them, he only brought them into the desert to kill them. Now, neither Egypt or any other people will be able to say ill about God or His people because the Israelites were now camped in the Promised Land, just as God promised. (See Numbers 14:13-16 and Deuteronomy 9:28)

It appears that the Israelite men were circumcised on the tenth day of the first month. This was the day that the lambs were selected for the first Passover, which was held in Egypt. Being circumcised then gave the men enough time to recover from the surgery to celebrate the first Passover in their new land on the fourteenth day of the first month while still camped at Gilgal. Just as all the Israelite men in Egypt were circumcised before the first Passover, all the Israelite men in Canaan were circumcised before the first Passover in the Promised Land. It appears that the author deliberately meant for the reader to draw the parallel. (Joshua 5:10)

The next day, the Israelites ate unleavened bread and roasted grain, made from harvesting what was grown in Canaan. The manna that God had provided for 40 years stopped the day after. The Israelites then ate of the grain of Canaan for the next year. (Joshua 5:11-12)

b. Fear Shreds the Resolve of the Enemy

Even when the Israelites were still east of the Jordan River, the spies learned from Rehab that the people of Jericho were sick with fear. However, when word spread that God had dried up the Jordan River to allow the Israelites to cross dry land into Canaan, the entire region became alarmed. All of "the Amorite kings west of the Jordan and all of the Canaanite kings along the coast" had been informed about what God had done to allow the Israelites to enter Canaan at a time when the wide and turbulent Jordan River should have kept the Israelites out for several more months, at the least. The hearts of the kings "melted in fear" and any courage they had to face the Israelites vanished. (Joshua 5:1)

c. Joshua Meets the Angel of the Lord

As the Israelites, led by Joshua, begin their march towards Jericho, Joshua encountered a man whose appearance was puzzling to Joshua. The scripture is not clear as to how the man came to be in front of Joshua. A case can be made from the language of the scripture that the man appeared suddenly, as if the man was not there one moment and then the next moment was standing before Joshua. In any event, the man had a drawn sword in his hand. Normally, such a posture would suggest that the man was armed and ready for combat. However, there must have been something about the man that made Joshua wonder about the man's intentions. And, instead of keeping his distance, Joshua approached the man. There is no indication that the man changed his posture at all when Joshua approached him. Finally, Joshua asked the man, "Are you for us or for our enemies?" The man then answered the question with an enigmatic "neither." If the man was neither for the Israelites or for their enemy, why was he there at all? The meaning behind the "neither" answer seems to be this: "I am not here as a combatant. I am here on another mission." The man then completed his sentence by revealing that he had come as commander of the army of the Lord. (Joshua 5:13)

Joshua's reaction showed that he believed what the man had to say. There must have been something about his sudden appearance, his countenance, his stance, and his bearing that caused Joshua not to doubt what the man said. Joshua immediately fell prone with his face to ground. It appears to have been a voluntary reaction because it was done "in reverence." Also, Joshua was not in such a state that he was speechless. He asked the man, "What message does my Lord (or lord) have for his servant?" The word in the question rendered Lord can also be rendered lord. Even if the word is "lord," the impact is the same: the "lord" had a message from the "Lord" for Joshua and he was about to give it. (Joshua 5:14)

The message was this: "Take off your sandals, for the place where you are standing is holy." What could the message mean? Did the captain of the Lord's army mean that the spot where Joshua had been standing was somehow dedicated to God's use or God was claiming it for some special purpose and Joshua needed to revere it? Actually, the statement appears to mean that where Joshua was standing represented the entire Promised Land and Joshua needed to understand that God had set it aside as sacred and it always needed to be seen in that light and no other. It was God's land and it would be forever set aside for His use. Joshua understood what God was telling him and Joshua removed his sandals in obedience. (Joshua 5:15)

"Captain of the host of the Lord am I."
—Josh. v. 14.

136

It is reasonable to conclude that the author of the Book of Joshua included the appearance of the commander of the Lord's army in the narrative because it was meant to parallel the experience that Moses had with the burning bush while at Horeb, the mountain of God. (Exodus 3:1-2). Then, an angel of the Lord appeared in the flames of the bush that would not be consumed. When Moses approached the bush, God called to Moses from within the bush. God told Moses to take off his shoes for he was standing on holy ground. (Exodus 3:2-5) This event was significant to Moses because it was when God called him to bring God's people out of Egypt. God assured Moses that he would be with him. (Exodus 3:12) The appearance of the commander of the Lord's army was significant because it came at a time just after Joshua had been called by God to lead the Israelite nation and just before Joshua would face his first conflict in Canaan at Jericho. The message from the commander meant the same for Joshua as it had been for Moses: you are in the presence of God, the God who will be with you throughout everything that you will face.

CHAPTER SIX

a. The Conquest Begins

There is no evidence in scripture as to how much time passed after the crossing of the Jordan River until the conquest of Canaan began. However, a good military commander would always take advantage of any kink in the armor of the enemy as soon as possible and Jericho's kink was an absolute paralyzing fear of the Israelites. The faster the assault on the kink, the more likely the assault would have its intended effect, and that intended effect would be the destruction of the enemy. The kink in Jericho's army was a loss of will to fight. Every military force must have a will to win to prevail. Jericho did not have that. When the size of the armies on each side of a conflict are equal, when the means to fight a battle are equal, when the quality of the leadership is equal, then the side which has the greater will to win will win. When the other side has a melted resolve, then that side should be attacked as soon as possible. Joshua probably did exactly that.

When the Israelites reconnoitered Jericho, they found that the gates were securely barred and no on went in or out. (Joshua 6:1) This is a common situation that is found throughout history. When a city or even a nation is threatened and it does not have the means or the will to resist, then the city or nation draws in upon itself and hopes that time or some unexpected circumstance will cause the enemy to withdraw or to be defeated. Jericho was obviously unwilling to test the strength of the Israelite forces in open battle. The king sent no troops out the gates to confront the enemy because the king did not have the will or resources to fight. Interestingly, the king did not even send out an envoy to seek peace terms with the Israelites. It was discovered through Rahab that the people of Jericho were well aware of how the Israelites treated the Amorites east of the Jordan River after their kings were defeated in battle. Of course, they were eradicated because they chose to fight rather than surrender, per God's instructions.

The king of Jericho likely reviewed all of his options with his advisers and none of them even came close to being acceptable, except to close the gates and wait. One of their options was to close the gates and attempt to fight off the enemy if the Israelites attacked the city. Another option was to prepare for a siege and hope the Israelites got tired of the wait and moved on to another part of Canaan. The king obviously had no realistic options because it does not appear that he had a treaty of mutual support with any other Canaanite city since none ever came to his rescue. It is likely he sent out a message to nearby cities for aid, but it was clear at that point that none was coming. What finally happened to the people of Jericho was probably not even on the list of possible strategies or outcomes drawn up by the king's advisers.

Joshua likely called upon the Lord, asking for guidance in the battle to take Jericho. From a military perspective, Jericho probably appeared formidable. Even if the enemy's will to fight was at its lowest point possible, there were two walls, one massive in height and width, that lay between those melted hearts and the point of an Israelite spear. Since this was the first battle of the Canaan campaign, it was very important that the morale of the Israelites remain as high as possible. Every Israelite soldier still had the Jordan River miracle, fashioned by God, still in his mind and that would tend to elevate the morale of the Israelites . The new nation of Israel, as a people, knew that God was with them. Every Israelite believed that God had elevated Joshua to the same status once held only by Moses. A defeat at the hands of the people of Jericho would shake the confidence of a newly-united people that still had a vast amount of territory yet to conquer. It was a magnificent idea to consult with God and to ask Him for insight on how to bring about victory.

Even though the Israelites had taken the cities of the Amorites east of the Jordan River, it appears that those conquests had occurred after the Amorite armies had been slaughtered by the Israelites. The cities then were without any effective defense. Jericho was different. It could be attacked, but the Israelites did not have the siege equipment to accomplish their objective without a significant loss of life. The Israelites had no battering rams and they had no siege towers whereby archers could shoot down at defenders on the walls of the city. Also, they had no catapults that could be used to toss large stones into the city, causing destruction of property and death. In addition, it is likely the Israelites did not have ladders for scaling the walls or digging equipment to be used to undermine a section of the city wall, causing it to collapse. To assault the city without the necessary siege equipment would violate one of the major axioms of warfare: never attack the enemy on the enemy's chosen ground.

b. God's Plan to Capture Jericho

When Joshua consulted with God, God had a plan and He gave that plan to Joshua. The fact that Joshua carried out the plan to its fullest shows how much faith Joshua had in God as the plan was one that even Joshua could not have expected. The plan was simple in its explanation and simple in its proposed execution. However, it was a plan never devised in the mind of any commanding officer in the history of warfare. God prefaced his plan by giving Joshua the outcome. God told Joshua that He had delivered Jericho into Joshua's hands. And, that included the king and all of his fighting men. (Joshua 6:2). Joshua was likely very pleased with this pronouncement. It was a good way to start any talk about an upcoming battle. The details were to come and they had to be somewhat surprising.

God told Joshua that the defeat of Jericho would take seven days. However, unexpectedly, God revealed that the taking of the city would not involve any fighting whatsoever. The archers would not have to fire one arrow. The spearmen would not have to throw one spear. And, the swordsmen would not have to engage in any hand-to-hand combat.

God gave Joshua the details for the destruction of Jericho. For the first six days, the ark of the covenant would be carried around the city walls of Jericho once. The ark would be preceded by seven priests, with each priest blowing on a trumpet made of a ram's horn. The entire Israelite army, armed for battle, would also march with the ark and the trumpeters, with half of the army behind and half in front. On the seventh day, the ark, the trumpeters with their blaring horns, and the army would march around the city as they did on the first six days, with a few important differences. On the seventh day, they would march around the city seven times. After the seven encirclements were concluded, the trumpeters would sound one long blast. When they blew their horns, the whole army was to give a loud shot. At that moment the wall of the city will collapse and the army would go in and capture the city. (Joshua 6:2-5)

If anyone but God had proposed such a plan, he or she would have been laughed out of the war council and banned from speaking in public ever again. The plan did not appear to speak to any of the usual tactics of a battle, except for the wall falling down at the end. However, walls usually fall down after they have been undermined so severely there is no support to hold them up. If the walls cannot be undermined, then holes have to be battered in them. If holes cannot be battered in them, then they have to be scaled by infantry using ladders. If the walls cannot be scaled, then the gates have to be breached somehow. None of the usual tactics were mentioned by God whatsoever.

c. The Execution of God's Plan

There is no scripture that indicates how Joshua viewed God's plan. All we know is that he passed the information along in the form of commands to the priests and to the army. And, it appears he made the commands immediately after being given the plan by God. Scripture records that Joshua told the priests to take up the ark of the covenant and to have seven priests with seven trumpets walk in front of the ark. He ordered an army guard to precede the priests. He told them to march around the city. He also commanded the army not to shout at any point until Joshua made an order to do so. (Joshua 6:6-7, 10)

Jericho was about the size of most cities of this period in history (around 1400 BC), which meant it was not large. According to some archaeologists, Jericho was about 740 feet long and 265 feet wide. In other words, the city was about 4.4 acres in size. (Others put the size at about six acres for the city and another three acres between the upper wall of the city and the lower wall.) If the city were 4.4 acres in size, then anyone walking around the city would complete the walk after going about 2,000 feet. Of course, those walking around the city would walk further away from the wall and, therefore, would have a longer walk. If the city were about nine acres in size and rectangular in shape, anyone walking completely around the city would go about 2,650 feet or about one-half mile.

Jericho at the time of Joshua

The main part of the city was also located as much as 70 feet above the surrounding plain on a mound. This would make it even less vulnerable to attackers. The city even had its own water source. The water for the city came from a spring now called 'Ayn Al-Sultan. It was located inside the city.

The usual population of the city was probably around 1,200 people, but, if the rural people had gone to the city for refuge, the population may have swelled as high as 2,000 people.

Archeologists have determined that the main city was on a mound surrounded by a red brick wall. The wall that surrounded the top of the mound was about 20 feet above the height of the lower wall. At the bottom of the slope where it met the plain of Jericho, there was a mud brick retaining wall about 12 to 15 feet high and over six feet thick. On top of the retaining wall was another wall made from mud brick. It was about six feet thick and was from 20 to 26 feet high. Therefore, the highest wall at the bottom of the mound was about 41 feet above the plain. Houses were built between the upper and lower walls. It is likely that Rahab's home was in the area between the two walls and it was likely on the north side of Jericho because some of the inner and outer walls did not collapse on that side.

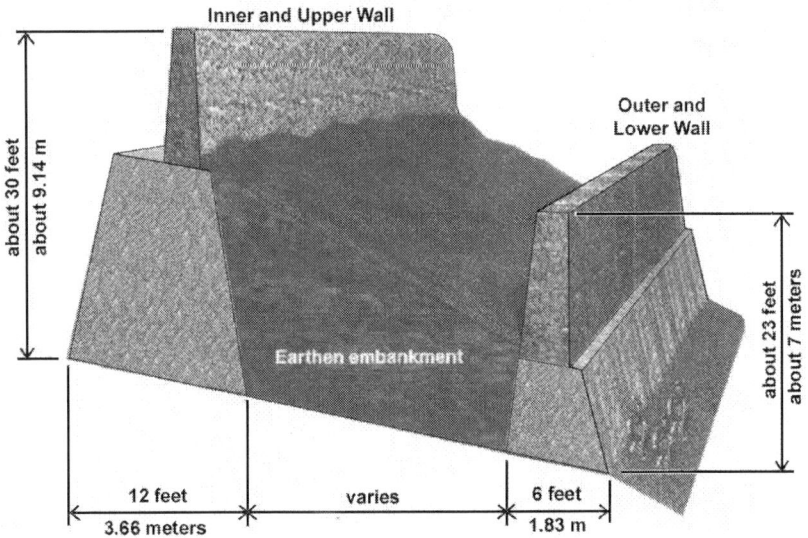

DOUBLE REDOUBTABLE WALL FOR THE ANCIENT CITY OF JERICHO

Joshua must have given the Israelites more information than was recorded in his recorded instructions, because, when the marching started on the first day, the seven priests started blowing their trumpets and the army split into two units, providing an armed guard in the front of the priests and an armed guard behind the priests. (Joshua 6:8-9) They marched around the city once. (Joshua 6:11a)

After the priests and the army marched around the city on the first day, they returned to camp. (Joshua 6:11b) Early the next morning and each morning thereafter for five more days, the priests and the army marched once around the city as they had done on the first day. (Joshua 6:12-14)

The seventh day started at daybreak. The priests and the army once again headed for Jericho. Before they arrived, they knew the day was going to be different than the previous six days. Joshua had given them instructions as to what should happen. He told them that when the wall collapsed, the city and all that was in it was to be devoted to the Lord. This meant that all the silver and gold and any articles of bronze and iron found within the city was sacred to God and must go into His treasury. (Joshua 6:19) It also meant that all the people in the city were to be killed, except for Rahab "the prostitute" and all the family within her house. She was to be rewarded for hiding the spies sent by Joshua. (Joshua 6:17) Joshua also told the soldiers that they must not to keep any of the precious metals as they were devoted to God. This was a nice way of saying that they should not take any of the precious metals for themselves or it would bring about their own destruction. It also would make all of God's people liable for destruction and would bring trouble on them. (Joshua 6:18) This was a foreshadowing of what will follow in Chapter 7 of Joshua.

For the entire army of the Israelites to be able to fit in a column marching around the city, there had to have been many of them walking abreast with each other. Perhaps what was really meant by the entire army is that there were representatives from every fighting unit in the march. In any event, it would not have taken the column of men very long to get around Jericho. What is amazing about each day's march is that there was no attack on the Israelites from the wall surrounding the city. The Israelites were allowed to march in absolute peace. There is a logical explanation for this. The king's men were probably told not to attack the Israelites because the king did not want to antagonize the them. After all, the Israelites were not attacking the city. It appeared that they were engaged in some sort of ritual exercise that could very well have been a prelude to peace talks. Maybe the Israelites were engaged in a practice whereby they were attempting to divine the will of their god as to how to proceed further. Maybe their god would tell them to leave Jericho alone and move on. If so, why risk the wrath of their god by attacking them while they were not attacking us? Seems reasonable, if that was really what the

Israelites were doing. So, why take a chance? There was nothing for the people of Jericho to do but to wait for the outcome.

On the seventh day, once the priests and the army was at Jericho, they marched around the city seven times instead of just once. However, they stayed in their assigned positions while the priests blew on their trumpets. At the end of the seventh time around the city, as prearranged, the priests blew their trumpets in one long blast. When that happened, Joshua commanded the men of the army, "Shout! For the Lord has given you the city!" (Joshua 6:15-16) The army then shouted as one and the walls of Jericho collapsed.

The soldiers immediately ran up the mud bricks from the fallen wall, entered the city, and killed every living thing in the city, whether human or animal, except for Rahab and her family. Joshua personally made sure Rahab and her family would be safe by sending into Jericho the two young spies Rahab had protected. The two young spies did as they were instructed. (Joshua 6: 20-23) It was an inspired move on Joshua's part to send the two young spies to rescue Rahab and her family. One, they knew where Rahab lived and, two, Rahab knew the two young spies by sight and by their voice. The two spies would not have to waste any time getting to her home because they knew where it was and she would probably only open her door to the two spies for fear of being killed by someone who did not know her. Likely, Joshua instructed the two spies before the wall collapsed and they were probably a part of one of the two contingents of army marching with the priests. One might even suspect that Joshua allowed them to be in the area of Rahab's home when the outer wall of Jericho collapsed so they could rush in to protect her and her family.

Obviously, when the city wall collapsed, the outside wall of Rahab's home did not fall. Neither did the wall above Rahab's home. Otherwise, everyone in Rahab's would have been crushed by the stones of the outer wall or the stones cascading down from the upper story. Further, since no soldier going into the city would have been able to see the scarlet cord in the window, which faced outward, one wonders why it was there. It was there for two reasons. One, it was a symbol of the faithfulness of both Rahab and the two spies to their agreement. She gave them valuable information as to the collective psyche of the city and she gave them protection from the king and the king's men. Two, it was also, as noted before, a shield from the destructive forces that God was about to release upon the city of Jericho. Rahab and her entire family were saved because of her loyalty to the two spies and the author of the

Book of Joshua noted that she was still living with the Israelites when the history was being written. (Joshua 6:25)

The part of the wall that did not collapse

The precious metals from the city were placed "in the treasury of the Lord's house" and the entire city of Jericho was put to the torch and burned. (Joshua 6:24) Archeologist have found evidence that the walls of Jericho collapsed, except for a part of the north side, and that Jericho was burned. They have also found that the city

contained large jars full of grain. It appears that the people
of Jericho were preparing for a long siege.

(See **https://answersingenesis.org/archaeology/the-walls-of-jericho/** for a very interesting overview of the
destruction of Jericho.)

Rahab spared

Joshua then pronounced an oath that it would cost anyone
dearly if he or she ever attempted to rebuild the city. The
cost would be this: his firstborn to lay the foundation and
his youngest for the city gates. (Joshua 6:26) Although

communities have been built nearby and called Jericho, the site of the original Jericho remains unoccupied to this day, except for probing archeologists.

"So the Lord was with Joshua, and his fame spread throughout the land." (Joshua 6:27)

CHAPTER SEVEN

a. The First Battle of Ai

After God handed Jericho into the hands of Joshua and the Israelites, Joshua immediately devoted his attention to his next objective. The plan was to attack and capture the city of Ai, which was probably located to the northwest (or north northwest) of the ruins of Jericho. Just as he had sent spies to reconnoiter the city of Jericho and the surrounding area, Joshua now sent spies to look over the region around Ai. (Joshua 7:2) The men did as Joshua commanded them. When the spies returned, they gave a report that did not flatter Ai at all. The spies were unimpressed with the city ("only a few people live there") and its defense. The spies suggested to Joshua that only two to three thousand man could do the job of destroying Ai and it certainly would not take the entire Israelite army. **Without consulting God**, as he did before approaching Jericho, Joshua accepted the recommendation of his spies and dispatched "about" 3,000 men. (Joshua 7:2b-4a)

Unfortunately, something went wrong. The Israelites attacked the men of Ai, but they were routed. "About" 36 Israelites were killed in the battle and its aftermath. Not only were the Israelites beaten badly in the battle, they were chased by the men of Ai from the city gate as far as the stone quarries in the area. Either the spies were incompetent or there was something else behind the disastrous defeat of the Israelite forces. Maybe the Israelites did not establish a good plan of attack. Maybe they were too confident because of Jericho and they figured the enemy would scatter with fear at the sight of the Israelite soldiers. Or, maybe Joshua should have consulted God before he sent the men to attack Ai. When the people in the camp heard the upsetting news, their hearts "melted in fear and became like water." (Joshua 7:4b-5)

b. Joshua in Anguish Over the Defeat

In anguish over the disheartening news, Joshua tore his clothes in despair and fell facedown before the ark of the covenant ("the ark of the Lord"). Scripture is not clear as to how long he lay on the ground, but it was until the evening hours. The elders followed the lead of Joshua and, in addition, sprinkled their heads with dust as a sign of mourning. (Joshua 7:6) Joshua addressed God about the military defeat, but the words were not that of a humble man seeking Lord's will. **First**, in the form of a question, he accused the Lord of bringing the Israelites across the Jordan River to deliver them into the hands of the Amorites. He sounded a lot like the Israelites right after they left Egypt. **Second**, in the form of an exclamation, he lamented the fact that they had obeyed God instead of staying on the east side of the Jordan River. **Third**, thinking that he could continue his attack on God by pardoning myself, he wondered what he could possibly say now that the Israelites had been routed by their enemy. It is unclear as to whom he should be addressing, but it could be both to his people and to God. **Fourth**, Joshua kept the same line of attack going by stating that the Canaanites would now surround them and wipe them off the face of the earth, thereby implying that God could not or would not prevent it. **Fifth**, he then tried to shame God by asking God what he would then do to redeem himself in the eyes of the world. (Joshua 7:6-9)

When God had heard enough from the impudent Joshua, He said to Joshua, "Stand up! What are you doing down on your face?" God's question carried a boat load of meaning.

First, God was demanding to know how Joshua could appear to be addressing God, but use such insulting language. If Joshua was going to speak to God that way, then he needed to get back to his feet and shut up. **Second**, God was upset at Joshua because Joshua did not consult with God before sending the troops off to Ai. If Joshua had done so, then God would have told him he was making a monumental mistake or God would have given him a plan that would have succeeded. **Third**, God wanted Joshua to understand that Joshua was the source of the defeat and not God. He had failed in his role as God's human representative on earth. **Fourth**, God did not want to be blackmailed by the man whom God had placed as the leader of the Israelites. Joshua had tried to use God's reputation against him to get what Joshua wanted and it did not work. **Fifth**, God did not want to be blamed for what happened. He warned the Israelites that they needed to obey him in everything he commanded and one of them failed to do that and that one was Joshua. God said when that happened there would be consequences. (Joshua 7:10)

c. God Revealed the Sin

In all humility, Joshua should have asked God after the defeat this question: "What had the Israelites done to cause the defeat?" Joshua, for his people, should have taken the blame. Instead, he tried to place the responsibility squarely on God's shoulders. God then revealed what He would have shared with Joshua if Joshua had only asked, either before the defeat or after the defeat. He put the shame right where it belonged (**bold** added for emphasis): "Israel has sinned; **they** have violated my covenant, which I commanded **them** to keep. **They** have taken some of the devoted things; **they** have stolen, **they** have lied, **they** have put them with their own possessions." (Joshua 7:11) He then explained in detail what caused the defeat at Ai. God commanded that all of the bronze, iron, silver, and gold be devoted to God and turned over to the treasury. God accused **"they"** of taking some the metal and placing the "stolen" items with **their** own possessions. God said He would not be with the Israelites if they did not devote all the bronze, iron, silver, and gold to him. Because God was not with the soldiers at Ai, the soldiers could not stand against their enemy. If Joshua wanted God to continue to be with the Israelites and to help them defeat their enemies, then Joshua would have to find out who violated the command God made before the attack on Jericho. (Joshua 7:10-12)

God went even further with his comments to Joshua. He commanded Joshua to consecrate the entire camp of Israelites. He wanted them to once again set themselves apart from the way of the world and once again submit to the will of God. They were to consecrate themselves because the next day they would have to cleanse themselves of the wrong that had been committed against God. In the morning, God would direct the proceedings, narrowing the violator or violators by tribe, then by clan, then by family, and then by the guilty person or persons. Whoever violated God's command shall suffer the "fire" of death. Not only will the offender or offenders be killed, everything, animate or inanimate, that belongs to him or them shall be destroyed also. (Joshua 7:13-15)

d. The Sinners Are Exposed

The next morning, Joshua had each tribe come forward. When the tribe of Judah, probably represented by the leader of the tribe, who may have been Caleb, came forward, God chose that tribe as the offending tribe. One can almost hear a sigh of relief coming from the other tribes, as they took one step backward to get out of the line of fire. When the clans of Judah, again, probably represented by the elders, stepped forward, the clan of Zerah was chosen. When the families of the clan of Zerah came forward, the family of Zimri was chosen. Joshua was from the family of Zimri. So, he and all the members of his group came forward man by man. When Achan, son of Karmi, stepped forward, God chose him as the person who had brought defeat on the Israelites that resulted in the death of about 36 of his fellow comrades in arms. (Joshua 7:16-18)

Joshua then addressed Achan, a man he had probably known all of his life as they were both members of the family of Zimri. It is possible that Achan's father Karmi was a brother to Joshua's father Nun. If so, then Achan was in the 60 to 70 year old range. This would make all of Achan's sons and daughters in the 40 to 50 year old range. Whatever the nature of the relationship, Achan's sin had to have been distressful to Joshua. He had tried to blame God for the defeat at Ai and the defeat was caused by a member of Joshua's own family. If Joshua had not felt humiliated by God before, he certainly had to be feeling severely humbled at this moment. Joshua told Achan to give glory to God and to honor Him by telling Joshua what he had done, keeping nothing to himself. Achan responded to Joshua by giving every detail of the sin he had committed. He first admitted to the fact that he had sinned against God's direct command regarding all the valuables found in Jericho. He sinned by keeping to himself a beautiful robe from Babylon, two hundred shekels of silver (about five pounds), and a bar of gold weighing fifty shekels (about 1.25 pounds). He had hidden the items in the ground inside his tent, with the silver under the other items. Joshua then sent messengers to Achan's tent, where they found the items and brought them to Joshua. The items were then spread out before everyone in the camp and before God. (Joshua 7:19-23) Achan had been indicted by God. Achan then provided verbal evidence against himself. The items he took, which were found hidden under his tent, provided physical evidence of his guilt. The trial was then over. God had chosen the guilty person. The guilty person had confessed to his sin. And, the items that should have been devoted to God (the silver and the gold) and the item that should have been destroyed (the beautiful robe) were evidence against Achan by corroborating his confession.

There was no formal finding of guilt or pronouncement of judgement, but they were implied by what happened next. All that was left to do was carry out the sentence and it appears to have occurred without any delay. Achan, his adult sons, his adult daughters, his cattle, his donkeys, his sheep, his tent, all his personal possessions, the robe, the silver, and the gold were all taken to a nearby gully. Joshua then had these words for Achan: "Why have you brought this trouble on us? The Lord will bring trouble on you today." (Joshua 7:24-25) It is clear that Joshua was acting as Judge and Executioner. He put the blame for the "about" 36 deaths on the head of Achan. He put the blame for God turning his back on the Israelites at that time on the head of Achan. Joshua, by implication, then tied Achan's punishment to the fact that what was about to happen was a direct consequence of breaking God's command. In other words, Achan could only point a finger at himself for what he and his family and his possessions were about to suffer.

e. The Sin Is Eradicated

1. The Judgment Is Carried Out

Then the execution was carried out. Achan, his adult sons and adult daughters, and all of his animals were stoned to death. All of the bodies, the robe, and the precious metals were all burned. Everything was then buried beneath a large pile of rocks, which was still there at the time the Book of Joshua was written. The writer seemed to be saying that not only was the pile of rocks still there as a testimony to the people of Israel carrying out a punishment for a violation of God's command, it was also a testimony to the fact that God was still being honored because no one had disturbed the pile since the execution. (Joshua 7:25b-26a) The place was called the Valley of Achor ever since because Achor is the Hebrew word for "trouble." (Joshua 7:26b)

"Then the Lord turned from his fierce anger." (Joshua 7:26b)

2. Why Stone Achan?

Some people wonder why Achan had to be stoned to death just because he took some items that should have gone to the Lord's treasury. The answer is simple: discipline. God's people were entering a land occupied by people who would oppose the Israelites with everything they had. In all, they outnumbered the Israelites and, if they ever united, they would be a formidable force. To defeat any and all foes, the Israelites had to be united. They had to have one focus and that was on the job ahead and, most importantly, their focus had to be on God and his commands. Not only did they have to focus on God's commands, they had to carry them out, no matter what they were and no matter how much they might think they had a better way. The focus and the obedience would require a discipline of steel. Without it, the Israelites faced certain defeat.

3. Why Stone Achan's Adult Children?

(a) No Dissent from Judgment

More people wonder why Achan's adult sons and adult daughters had to be stoned to death. It should be clear from the totality of the circumstances that they were also involved in their father's sin against God. The author of Joshua did not go into any detail regarding the adult sons and adult daughters, but the entire assembly of Israelites would not have allowed the children to have been killed unless there was clear evidence of their implication in their father's sin. And, the fact that scripture does not record any outcry from the sons and daughters, nor from any of the other Israelites, seems to be good evidence that the children shared in their father's guilt.

(b) Children Were Like Achan

Also, there is another thought that has to be considered regarding the children of Achan and it harkens back to the time of Noah. Remember that Noah had three sons and one of them was Ham. Remember that Ham had a son named Canaan and the Biblical record clearly implies that Canaan was just like Ham and, perhaps, was even worse. (See the discussion in the Introduction.) It was the descendants of Canaan that God cursed to be slaves to the descendants of Japheth and Shem. It is likely that the sons and daughters were just like Achan and, perhaps, even worse. It should be noted that there is no mention in the scripture of any dissent to the stoning of the sons and daughters. It should also be remembered that the Book of Joshua was written at a time when the stoning of Achan and his children was still fresh in the minds of the Israelites. The author, therefore, was not inspired to go into any more detail than is found today. It would appear that the detail would have included volumes of material about the misdeeds of the sons and the daughters. After all, if the children had been put to death merely because their father had sinned, the action would have violated God's commandment He made during the time of the wandering in the wilderness. God gave the Israelites this law: "Fathers shall not be put to death for their sons, nor shall sons be put to death for their fathers; everyone shall be put to death for his own sin." (Deuteronomy 24:16) God also said, "I, the Lord your God, am a jealous God, visiting the iniquity of the fathers on the children, on the third and fourth generations of those who **hate** Me, but showing lovingkindness to thousands [of generations], to those who **love** Me and keep My commandments." (emphasis added) (Exodus 20:5-6.) It should be clear that the sons and the daughters were somehow complicit in the crimes of their father and they were being punished for their own part. After all, God did use the word "**they**" when he was speaking about the perpetrators. (See Joshua 7:11.)

See this article, written by John Piper, for a brief discussion on the topic of the sins of the fathers are visited upon their sons: **https://www.desiringgod.org/articles/does-god-visit-the-sins-of-the-fathers-on-the-children**.

(c) Perpetuation of Sin

Also, Achan's sons and daughters represented the perpetuation of his name and, therefore, his sin into the future. God did not want that distraction from the goal he had set for His people. It is unfortunate that a father has to implicate his children in his acts that leads to their destruction. However, the reader needs to keep this principle in mind: the Israelites were a united people, a common entity. They were not a group of individuals who made up the group, their identity came from being a part of the group. The group came first and the individual amounted to nothing in comparison. That is a hard concept for Americans to understand because of our focus on individual freedom and the rights of the individual under our state and federal constitutions. However, such a future outlook was foreign to the Israelites because, at this juncture in history, God demanded obedience to his unifying commands and that left no room for any contrary thoughts or actions.

(d) Achan and Rahab Contrasted

There is another interesting angle to the stoning of the sons and the daughters and it has to do with Rahab. There appears to be a parallel between the story of Rahab and the story of Achan. Rahab was aware of who God was and what was likely to happen with the Israelites crossed the Jordan River to claim the land God promised to them. Rahab became involved when the two spies sought her out and she protected them by lying to the king's men. She not only protected them, she provided them a way to escape Jericho and she gave them advice as to how to avoid capture. In other words, Rahab was faithful to the men who represented the God she had come to know and she trusted their word that they would rescue her and her family. And, God (by keeping the wall of her home intact), Joshua (by remembering about Rahab and sending in the spies to protect), and the two spies (by bringing Rahab and her family to safety) made sure that Rahab would live to marry and, have a descendant as a king (David), and have a descendant as the Savior of the World (Jesus).

Achan, on the other hand, was raised in the wilderness with all the other men his age. He knew about God and all the miracles God had provided for His people the Israelites. He had been there when God stopped the flow of the Jordan River. God was there in their midst and Achan knew that. Even with all he knew about God, Achan allowed his greed to have greater weight in his mind than God's command that certain items be turned over to God's treasury and the rest be burned. Not only did he take the items, he had to have secreted the items in such a way that he could not participate with the rest of the troops in following through with the subduing of the city. Not only that, he had to use stealth and chicanery to get the items to his tent and bury them. If this was the kind of man Achan was, then he certainly was passing on these characteristics to his children and the Israelite community did not need or want these kind of people in their midst at this juncture of their attempts to conquer Canaan. Therefore, they had to die and the verdict of God and the community was carried out. In short, Rahab was faithful and she and her family survived. Achan was not faithful and he and his family did not survive.

(e) Closing Comment

One last comment. The reader should have noticed that Achan's wife was not included amongst those who were stoned to death. Even though she was married to Achan, she was not a member of Zimri's family. Therefore, she was not condemned with the rest. In addition, she was not included as a part of his personal possessions. She was seen as a separate and distinct person from Achan in the eyes of God. It could also be said with certainty that she was not involved in the crimes of Achan and her children.

CHAPTER EIGHT

Part One

a. Problems with Chapter Eight

There are some problems with Chapter 8 of the Book of Joshua that several evangelical authors ascribe to scribal error. There is one glaring problem and one minor problem that stand out that cannot be reconciled within the text. One has to do with the number of men who Joshua sent to the area between Ai and Bethel to serve as an ambush and the other has to do with the timing of the battle between Joshua's main army and the army of the king of Ai.

The glaring problem should be dealt with first. In verses 3 through, and including, 8, Joshua speaks to the men he will send out to take part in the assault on Ai. The text indicates at verse 3 that he chose 30,000 of his best fighting men to be a part of the ambush. However, at verse 12, the text indicates that Joshua had selected 5,000 men for the ambush party. Only one of the numbers can be correct and it appears that the ambush party most likely contained 5,000 men. This choice is based on two factors. One, 5,000 men would be easier to hide in the area between Bethel and Ai than 30,000 men. Two, it would appear that 30,000 was the total number of men that Joshua had chosen for the entire mission, including both the men in ambush and the men who would openly challenge the forces at Ai to battle.

The minor problem needs some explanation. In verses 10 through, and including, 13, the text indicates that Joshua mustered his army the next morning after the ambush party had set up their position between Bethel and Ai. The main army then marched to a raised area north of Ai where it camped. The text then makes reference to the ambush party of 5,000 men. When the text looks back to Joshua and his contingent of men, there is a reference to Joshua going into the valley "that night" with the battle taking place after sunrise the next day. On May 1, the approximate date of the attack, sunrise would be about 6:00 am. The minor problem has to do with the timing. If the ambush party arrived at their location around 11:00 pm one day (see the discussion in the next section) and then had to remain hidden until 6:00 am on the third day, that is a period of time of approximately 32 hours. It just seems unrealistic that the ambush party of 5,000 men could remain undetected for that long a period of time. This is especially true with Bethel so close to Ai to the west and the likelihood of agents from Ai roaming the area looking for Israelite spies or approaching soldiers. After all, one battle had already taken place at Ai and likely the king of Ai expected another soon.

As to the minor problem, there is an explanation that would satisfy most believers. God is the one who planned the battle that included the ambush party. If God planned the battle, he could easily protect the ambush party from detection and that may have been what He did.

b. The Location of Ai

Where was Ai at the time the Israelites entered Canaan to claim the Promised Land? This question has been difficult to answer. At Joshua 8:1, God told Joshua to go "up" to Ai. Since Joshua was then encamped at Gilgal, which was in the Jordan Valley about 1,000 feet below sea level, just about anything was "up." However, Joshua filled in some of the ambiguity by indicating that the ambush party was to lay in wait between Bethel and Ai. Eusebius of Caesarea, also known as Eusebius Pamphili, became a bishop in or about 314 AD. In his writings, he identified Bethel as being a small village that lay about 12 Roman miles north of Jerusalem. Ai would then have been east of Bethel. Based on what is known about the approximate location of Ai, it may have been as much as 2,500 feet above sea level. The climb from Gilgal to Ai would then have been about 3,500 feet.

Edward Robinson, who lived from 1794 to 1863, identified Ai with a place then called Et-Tell. He based his conclusion on the fact that Ai is easily translated into the Arabic as Et-Tell. However, the excavations of Et-Tell, which started in the 1930's, have not been successful in confirming Robinson's hypothesis.

Dr. Bryant Wood has identified a site nine miles north of Jerusalem as the location of Ai. It is called Khirbet el-Maqatir. (See **https://answersingenesis.org/archaeology/ getting-archaeology-right-at-ai/**)

Khirbet el-Maqatir fits every description given in the Biblical account. **First**, in Joshua's account of the battle, his army encamped on the north side of Ai with a valley between his army and Ai. North of Khirbet el-Maqatir is a hill called Jebel Abu Ammar. It is the highest hill in the area and it would provide an excellent view of any activity in the valley below. **Second**, while on the north side of the city, Joshua could see the "front" of Ai. This is where the gate to the city would be located and Dr. Wood and his team found such a gate on the north wall. **Third**, the ambush party hid in a location west of Ai. Due west of the ruins at Khirbet el-Maqatir is a steep valley called the "Wadi Sheban." It is close to Ai and deep enough to hide Joshua's ambushers. **Fourth**, many of the items found within the site are similar to items known to have been used at the time of the Israelite invasion. These include storage jars, jar rims, and sling stones. Pottery found near the west wall matches pottery found elsewhere that was known to be used at the time of Joshua. **Fifth**, the west wall was found to be up to 12 feet thick. This is similar to other walls in other cities at the time of Joshua. **Sixth**, Ai was burned on the orders of Joshua. At Khirbet el-Maqatir, there is substantial evidence that the city that was once there was burned. There are layers of ash, heated bedrock, burned stones, and pottery that had been "refired." Pottery that had once been baked in a kiln will become like concrete when refired or exposed to intense heat once again. See also: **http:// aa9f7364abaa148daf52-1f98f729ef50ec6a5be3e846616ef 691.r65.cf2.rackcdn.com/uploaded/p/ 0e7527232_1530645669_problem-of-ai-2018-bible-and- spade.pdf**

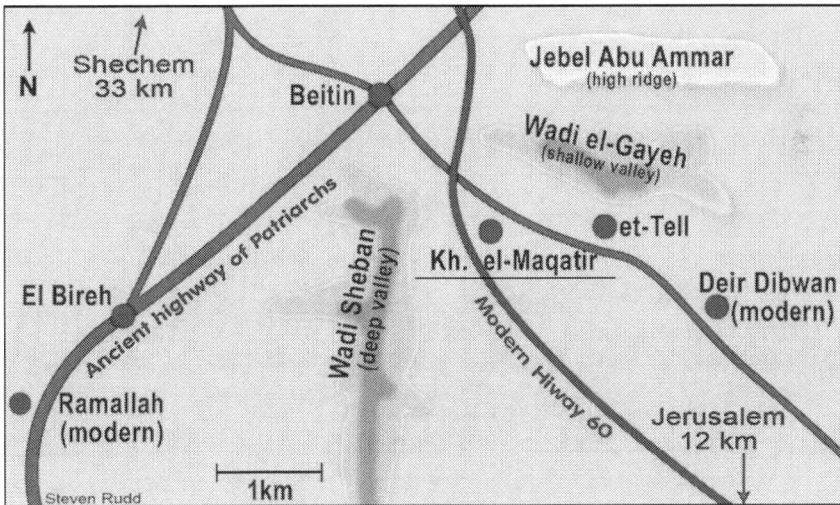

Khirbet el-Maqatir (ancient Ai) is underlined

c. God's Plan to Attack Ai

After the judgment was passed on Achan and his troublesome children, the Lord went to Joshua to counsel him about the city of Ai. It appears from God's words to Joshua that Joshua was unsure of what to do about a renewed attack on the city of Ai. The first assault had been a disaster, despite the confidence of the Israelite warriors that victory was within their grasp. The defeat left the Israelites quaking about their future. Yes, they may have crossed the Jordan River by a miracle of God and, yes, they may have destroyed the city of Jericho with the help of a miracle by God, but they had been crushed by a foe in their first hand-to-hand battle in Canaan. The rout left the Israelites with too much time to ponder about the future and that future looked bleak. They were now bottled in by the raging Jordan River to the east and Canaanites to the west. If something positive did not happen soon, the Israelites would be forever cornered in a small section of land, at best, or annihilated by a combined force of Canaanite peoples, at worst.

God told Joshua, "Do not be afraid; do not be discouraged." (Joshua 8:1a) God was attempting, with his words, to build confidence in Joshua. Even though God would be behind the Israelites, he still wanted them to initiate the battle. Just as he did not stop the flow of the Jordan River until the priests put their feet in the water, God was not going to aid the Israelites until they moved into action. Also, Joshua needed to stop showing fear because he was the leader of the Israelites. They were looking to him for leadership and he appeared not to be providing it. Remember God's words when he chose Joshua to be the leader of the Israelites. He told Joshua to be "strong and courageous." He was again telling Joshua to have those same characteristics. Joshua was not being strong and courageous and God needed to prompt him into action. And, what is the best cure for the "mopes," it is movement, and especially movement in the direction that God wants every believer to go. Therefore, God commanded Joshua to take the "whole" army with him, go up to Ai, and attack that city. (Joshua 8:1) Why did God command Joshua to take the entire army with him? He did it for at least two reasons. **One**, the original force was about 3,000 men and it did not live up to expectations. **Two**, the use of the entire army at Jericho was a brilliant victory. Therefore, since the entire army had been used at Jericho and that expedition was a success, then the people needed to know that the troops were going to build on the success of Jericho and not the failure of Ai.

God told Joshua to take his army "up" to Ai. There is a good reason for that as Ai truly was up from Gilgal, where the Israelites were camped. Gilgal was on the edge of the Jordan Valley and it may have been around 1,000 feet below sea level. God further told Joshua that He had already delivered into Joshua's hands (1) the king of Ai, (2) the king's people, (3) the king's city, and (4) the land of the king. All Joshua had to do was get the army together, advance to Ai, and then God would do the rest. (Joshua 8:1) These were similar words God told Joshua on the eve of the taking of Jericho. He told Joshua then, "See, I have delivered Jericho into your hands, along with its king and its fighting men." (See Joshua 6:2.) God commanded Joshua and his army to do to Ai as it had done to Jericho. In other words, the Israelites would kill everyone within and without the city. No one would be left alive to ever trouble the Israelites again. God made an exception as to anything of value within the city and as to all the livestock. God told Joshua that all the bronze, iron, silver, and gold could be plundered by the troops and, by implication, not given to God's treasury. God told Joshua that his men could keep all the livestock for themselves. God also gave Joshua a plan that involved setting an ambush. (Joshua 8:1b-2) The details of the plan were revealed by Joshua to his soldiers. The plan given by God would correct all the mistakes made in the original assault and would actually take advantage of that disaster. It was a brilliant plan and it was well executed.

Here is a summary of the battle plan. (1) Israelite troops would hide at night in ambush in the area between Ai on the east and Bethel to the west. (2) The next day, Joshua would bring the bulk of his troops to a position on a hill north of the city gate of Ai. (3) Later, Joshua would bring some of his troops off the hill and into the valley where Ai was located. (4) The king of Ai would then bring his troops out and array them for battle. (5) Joshua and his troops would then flee in feigned disarray. (6) The king of Ai and his troops would then chase after the fleeing Israelites. (7) The troops in ambush would then go into the city of Ai, capture it, and then set it on fire. (8) Joshua and his forces would then turn and fight the army of the king of Ai. (9) Soon, Joshua's troops would be joined by those who captured the city and others coming from the north. The king of Ai and his men would then be surrounded and killed. (Joshua 8:4-8)

d. Joshua Executes God's Plan

1. The Ambushers Are Dispatched

The main point of the scripture of Chapter 8 is God's guidance and God's encouragement. This has to be the focus because there is much about the description of the second battle of Ai that is troublesome to any researcher who approaches it. The story line is simple; it is the details that present problems. And, it starts right from the beginning. Verse 3 indicates that "Joshua and the whole army moved out to attack Ai." This has to be seen as a summary of what happened later, as Joshua and the whole did not move out at that time to attack Ai. In addition, scripture then indicates that Joshua chose 30,000 of his best fighting men to go to Ai that night to set up an ambush behind the city of Ai, which would have been west of Ai. (Joshua 8:3) Later, the fighting men sent out by Joshua was set at 5,000, rather than the original 30,000. The 5,000 were to set up between Bethel and Ai and west of Ai, the same place the original 30,000 were sent. (Joshua 8:12) When the men arrived in the vicinity of Ai, they lay in wait between Bethel and Ai. (Joshua 8:9)

The men probably hid in the Wadi Sheban, which was west of Ai. The men probably were not completely between Bethel and Ai, as the Wadi Sheban only extends northward for a short distance past Ai. However, the men were certainly in a position to intercept any troops that might be sent from Bethel to Ai. As previously discussed, it is likely, as one evangelical commentator noted, that the number 30,000 is a scribal error, as 5,000 men would be easier to hide than 30,000 men. It is probable that the number 30,000 applied to how many men were in the entire force that Joshua had selected to capture Ai. This would be a good number for Joshua to have chosen, as it represented a force that was ten times what was sent to Ai earlier. Such a number would be impressive both to the people at the camp and for the soldiers making the hike to Ai. And, it would be enough to overcome any resistance by the enemy at Ai.

The men selected to form the ambush party were to go to their position between Ai and Bethel during the hours of darkness and to remain hidden at all times. (Joshua 8:3b-4,

9) This tactic had three advantages. **One**, the troops would travel at night to cover the 10 miles or so from Gilgal to Ai. The change in altitude would be about 3,500 feet or a rise of 350 feet per mile or one foot every 15 feet. Such a climb would tire even the sturdiest of soldiers. The average person can walk a leisurely mile in 20 minutes. If the distance were flat, then the average person could walk from Gilgal to Ai in 200 minutes or three hours and 20 minutes. Therefore, a trained soldier could easily go the same distance, even with the rise in elevation, in about four hours. If the soldiers left Gilgal at 8:00 pm, they could be at Ai around midnight or 1 am at the worst. They would then be well rested in the morning. **Two**, leaving at night would mean that anyone sent from Ai to Gilgal to spy on the Israelites would probably had left their positions by 8 pm to return to Ai for the night. **Three**, if there were any unforeseen delays, the soldiers would still get a decent night's rest before daybreak.

2. Joshua Stayed with the Main Army

Joshua spent the night at Gilgal. (Joshua 9b) The next morning, Joshua brought together the rest of army. The number of soldiers available to Joshua at this point was not mentioned in scripture. However, it was likely 30,000 minus the 5,000 already sent up to Ai the night before. This would make 25,000 troops available to Joshua as his main attacking force. This was a substantial number of fighting men. Of course, considering the forces available to Joshua, he would be leaving even more men behind to guard the camp at Gilgal. It would have been eminently foolish of Joshua to have left the camp unguarded.

3. Joshua and His Men Marched to Ai

Joshua, the leaders of the tribes and families, and the foot soldiers marched to Ai. They did not go up the valley to the east of Ai. They took a position on the hills to the north of Ai, facing the city gate, with a valley between the Israelites and the city of Ai. (Joshua 8:10-11, 13) The summit of the hills to the north of Ai are called Jebel Abu Ammar today. The the shallow valley between Ai and the hills is called the Wadi el-Gayeh today. The text implies that Joshua's men spent the night in their encampment and that they entered the valley or wadi before sunrise. The language used was this: "That night Joshua went into the valley." (Joshua 8:13b) Since Joshua and his warriors went to the hills during the daylight hours, Joshua would have gone down into the valley the next morning while it was still dark. In addition, it would be absurd to interpret this scripture to mean that only Joshua entered the valley. Joshua was the leader of his men and, by using his name, it was a way of describing that Joshua's army was with him. This is especially true when the king of Ai's response to Joshua being in the valley was to bring his men out of Ai to meet the Israelites. (Joshua 8:14a)

The question at this point was how many men did Joshua bring with him in the valley? Scripture does not give the answer so the situation needs to be looked at logically. Even though the men of Ai had defeated a force of 3,000 men earlier, it is illogical to assume or even conclude that the king of Ai would consider bringing his men out to face 25,000 Israelites. No leader would have been that stupid or foolhardy, no matter what the past had shown. Even though it is likely that the king had been given reinforcements to help in the defense of Ai, there would have been no good reason to go outside the city gate to face an army so much superior. A fair interpretation of scripture indicates that there were men from both Ai and Bethel in the city. (See Joshua 8:17.) Since the Israelites had attacked Ai once, there was a good chance they would be back, but with a larger force the next time. Therefore, it is highly likely that Ai had been reinforced by troops from Bethel. The fact that there were troops from Bethel would suggest one of two possibilities: (1) Ai was an outpost for Bethel and the key to preventing the Israelites from attacking Bethel directly or (2) Ai and Bethel had a strong alliance, whereby each king swore to help the other in the event of an attack on either city. Researchers tend to lean towards the first possibility because the name "Ai" means ruins. In other words, Ai may have been a stronghold at some point in the past and what remained was a shadow of the former city. The fact that the city may have been vulnerable in the event of a siege is why the troops from Ai came out to meet the first wave of 3,000 Israelites in open combat. However, it is also a good possibility, as some researchers suggest, that Ai was named later.

In any event, Joshua and 25,000 warriors spent the rest of the daylights and the following night on the hills north of the city gate of Ai. It would have given Joshua and the commanders with him to consider the tactics to be used to carry out the detailed plan God had given to Joshua. God likely told Joshua everything Joshua was to do in attacking Ai. Scripture just does not reveal all the details of the plan as told by God. Much of this is revealed during the battle itself. This would not be the first time scripture revealed the details of the plan while the plan was being executed. Prior to the conquest of Jericho, God gave Joshua the plan. When the plan was being carried out, scripture revealed details in the execution not mentioned earlier when God gave the plan to Joshua. It appears that there is a similar situation in the plan to conquest of Ai. Joshua likely spent the daylight and evening hours reconnoitering Ai from his vantage point on the hill. He would have been able to see that the city had more troops in it than were there during the First Battle of Ai. He would have seen this during the day and by campfire at night. It is likely that Joshua estimated the military strength of the enemy at around 10,000 men before the battle took place since 12,000 men and women in and outside Ai were killed by the Israelites during the Second Battle of Ai. (See Joshua 8:25.)

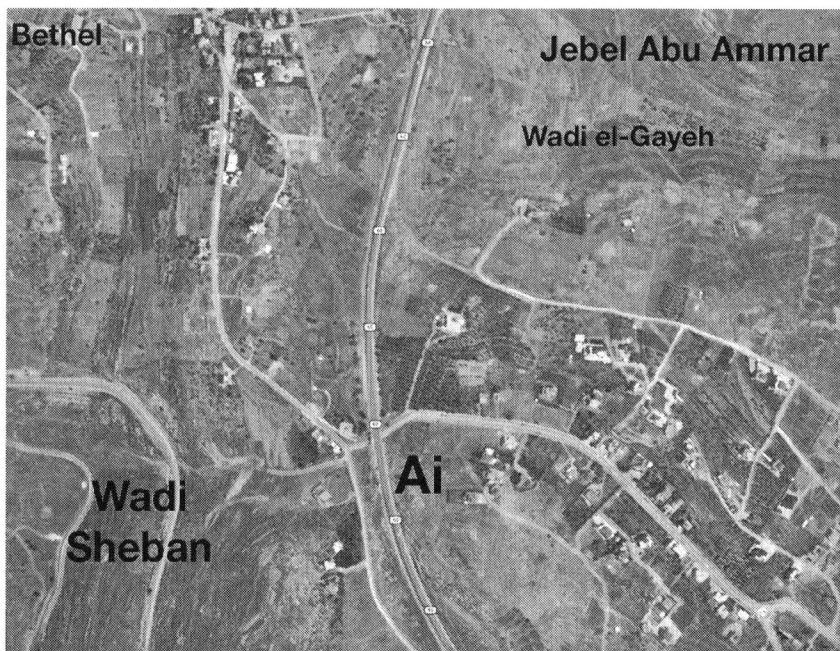

This map shows where Ai was located at the time of Joshua. The Wadi Sheban (lower left) is where the ambushers were hidden. The mountains to the front of Ai (now called Jebel Abu Ammar) are at the upper right. The shallow valley where Joshua stationed his troops is now called Wadi el-Gayeh. It is at the base of Jebel Abu Ammar.

It is easy to conclude that Joshua brought down less than half the men he had available to face the king of Ai and his army and that number was probably about 10,000 warriors. The whole idea was to have the king of Ai attack Joshua's forces, who would then turn and flee, just as they had done in the first battle. Since this was going to be the case, then Joshua would not want his fleeing men falling all over themselves. Therefore, he would want a force of men large enough to make it appear that he was asking for a battle, but small enough so that Joshua's men could flee easily and not be caught by the pursuing Canaanites. If Joshua brought a force of 10,000 men into the field, then he would have left about 15,000 men up on the hills north of Ai. Whatever the number in the valley, there would have been a greater force in the hills and these men would stay out of sight until needed. And, based on what Joshua did with his javelin, there was probably someone on the hills north of Ai to transmit whatever signals Joshua gave to the men in the hills and to those men in ambush west of the city. In fact, it may have been the monitor on the hills who transmitted Joshua's signal to the men in ambush.

This is probably the best time to discuss two issues: (1) was Joshua with the troops who were down in the valley and (2) how did the men in ambush know when to come out of hiding? Scripture does not make it clear if Joshua was on the field of battle or not. The scripture that reads "That night Joshua went into the valley" is ambiguous. Obviously, it does not mean that Joshua went into the valley all by himself. If not, does it mean that the Israelites went into the valley and the name "Joshua" is symbolic of their presence? It would seem that Joshua and the Israelites went into the valley together and their combined presence was represented by the name "Joshua." This appears to be the best interpretation for another reason. The primary motive for sending the Israelites into the valley was to fool the army

176

within Ai. What better way to motivate the men of Ai to come out than to have Joshua as an alluring target. If the Israelites were again beaten, then maybe Joshua would be killed or captured. If so, then the Israelites would have lost their leader and, often times, when a leader is killed or captured, the people never rally from such a loss. Therefore, it seems likely that Joshua was with his army in the field to further motivate the king of Ai to want to engage the Israelites in battle. It is likely the Israelites made it very clear who the most important person on the battlefield was, just as the people of Ai did the same with their king.

If Joshua were in the field with his army, then how could he communicate with the ambush party in the ravine west of Ai? The men in the ravine would not even have been able to see what was happening in the valley northeast of Ai. It would appear that Joshua was going to do the communicating with the blade of his javelin. Since the Second Battle of Ai took place shortly after sunrise, the sun would still be in the east and behind Joshua and the Israelite troops. At the appropriate time, Joshua would use the blade of his javelin to flash a signal to someone on the hills where Joshua and his men had spent the night. The person on the ridge would then relay the signal, using another javelin, to the men in hiding west of Ai. This technique, when used successfully, can relay a signal for miles. In fact, it was used by the Israelites throughout their history and by the Maccabees in the second century before Christ. Of course, this method of communicating with the ambush party would have been set up ahead of time. And, now to the battle.

e. The Second Battle of Ai

When the king Ai saw the Israelites in formation in the valley "overlooking the Arabah (the Jordan River Valley)," he and

177

his men hurried out of Ai to engage the Israelites in battle. Scripture makes it clear that he had no idea what lay in store for him. Once his men were in position, which would have taken some time, there was usually a short time when two armies would "posture" in front of each other. This was usually done to show the weapons on each side and to show each side how confident of victory each side was. Whether this happened or not, the king of Ai eventually pressed the fight with the Israelites. When the battle was joined, the Israelites put up a token resistance ("let themselves be driven back") and then they ran toward the "wilderness." (Joshua 8:14-15)

The Israelites most likely ran to the east, toward the Jordan Valley. They would not have run west, because his would have taken the enemy back towards their own city gate. In addition, that is direction from where the ambushers would be coming. The Israelites would not have run north, as they would have been trapped between the valley and the hills and, in addition, this is where the remainder of the Israelite warriors were hiding. The logical direction was east. This would be perfect, as it would take the men of Ai away from their city, which was part of the plan, and it would make them vulnerable to an attack on their left flank from the Israelites left on the hill.

The plan to lure the men of Ai away from the city worked perfectly. Thinking he had a repeat of the earlier battle, the king of Ai either ordered his men to pursue the Israelites or the men reacted instinctively and pursued on their own. In any event, the men of Ai and Bethel were lured away from Ai. This left the city completely unprotected as there was not a single man left inside. (Joshua 8:16-17)

It was time to put into play the next step of the plan. It was God who told Joshua to hold out his javelin (a light spear designed for throwing) and point it toward Ai. It was God who knew the perfect time to spring the trap. God then promised that Ai would soon be in the hands of the Israelites. What Joshua did with his javelin was obviously a pre-arranged signal that Joshua would use to alert the troops hiding in ambush west of Ai. The fact that God told Joshua when to do it, shows that God was, in fact, completely in control of the entire battle, from the planning to the execution. As soon as Joshua pointed his raised javelin toward Ai, the Israelites who had been waiting in ambush moved quickly into action. They rushed forward toward the open gate of Ai. When they reached the open gate, they entered the city unopposed, captured it easily (because there were no men present), and then set it on fire. (Joshua 18-19)

When the men of Ai saw the smoke coming from the city, they realized immediately that they had been fooled into leaving the city and they were now trapped between the Israelites behind them and the Israelites in front of them. It also seems likely that the Israelites on the hill also joined the fray, reinforcing the Israelite warriors who had "fled" towards the wilderness. The men of Ai had nowhere to go. The Israelites who had captured Ai then joined the battle. The Israelites who had been running to the east had stopped and had turned around. There was nothing that the men of Ai and Bethel could do but to run or to stand and fight to the death. And, that is what happened. The men of Ai had no other choices and God soon delivered them into the hands of the Israelites. Every enemy soldier was killed but the king of Ai. He was captured and brought to Joshua. (Joshua 8:20-23)

Once all the men of Ai and Bethel were killed, the Israelites went into the city and killed everyone there. As already mentioned, 12,000 men and women "fell" that day before God and his people. Every person who had been in the city of Ai that very morning were now dead. The last person to die was the king of Ai. Joshua impaled the king and then left the body hanging until evening. At sunset, Joshua ordered the body taken down and thrown at the entrance of the city. Once that was done, the Israelites covered the body with a large pile of rocks. (Joshua 8:24-26, 29)

Joshua ordered the entire city to be burned, making it a "permanent heap of ruins." However, before the city was burned, the Israelite soldiers were allowed to go through the city and take anything they could find of value, including livestock. (Joshua 8:27-28)

Joshua burning the city of Ai

It is interesting that none of the other city-states around Ai did anything to help the city and its people except Bethel and one commentator even suggested that Ai was actually an outpost of Bethel and they were obligated to defend it. Jebus, which later became Jerusalem after David conquered it, was only a day's march to the south of Ai and the king of that city did nothing to aid Ai. Maybe the kings of the cities in the area thought the threat of the Israelites would go away once the Israelites conquered some territory and settled down. It is likely that the Jebusites were not in league with Bethel and Ai and felt no compunction to go to the aid of those two cities. In addition, the Amarna Letters (see Appendix) give yet another picture of the times. If the cities of Bethel and Ai were a competing league of cities with the Jebusites and their allies, then the Jebusites would have deliberately not intervened in the conflict, perhaps hoping that Bethel and Ai would be defeated and a deal could be made with the Israelites. The Jebusites would later regret the decision to not get involved at an early stage of the Israelite invasion of Canaan.

Even though God had to urge the Israelites to carry out His plan, the author of the Book of Joshua made it very clear that it was God's victory from start to finish. It was God who encouraged Joshua. (Joshua 8:1a) It was God who revealed to Joshua that God had already delivered the king of Ai and all that he owned and controlled into Joshua's hands. (Joshua 8:1b) It was God who changed the reward system for the battle to allow the Israelites to profit materially from the victory. (Joshua 8:2, 27) It was God who developed the entire plan for the battle to take Ai. (Joshua 8:2b, et sequence) Joshua told his troops that it was God who would hand Ai over to them. (Joshua 8:7b) It was God who told Joshua the exact moment the troops waiting in ambush needed to be brought into the battle. (Joshua 8:18) God told His people he would be there with them when they obeyed his commands and He was.

f. The Second Battle Of Ai Duplicated

The Second Battle of Ai was duplicated at the Battle of Cowpens by an American general during the American Revolution. The strategy used by Brigadier General Daniel Morgan was so similar to that used by Joshua, it appears that the American commander must have read about the Second Battle of Ai in his Bible. He used a ruse that helped him defeat the British troops opposing him. He set the scene nicely. He picked a spot on a road which had a ravine on one side of the road and a swamp on the other side. The spot was obviously chosen to funnel the British troops towards him and to prevent being enveloped on his flanks. He then sent his militia ahead on the road to face the first onslaught of British troops. He positioned the militia where they would be seen by the advancing British soldiers. Militia were made up of troops drawn from counties and were not a part of the regular army. They had a well-deserved reputation for retreating briskly when under fire. "Retreating briskly" is a nice way of saying that they ran from the battle as soon as they were confronted by British regulars. Behind a slight rise in the road and hidden from the approaching red coats, the American commander put his Continental troops, all well-trained, well-armed, and well-disciplined. The militia had these orders: fire a couple of rounds when the British got close enough and then run away in a disorganized and haphazard manner. The militia did as they were ordered. The British troops, thinking that the militia had panicked once again and were in full flight, broke ranks and chased after the militia. In the meantime, the militia ran up the rise in the road and then ran behind the waiting Continental troops. Thinking they had won yet another battle against an ill-trained and motley militia, the British troops continued to run after the militia. However, once they got to the top of the rise, the only thing they found were Continental troops, who then opened fire, killing a large number of the British soldiers. The remainder of the British regulars abandoned the battlefield soon after and were captured. Lieutenant Colonel Banastre Tarleton, the British commander, was barely able to escape. His military force suffered an 86 per cent casualty rate, which included dead, wounded, captured, and missing in action. The heavy losses by Tarleton forced

General Conwallis to retreat to Yorktown, Virginia, where he eventually surrendered to General George Washington.

Part Two

f. Mount Ebal and Mount Gerizim

There is no doubt that Joshua took the Israelites to Mount Ebal and Mount Gerizim at some point after the Israelites went into Canaan, but it may not have been right after the victory at Ai. For the Israelites to have gone unhindered to the two mountains, the central region of Canaan would have had to have been subdued and there is no evidence of that. In addition, there mention of any capture of Shechem, which lay between the two mountains. Also, it would seem that the destruction of the cities in the southern and central regions of Canaan, as set forth in Chapter 9, would logically follow the Israelite victory at Ai and the Israelite journey to Mount Ebal and Mount Gerizim does not. It is likely the author inserted it after the battle at Ai because it seemed like a good place to bring up Moses' admonition to the Israelites, which will be discussed below.

Whatever the timing might have been, Joshua definitely took the Israelites to Mount Ebal and Mount Gerizim. It appears Joshua did this because of a command from Moses, who gave these instructions to the Israelites:

"If you carefully observe all these commands I am giving you to follow—to love the Lord your God, to walk in obedience to him and to hold fast to him— then the Lord will drive out all these nations before you, and you will dispossess nations larger and stronger than you. Every place where you set your foot will be yours: Your territory will extend from the desert to Lebanon, and from the

Euphrates River to the Mediterranean Sea. No one will be able to stand against you. The Lord your God, as he promised you, will put the terror and fear of you on the whole land, wherever you go. See, I am setting before you today **a blessing and a curse**— the blessing if you obey the commands of the Lord your God that I am giving you today; the curse if you disobey the commands of the Lord your God and turn from the way that I command you today by following other gods, which you have not known. When the Lord your God has brought you into the land you are entering to possess, you are to proclaim on Mount Gerizim the blessings, and on Mount Ebal the curses." (Deuteronomy 11:22-29)

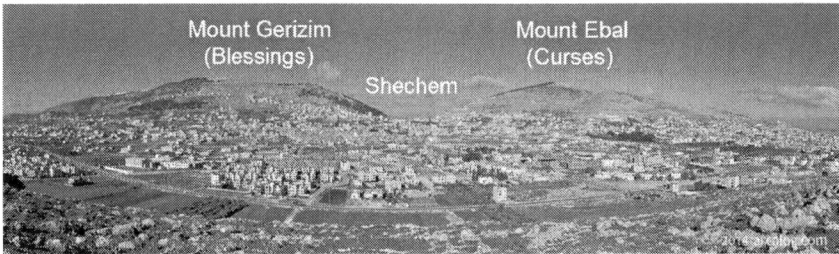

After the victory at Ai, the path to go to the two mountains may have been clear. Mount Gerizim was located to the south of Mount Ebal. The valley between the two mountains is 1,500 feet wide. The tops of the two mountains are about one and two-thirds miles apart. The town of Shechem lay between the two mountains. Mount Gerizim was covered with grass and shrubbery, and many kinds of food were grown on it. It had an abundance of flora. It was truly "blessed" with vegetation. Mount Ebal was just the opposite. It was devoid of all plant life. The word "Ebal" means "bald stone." It was truly "cursed" with barrenness. Both mountains had the same soil, the same rains, and the same winds, but it did not produce the same result. Mount Gerizim was closer to Jerusalem than was

Mount Ebal. This may later have had some symbolic meaning for the Jews and it certainly did for the Samaritans, who worshipped on Mount Gerizim. The Samaritans believed that Mount Gerizim was taller than Mount Ebal, which is not true. Mount Gerizim is 2,890 feet above sea level, with Mount Ebal being taller at 3,080 feet above sea level. See this website for more information: **https://bibleatlas.org/mount_ebal.htm**

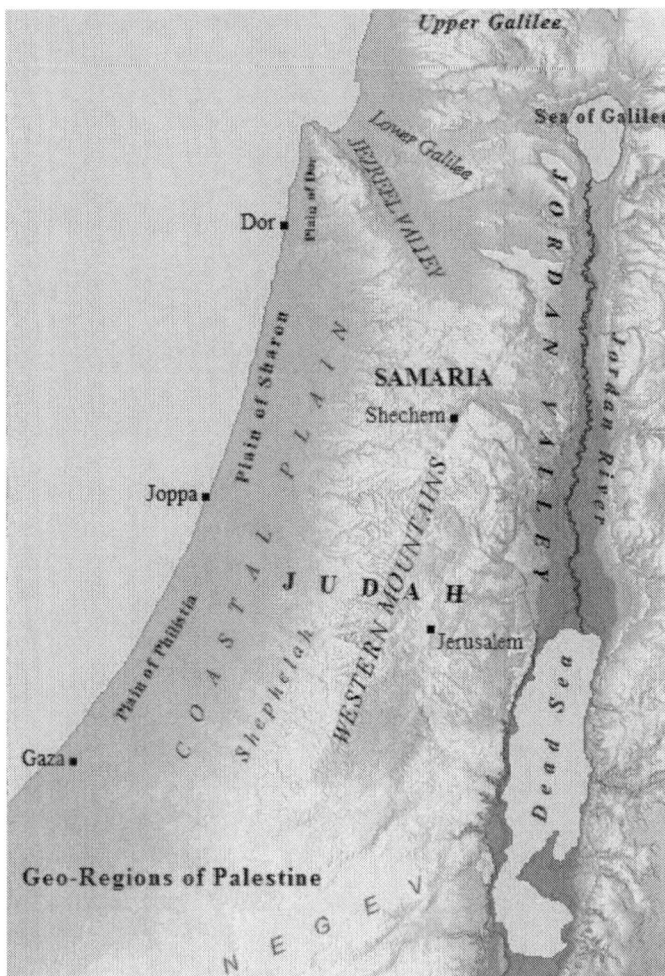

Location of Shechem.

Mount Gerizim was about 25 miles northwest of Jericho. It is not known what route the Israelites took to get to Mount Gerizim and Mount Ebal. However, it is likely that the Israelites went to the two mountains by going north up the west side of the Jordan River and then heading west at some point. How they convinced the Canaanites they met along the way to allow them to pass is not mentioned. Perhaps the defeats the Canaanites suffered at Jericho and Ai (and, perhaps Bethel) persuaded the locals to give the Israelites safe passage. Or, it is possible that the Israelites did not travel to the two mountains until after the southern and the middle regions of Canaan had been subdued.

g. The Reading of the Law

Once the Israelites reached Mount Ebal and Mount Gerizim, they performed certain acts and certain rituals that did not seem to bear any relationship with setting about conquering Canaan. Why did they interrupt their pursuit of securing the land and go to two mountains in the central part of Canaan? It has already been noted that they went to the mountains because Moses had commanded it. But, why the rituals? Well, it again had to do with Moses.

While the Israelites were still east of the Jordan River, Moses gave the Israelites the law that was to govern them when they were in possession of the Promised Land. While giving the law, Moses and the elders instructed the people to keep all the commands that Moses had given them that day. In addition, Moses gave them instructions to go to Mount Ebal and to Mount Gerizim. While there, Moses said (bold added for emphasis), "When you have crossed the Jordan into the land the Lord your God is giving you, set up some large stones and coat them with plaster. Write on them all the words of this law when you have crossed over to enter the land the Lord your God is giving you, a land flowing with milk and honey, just as the Lord, the God of your ancestors, promised you. And when you have crossed the Jordan, **set up these stones on Mount Ebal**, as I command you today, and **coat them with plaster**. **Build there an altar** to the Lord your God, **an altar of stones**. Do not use any iron tool on them. Build the altar of the Lord your God with field stones and **offer burnt offerings on it** to the Lord your God. **Sacrifice fellowship offerings there**, eating them and rejoicing in the presence of the Lord your God. And you shall **write very clearly all the words of this law on these stones you have set up**." (Deuteronomy 27:2-8)

Joshua built an altar on Mount Ebal. The altar was made of uncut (or natural) stones that were not reshaped in any way. The Levites then presented to the Lord burnt offerings and sacrificed fellowship offerings on the altar. Joshua wrote a copy of the law of Moses on the stones. The text is not clear as to whether Joshua wrote on the stones of the altar or on different stones, but, following the command of Moses, Joshua most likely wrote on different stones. It appears from the text that while Joshua was writing on the stones, all of the Israelites were present somewhere. It is likely, based on the topography of the area, that they were standing in the valley between Mount Ebal and Mount Gerizim. They were standing on both sides of the ark of the covenant, which was being held up by the priests from the tribe of Levi. The assembled people included both descendants of the twelve tribes and foreigners who had joined the tribes at some point prior to the tribes entering Canaan. One half of the group was standing "in front of" Mount Gerizim and one half "in front of" Mount Ebal. It appears that the ark of the covenant was being held up between the two groups. The only way to make sense of what all of this meant was to find out what Moses wanted the people to do when they arrived at Mount Ebal and Mount Gerizim.

The altar Joshua built on Mt. Ebal

Moses gave further instructions as to what the people should do at Mount Ebal and Mount Gerizim. He commanded, "When you have crossed the Jordan, these tribes shall stand on Mount Gerizim to bless the people: **Simeon**, **Levi**, **Judah**, **Issachar**, **Joseph** [**Manasseh** and **Ephraim**] and **Benjamin**. And these tribes shall stand on Mount Ebal to pronounce curses: **Reuben**, **Gad**, **Asher**, **Zebulun**, **Dan** and **Naphtali**." (Deuteronomy 27:12-13.) The curses can be found at Deuteronomy 27:9-26 and the blessings can be found at Deuteronomy 28:1-13.

The list of the tribes in Deuteronomy 27:12-13 who made up the two groups is interesting. Those nearest or on Mount Ebal, the mountain of cursing, are the tribes of Reuben, Gad, Asher, Zebulun, Dan, and Naphtali. They were the descendants of the sons, with one exception, of Bilhah and

189

Zilpah. Of course, Reuben is the exception. He was one of Leah's legitimate sons, but, he was cursed because he had sexual relations with Bilhah, his father's concubine. (Genesis 35:22) Bilhah and Zilpah were the slaves of Leah and Rachel, the women Jacob married.

The tribes nearest or on Mount Gerizim, the mountain of blessing, were the descendants of Simeon, Levi, Judah, Issachar, Joseph, and Benjamin. The men named were the children of Jacob's lawful wives, Leah and Rachel. (See Genesis 35:23-26.) It appears that the groups were deliberately arranged by Moses based on the mothers who gave birth to the original sons of Jacob. The people standing on Mount Gerizim were the ones who shouted blessings to the ones on the barren slopes of Mount Ebal. The people standing on rocky Mount Ebal were the ones who shouted curses to the ones on the verdant slopes of Mount Gerizim.

Once all that was commanded by Moses was done, Joshua then read the entire words of the law regarding the blessings and the curses as they were found in Deuteronomy (The Book of the Law). Joshua not only read the law to the men, it was also read to the women, the children, and the foreigners who lived among the Israelites. (Joshua 8:34-35) The people on or about Mount Gerizim could hear Joshua speak because of the natural amphitheater that existed between the two mountains. The people now had no excuse for any deviation from God's commands. Joshua told each and everyone of them what the results would be of obedience to God's law and what the results would be of disobedience to God's law. It was now up to the people to follow the right path and not deviate from it.

CHAPTER NINE

a. The Enemy Unites

When the kings in southern and central Canaan heard about the Israelite victories at Jericho, Ai, and probably Bethel (Bet-el), they decided it was time to unite against a common foe. Therefore, the people of the three areas of Canaan (the hill country, the western foothills, and coastal region) came together as one. This included the kings of the Amorites, Canaanites, Hittites, Hivites, Jebusites, and Perizzites. However, the people of Gibeon, who were Hivites, had a better idea.

b. The Gibeonite Deception

The city of Gibeon was part of the Hivite people. Its king normally would have stayed allied with the other kings of the alliance. However, the Gibeonites had what they thought was a better idea. It was obvious that the Gibeonites were aware of the fact that the Israelites could entry into treaties with people east of the Jordan River, but not with nations west of the Jordan River. The people west of the Jordan River either had to be forced out of Canaan or eliminated. God gave no other option. And, it was clear from what happened to the people of Jericho and Ai that the Israelites were obeying God's command. The people of Canaan could either surrender and leave Canaan or they could resist the Israelites and be eradicated. Not wanting to leave Canaan and not wanting to be completely wiped out, the Gibeonites chose the middle road: deception.

The plan of deception was simple. The Gibeonites would pretend to be a people from "a very distant country." They would attempt to induce Joshua to enter into a treaty with their "nation." However, pretending would not be good enough. They had to have some proof of a very long journey from some land beyond Canaan. They would even have to pretend to have started their journey either north or east of the land already conquered by the Israelites on the east side of the Jordan River and already distributed to Reuben (in the south adjacent to and north of Moab), Gad (north of and adjacent to Reuben), and the half-tribe of Manasseh, (north of and adjacent to Gad). The area distributed to Reuben, Gad, and Manasseh stretched from the north half of the Dead Sea to the land of the Hittites, which was past Lake Huleh.

To make the ruse a successful one, the Gibeonites decided to make their carriage, their clothing, and their food appear to have aged from traveling an extended distance. They loaded donkeys with worn-out sacks and old wineskins, both of which were cracked and mended. They wore old clothes and put well-used and patched sandals on their feet. They then gathered a full supply of bread that was dry and moldy. They probably took additional steps to make it appear the trip they had been on was long and arduous. No doubt, they took powdered dirt and threw it on the bottoms of their cloaks. They may even have put items of dried vegetation in their hair and beards to add to the effect. In the end, they assured themselves that their lie would give them the protection they needed from the Israelite juggernaut. (Joshua 9:3-5)

c. The Ruse into Action

Now it was time to put their deception into action. It is likely that the Gibeonites took a round-about route to get to Gilgal, where the Israelites were camped. Gibeon was about 15 miles due west of Gilgal, but the Gibeonites could not be see coming from the west. If so, their deception would have been uncovered at the start. The Gibeonites had to either go north of Gilgal, which would have been the shorter route and less populated or go south of Gilgal by the major trade routes and into more populated regions. It is likely that the Gibeonites took the northern route to avoid unnecessary questions from people who might recognize them. Whichever route the Gibeonites took, they would have to appear to be coming from the east or the north.

The Gibeonites want a treaty with the Israelites.

Once the Gibeonites reached Gilgal and after the necessary formalities, the Gibeonites got down to the reason for their contact with the Israelites. The spoke directly and bluntly to Joshua: "We have come from a distant county; make a treaty with us." (Joshua 9:6) The Israelites, not Joshua, responded with a note of suspicion in their question: "But perhaps you live near us, so how can we make a treaty with you?" (Joshua 9:7) This question surely caused a tense moment in Gilgal. The Gibeonites likely thought their masquerade was an excellent one. They obviously did not

193

have much respect for the Israelites in the first place for them to think that such a ruse would work. Now, they were being asked a question that they might not have been prepared to answer.

At this juncture, Joshua should have taken the lead. He should have latched onto the Israelite's suspicion and carried it to God. After all, whenever the Israelites as a whole and Joshua in particular made any important decision without consulting God, the situation turned from what seemed an acceptable situation to disaster very quickly. The First Battle of Ai should have been in the forefront of Joshua's thinking. The Gibeonites responded to Joshua personally, "We are your servants." In other words, we are at your mercy, why would we lie to you and cause ourselves some serious problems? Unfortunately, the response of the Gibeonites did nothing to move Joshua in the right direction. Joshua now wanted some particulars to help him decide whether to deal with these people or not. Joshua wanted to know who they were and where was this place whose people wanted a treaty with the Israelites. (Joshua 9:8)

It should be remembered that this was the first time that Joshua had personally conducted international relations with a foreign people. He may have assisted Moses in Moses' negotiations with nations such as Moab and Edom, but Joshua had never made any treaty decisions on his own. This was an even greater reason for Joshua to have halted the discussions and turned to God for guidance. However, he did not do so and the negotiations continued.

The Gibeonites wisely did not name the king who had sent them or the name of the nation to which they belonged. They resorted to stealth, evasion, and flattery. Their first response contained the phrases "your servants" (referring to themselves), "from a very distance county" (unnamed), "because of the fame of the Lord your God" (flattery). They then continued their praise of God by listing all they had heard about Him: (1) what God did in Egypt; and, (2) what God did to Sihon, king of Heshbon, and Og, king of Bashan, who reigned in Ashtaroth (now controlled by the half-tribe of Manasseh). (Joshua 9:9-10)

The Gibeonites continued with their charade, either because they were not interrupted or because the Israelites seemed to be taking the bait. In any event, the Gibeonites gave a short history of being selected to travel to meet up with the Israelites to secure a treaty. They were ordered to take provisions for the journey. To make their point, the Gibeonites brought out samples of the bread they had with them. They pointed out that the bread was still warm (meaning fresh) when they packed it up on the day they left their country on the journey to the Israelites. They had the Israelites look at the condition of the bread as they spoke. It was then dry and moldy. They then drew attention to the wineskins on their donkeys. They explained that they were new and completely full when they started out, but they were now cracked. Lastly, they pointed to their clothes and sandals to shown how much they had worn out while on their travels to meet up with the Israelites. (Joshua 9:11-13)

The Israelites were not completely convinced by the latest spiel by the Gibeonites, but their resistance was slowly being eroded. The Israelites had no argument against the look of the wineskins or the appearance of the clothes or the shoes, but they could test the condition of the bread. The Gibeonites waited anxiously as the Israelites sampled at least the bread and determined that it certainly seemed to have been baked a long time in the past and had reached its prime some time earlier. Joshua then imprudently made a treaty with the Gibeonites without once asking for God's input into the matter. (Joshua 9:14-15) What the Israelites did was swear by the Lord, the God of Israel, that they would not attack the Gibeonites and, likely, the Gibeonites would not attack them. Interestingly, the reader will find later that the treaty with the Gibeonites worked to the advantage of the Israelites. But, that is getting ahead of the story.

d. The Deception Was Discovered

No detail is provided in the text as to how the Israelites found out that they had been bamboozled by the Gibeonites, only that the Israelites heard three days after the treaty was solemnized that the people from a far away country were actually people from Gibeon, a "neighboring" town. ("Neighboring" might be too strong of a word as the Israelites had to travel three days - without haste, no doubt - to get to Gibeon from Gilgal.) (Joshua 9:16) When Joshua heard that the Gibeonites had tricked him and the rest of the Israelites into a treaty, "the Israelites set out." (Joshua 9:17a) It is highly likely that not all the Israelites made the trip from Gilgal to Gibeon. The most probable scenario is that Joshua was accompanied by a significant portion of his army. To have moved the entire camp to confront Gibeon about its deception would have been absolutely unnecessary. However, the army had to have been large enough for the Gibeonites to understand the Israelites were serious about why they were on Gibeon's doorstep and that they were ready to execute any decision that was made by Joshua.

After traveling for three days, Joshua and his army came to the cities implicated in the ruse. They were Gibeon, Kephirah (or Kefireh, five miles west southwest of Gibeon), Beeroth (or Be'eroth, two miles south of Gibeon?), and

Kiriath Jearim (five miles southwest of Gibeon). These small towns were apparently part of an alliance whereby they were under Gibeon's protection. However, before any assault on Gibeion or the nearby towns was attempted, a war counsel of the Israelites was held. The leaders argued that they had sworn on oath to the Gibeonites by "the Lord, the God of Israel." This meant that the Israelites should not attack Gibeon. The rank and file were not impressed with the argument of the leaders and they "grumbled against the leaders." (Joshua 9:17-18) So, the leaders fashioned a compromise that seems to have been accepted by the grumblers. Interestingly, Joshua's name was not brought up once during these discussions, which seems strange since he was the person who made the treaty. The import of the give and take of the war counsel seems to be this: Joshua may have negotiated the treaty, but it was evidently ratified by the leadership. In any event, the compromise consisted of these elements: (1) We gave our oath to them by swearing on the name of "the Lord, the God of Israel"; (2) We cannot touch (kill) them now; (3) We will let them live so the Lord's wrath will not fall on us; and, (4) We will force them into slavery and they will be woodcutters and water carriers for us. (Joshua 9:19-21) Once the decision of the leadership was made, Joshua summoned the Gibeonites and they came. Joshua accused them of deceiving the Israelites by claiming they lived a long way from the Israelites when they actually lived nearby. Joshua then pronounced their sentence. They were now under a curse and the curse was perpetual servitude to the Israelites. The Gibeonites would serve as woodcutters and water carriers for the house (sanctuary) of God. (Joshua 9:22-23)

The Gibeonites, feeling as if they had to justify what they did, even after sentence had been passed on them, told Joshua that they participated in the deception because they feared that they would all be killed by the Israelites. They had been informed exactly what God had commanded to Moses and, if the command were carried out, every Gibeonite would be wiped from the face of the earth. It was not a future they relished. After giving their explanation, they placed themselves in the hands of the Israelites to do as the Israelites thought right. (Joshua 9:24-25) Of course, they already knew what their future would be like and their telling the Israelites to do what was right only echoed the decision that had already been made.

In the text, Joshua is given credit for saving the Gibeonites. Perhaps this was a shorthand way of revealing that the leadership followed Joshua's feelings on the matter when they made the decision to not kill the Gibeonites. From that day forward, the Gibeonites would be woodcutters and water carriers. They would "provide for the needs of the altar of the Lord at the place the Lord would choose." That was what they were doing at the time the Book of Joshua was written. (Joshua 9:26-27) The ark of the covenant was then in Gilgal, but it was later relocated to Shiloh. (Joshua 18:1-2) Scripture also reveals that, by the time of David, the tabernacle of the Lord had been erected "at the high place in Gibeon." After the ark of the covenant had been taken to Jerusalem, David left Zadok "the priest" in Gibeon to "present burnt offerings to the Lord on the altar of burnt offering regularly, morning and evening, in accordance with everything written in the Law of the Lord." This demonstrates that Gibeon not only became subject to the Israelites, it also became a center of worship for the Israelites. It also suggests that Gibeonite culture also changed from the worship of idols to the worship of the true God. (1 Chronicles 16:39-40)

CHAPTER TEN

a. Gibeon Is Attacked

Adoni-Zedek, the king of Jerusalem, then called Jebus, was very much aware of the presence of the Israelites in Canaan. He knew that both Jericho and Ai had fallen to the Israelites. These events were of concern to Adoni-Zedek. The situation worsened when he learned that Gibeon, a city in the midst of the highlands and not more than a day's march from Jerusalem, had made a treaty of peace with the Israelites. This alarmed him and his people enormously because Gibeon was an important city, politically, economically, and militarily. Even worse was the fact that Gibeon was practically on the doorstep of Jerusalem and Jerusalem lay between the Israelites and Gibeon. It was so significant to the area because it was like a royal city. Not only that, it was larger than Ai and its men were good fighters. (Joshua 10:1-2) In short, Adoni-Zedek would not be able to eliminate Gibeon from being a developing threat to the highlands without help from his fellow kings.

Adoni-Zedek needed assistance dealing with the threat from Gibeon. He sent messages to his fellow Amorite kings, telling them that Gibeon had made peace with Joshua and the Israelites. He called upon **Hoham**, king of Hebron; **Piram**, king of Jarmuth; **Japhia**, king of Lachish; and, **Debir**, king of Eglon. Adoni-Zedek had to have been pleased when all four kings responded positively to his request for aid.

The cities of Hebron, Jarmuth, Lachish, and Eglon were all south of Jerusalem and Gibeon. Jarmuth was about 17 miles southwest of Jerusalem; Lachish was about 28 miles to the south southwest; Hebron was about 30 miles to the south; and, Eglon was about 37 miles to the south southwest. All of the cities were over a day's march from Jerusalem and, in the case of Eglon, almost a four-day march. It was a strange alliance of disparate cities. Jerusalem was in the hills, Hebron was in the southern hills, and Lachish, Jarmuth, and Eglon were in the foothills. If maps can be believed, the Hebron people were Hittites, and the rest were Canaanites and Amalekites, although they are referred to as Amorites in scripture. One would think that if Jerusalem could form an alliance with these cities, surely it could have allied with Jericho, Ai, and Bethel, which were much closer. Whatever their ethnic differences may have been, it was not long before all five kings joined their forces and attacked Gibeon. (Joshua 10:3-5) It is altogether likely that the four kings met with Adoni-Zerek in Jerusalem and a plan of attack was worked out ahead of time, with each king having a specific role to play in the siege of Gibeon. King Adoni-Zerek may have played the role of summoner and planner, but it is likely that the other kings, normally jealous of their prerogatives, would not have relinquished control over their armies. This would prove to be a liability when surprised by the Israelites.

b. God and Joshua Responded

The Gibeonites sent word to Joshua that they were being attacked by all the Amorite kings from the hill country. They appealed to Joshua to come quickly and to save them. They pleaded with Joshua not to abandon "your servants." Joshua appeared to have consulted God on the matter and God told Joshua, "Do not be afraid of them; I have given them into your hand. Not one of them will be able to withstand you." When God gave Joshua this assurance in the past at Jericho and Ai, the outcome was a positive one for the Israelites. Joshua then marched from Gilgal with his entire army, including all of the best fighting men. (Joshua 10:6-7) Again, it is likely that Joshua did not take every fighting man with him. The reference to the "entire army" probably meant the entire group of men he chose to go with him, otherwise the mention of the "best fighting men" has no meaning. If he had actually taken every fighting man, then that would have included those who were the best. The reason Joshua would have left fighting men behind would be to guard the older men, the women, and the children against any attack on the camp. After all, if the Gibeonites had deceived the Israelites on one occasion, what would keep them from doing it again. Perhaps the message was meant to pull the Israelites away from their camp so the Gibeonites, allied with others, could attack it after the fighting men left. It seems assured that Joshua consulted God before he gave the plea for help any credence.

Joshua had his hand-picked men march from Gilgal during the night. The night would have been from about 8 pm to about 5 am. To have gotten to Gibeon without mishap, it is likely that the moon was full that night. Even if the Israelites took the road that ran by Jerusalem, they still would have needed some light to negotiate that route. It is most probable that the Israelites used the quickest and most secretive route possible to get to Gibeon. That was probably the road that ran right by Ai and Bethel. What better way to rally the morale of your troops than to have them go by sites where God had given them victory. Whatever the route taken, the Israelites fell upon the combined armies of the Amorites in utter surprise. The sudden assault likely took place at the first hint of sun over the hills. This would mean the sun would be in the eyes of the enemy soldiers. It would also mean that the enemy combatants would be just rousing from a night's sleep and would not be in their battle attire. In addition, the units would not have been assembled under the command of an officer and would not be in any battle formation. The Amorites could not form any defense whatsoever to the sudden attack. In short, the enemy was not prepared in any way for an assault on their unprotected back side. When this has happened in other battles, the result is utter confusion on the part of the army being attacked. The utter confusion would normally not allow the enemy enough time to respond appropriately. The first response under these circumstances, even for a well-trained soldier, would be to stand and fight as individuals and be slaughtered or to retreat as fast as possible in the hope of regrouping in some other area. Unfortunately, an unplanned retreat not only causes confusion amongst those retreating, it causes panic in the other soldiers caught in the retreat. Senior officers who stand their ground in an attempt to rally their troops are then the first to be cut down, increasing the wild sprint to a hoped-for place of safety. (Joshua 10:9)

The Lord also aided the attacking Israelites. He threw the Amorites into complete disorder around Gibeon. This meant a total inability of the enemy to organize any defense. Whether the Lord actually threw the Amorites into confusion or whether he gave Joshua the knowledge of how to do it and Joshua accomplished it is not known. Either way, it was God who accomplished the victory. It is likely, and more consistent with God's method of operation, that he gave Joshua the battle plan that would work and Joshua and his chosen men got the job done. In any event, Joshua and his troops utterly defeated the Amorite forces, throwing them into a mindless and disorganized mass of fleeing people, not soldiers, who were hoping their feet could save them when their weapons couldn't and didn't. The Amorites fled northwest towards Beth Horon, which would indicate that part of God's plan was to cut off the road to the southeast to Jerusalem as a means of escaping the enveloping Israelites. Joshua had prevented the fleeing Amorites from reaching the safety of Jerusalem or any of their cities. The fleeing Amorites were killed one by one as they fled from Gibeon to Beth Horon to Azekah and, finally, to Makkedah, a distance of about 30 miles. (Joshua 10:10)

If He had not been so in the battle at Gibeon, the Lord was actively involved as the Amorites ran from Beth Horon to Azekah. He "hurled" hailstones down on the fleeing Amorites and killed more with the hailstones than the Israelites killed with their swords. (Joshua 10:11) Before the reader conjures up some image of a Greek god personally throwing down hailstones or other objects (lightening, for example), one has to consider the aim of the author of the text. It is evident that God, the ruler of the universe, caused the hailstones to be cast down on the hapless Amorites. However, it is not likely that the author of the text meant that God actually tossed the hailstones himself. Incidentally, the current official record for a hailstone falling to earth is huge. It was about two pounds in weight, eight inches in diameter, and eighteen and one-inches in circumference. It was large enough to kill a human being if struck in the head. It fell in South Dakota on July 23, 2010. Interestingly, an author believes that the battle for Gibeon occurred on July 22 of a year near 1400 BC. (See **https://www.biblestudytools.com/dictionary/beth-horon-the-battle-of/**)

Joshua then added the last miracle to the day of disaster for the Amorites. Joshua, in the presence of the Lord and the Israelites, gave the command for the sun and the moon to stop in their movement across the sky and both stood still. The sun stopped over Gibeon and the moon over the Valley of Aijalon. This was done to make sure there was enough daylight for every Amorite soldier to be killed. This event was recorded in the Book of Jashar. (Joshua 10:12-13). The Valley of Aijalon is on a route which is just out of the hill country where Gibeon was located and the route was probably used by some of the fleeing Amorites in their attempt to escape the swords, spears, and arrows of the pursuing Israelites. It was about 10 miles slightly southwest from Gibeon. It would be considered to be in the lower foothills.

The sun stopped at noon and did not go down for almost 24 hours after it halted its path through the sky. (Joshua

10:13b) This gave the Israelites enough time to finish the rout by dealing with the five kings of the Amorites who had attacked Gibeon. They had attempted to hid in a cave at Makkedah while on the run, but they had been seen doing it. Their attempt to avoid being captured was foiled when Joshua ordered some of his men to pile up rocks in front of the cave. Joshua then had guards posted at the entrance to keep the kings from escaping. Everyone else continued to run after the Amorites because, as Joshua declared, "The Lord your God has given them into your hand." (Joshua 10:16-20) Once the enemy was completely defeated, Joshua had the five kings taken out of the cave to where Joshua was in Makkedah. The author named the kings again to make sure his reader knew who they were as their defeat was a major step toward the conquest of Canaan. Every king was from an important city: Jerusalem, Hebron, Jarmuth, Lachish, and Eglon. (Joshua 10:20-23)

Joshua commanding the sun to stand still.

Once the kings were brought to Joshua, he had them sprawled on the ground. He then told the Israelite army commanders to put their feet on the necks of these kings and the army commanders did as they were instructed. Joshua next commanded his troops, as the Lord had commanded him on other occasions, "Do not be afraid; do not be discouraged. Be strong and courageous. This is what the Lord will do to all the enemies you are going to fight." Joshua killed the five kings and had their bodies hung on five poles, where they were left until the evening. The bodies were then thrown back into the cave where they had been hiding and large rocks were placed in the front of the cave. (Joshua 10:24-27)

c. The Aftermath

Either before he executed the five kings or while they were hanging on the poles, Joshua and his troops conquered Makkedah. Everyone in the city was killed, including the king. He was killed in the same manner as the king of Jericho. (Joshua 10:28) The Israelites then went to Lidnah and attacked. They killed all of the people in that city, including the king. (Joshua 10:29-30) They moved on the Lachish and captured that city on the second day. Their king had been dispatched earlier. Everyone in that city was killed. Joshua then turned his attention to Horam, the king of Gezer, who had brought his troops south to aid Lachish. Joshua defeated the king of Gezer and his troops and left no survivors. (Joshua 10:31-33)

Joshua then attacked Eglon, the city whose king had gone to help the king of Jerusalem in his fight with the Gibeonites. It fell to Joshua and his men on the same day and every single person in the town was put to the sword. Joshua then moved on to Hebron, another city that had aided the king of Jerusalem. Everyone, including the new king, was killed. This included people in nearby villages. The text is not absolutely clear on this point, but it appears that Joshua destroyed the cites of Eglon and Hebron. (Joshua 10:34-37) Joshua then went back to Debir and its villages and killed everyone in that area. This concluded the southern campaign for the Israelites. They had conquered the entire area from the Negev in the south to Gibeon in the north and from Kadesh Barnea (home of the Israelites for 38 years while they were in the Wilderness of Zin) in the east to Gaza in the west. Joshua and the Israelites left no survivors, as God had commanded. They were successful in their fighting because the Lord, the God of Israel, "fought for Israel." (Joshua 10:38-42)

Then Joshua returned with his army back to their camp at Gilgal. (Joshua 10:43) 1400 BC had been a good year for the Israelites.

CHAPTER ELEVEN

a. Northern Kings Unite

Word made its way north to **Jabin**, king of Hazor, about the unprecedented defeat of the kings of southern and central Canaan by the Israelites. The word may have come from a tidal wave of refugees fleeing the swords of Joshua and his men. Perhaps it came by the way of pleas from desperate kings who were in the path of the Israelite forces. Whatever the source, Jabin acted immediately to what he perceived as a threat to his reign and to the other kings of northern Canaan.

Jabin sent messages to every king and tribal group in the entire north to rally behind Jabin to fight and defeat the Israelites and to be rid of that invading pest. One king is mentioned by name in the text. He was **Jobab**, king of Madon. Two kings are unnamed, but their cities are mentioned. They were the kings of Shimron and Akshaph (Achshaph). Several other unnamed kings were from different regions in the area near the Sea of Chinnereth (later called the Sea of Galilee). They were the northern kings in the mountains or hill country; the kings in the Arabah (the Jordan River Valley) south of Chinnereth; the kings in the western foothills (the Shephelah); and the king in Naphoth Dor in the west. The tribal groups included the Canaanites in the east and west; the Amorites, the Hittites, the Perizzites, and the Jebusites in the hill country; and, the Hivites below Mount Hermon in the Valley of Mizpah. In short, Jabin attempted to bring together an overwhelming coalition to confront the Israelites. He wanted a massive show of strength because the five-king coalition in the south had not been able to overwhelm the Israelites. (Joshua 11:1-3) If there were just two kings from each region mentioned added to the cities noted in the scripture, then there was a minimum of 10 kings in the alliance put together by Jabin. Likely, the coalition was even larger. Certainly, it was many times more formidable than the troops Joshua and the Israelites faced at Gibeon.

Interestingly, the list of kings and kingdoms seemed to include those areas in the upper one-third of Canaan, except the Jebusites, who occupied Jerusalem. It is doubtful that the Jebusites sent any troops at all. There may not have been many left after the debacle at Gibeon. Joshua had conquered the lower one-third by this time and many of the cities in the middle one-third of Canaan. Also, see Chapter Fifteen for a full discussion of the Israelites' fight to capture Jerusalem. It is likely the Jebusites needed every soldier they could muster to defend their city. Some researchers have written that the northern coalition may have included the remnants of the Jebusite army, but this is not likely, considering the fact that the Biblical narrative indicates that the armies of the south, which included the Jebusites, were annihilated by Joshua's troops at the Battle of Gibeon.

The response Jabin got was probably greater than even he expected. The kings brought together an army of enormous size. It was "as numerous as the sand on the seashore." The army not only included men, it was comprised of a large number of horses and chariots, war implements the Israelites did not have but would need if they faced the enemy in a face-to-face, open-field battle. Chariots, in particular, were like modern-day tanks. They were designed to intimidate and demoralize an enemy that only had foot soldiers. All the forces of the north came together at the "Waters of Meron" or "Waters of Merom." (Joshua 11:4)

For the purposes of the discussion, the term Waters of Merom or Mount Merom will be used because Scripture used the term "Waters of Merom."

The exact location were the armies gathered is not known for sure, but some writers have placed the site at the southeast base of Mount Merom. Some researchers have focused on the area around Jebel Marun as the probable rallying site. The physical features of this region harmonize nicely with what is known about the battle. The road up from the southern part of Canaan went through the plain of Acco from Gath (in the south) to Merom. A northeastern route then went to Hazor and then to Kadesh of Galilee. A northwestern route went to Sidon. This location was generally a central point for all the armies that gathered. Unfortunately for the alliance, it was a site unsuitable for an army with chariots. The area abounded with water for the soldiers and for the horses, but it was no place to fight a battle using chariots or traditional formations. The land between Mount Merom and the Waters of Merom was a narrow strip of land bounded by low hills. It was a great place to gather an army, but it was a very poor place to fight a battle.

b. God Prepared a Response

There is no doubt that Joshua had his spies watching the arrival of king after king, each with their own troops. It had to have been a terrifying sight as the size of the army got bigger and bigger and more formidable than anything the Israelites could hope to match. No doubt, these spies had the same outlook about the size of the northern army that ten of the spies over 40 years earlier had of the people and their cities in Canaan. They probably told Joshua that it might not be a good time to attempt to invade the northern part of Canaan. Based on their likely recommendation, Joshua consulted God to see what should be done. After all, it was God who was the driving force behind the Israelite victories in the south. If the southern kingdoms could be attacked and defeated, why not the northern kingdoms. Of course, there was a major difference. Only five kings united against the Israelites in the south. Once they were defeated, Joshua and his men were able to defeat the other cities and villages in piece-meal actions. In the north, Jabin had brought together every kingdom in a united effort to thwart the Israelites once and for all.

The north presented an entirely different and bigger challenge than the south. However, God was not impressed. He told Joshua, "Do not be afraid of them, because at this time tomorrow I will hand all of them, slain, over to Israel." God had said something similar before the capture of Jericho and the Second Battle of Ai and the Battle of Gibeon and the God had fulfilled His promise each time. God only had one condition: "You are to hamstring their horses and burn their chariots." (Joshua 11:6) It is interesting that God made that a condition and it may have puzzled Joshua. However, it made sense to God. Joshua and his men needed to depend upon God in every decision. If the Israelites captured the chariots and the horses that were used with the chariots, then the Israelites might start depending on the tools of war rather than God. And, that would mean disaster for the Israelites, as Saul, the first king of the Israelites found out.

God understood perfectly what needed to be done. He applied two axioms of war in absolute harmony. Axiom One: never fight on the enemy's chosen ground. Axiom Two: when outnumbered, hit the enemy when it least expects it. God did not wait until the enemy was ready to fight. If God had waited, then the Canaanites and their allies

211

would have amassed their troops, talent, and tools of war at the Waters of Merom, developed a cohesive command structure and battle plan, and then decided on where and when to attack the vastly outnumbered Israelites. There should be no doubt that God knew what lay ahead and His plan of attack was to hit the northern armies when and where they least expected it. The text does not tell us when Joshua attacked the combined forces of the north, but it was likely while it was still dark, but during a full moon. At that time, the enemy soldiers would be asleep, out of their warrior garb, and the horses unyoked from their chariots. The only soldiers awake would be on guard duty, if there were any, and they would be dealt with easily enough.

The northern army had two weaknesses that come immediately to mind: (1) no unified command and (2) over confidence. As Civil War General Ulysses S. Grant once said, "Two commanders on the same field are always one too many." Whenever a number of different armies are brought together for a common goal, there is always the problem of command. Who was the commander-in-chief of the northern army? Likely, it was no one at this point. Even though Jabin had called the kings together, it is likely that no king wanted to be subordinate to any other king. These negotiations could drag into many days, if not months. How were the troops of the different kingdoms to be integrated with the other troops, many of whom had different training, different structures, different levels of competence, to name a few? This has always been a problem throughout history, as seen during World War I and World War II.

Even with the inherent problems of command and the integration of troops, these were probably not felt to be a problem because of the superiority of numbers of the combined northern armies. General Ulysses S. Grant once said something like this, "I have a two to one superiority over the Rebs. If I only lose one of my men for every one I kill, I will win the war." With the vast number of troops filing into the area day after day, there had to have been a corresponding swelling of confidence in each and every soldier. They had to have been sleeping peacefully at night, knowing that they would be called upon soon to slaughter the Israelites in battle and perhaps to kill each and every Israelite man, woman, and child to avenge what had happened in the south, and once again bring peace to Canaan. Their sleep was soon to be interrupted.

c. The Battle Was Joined

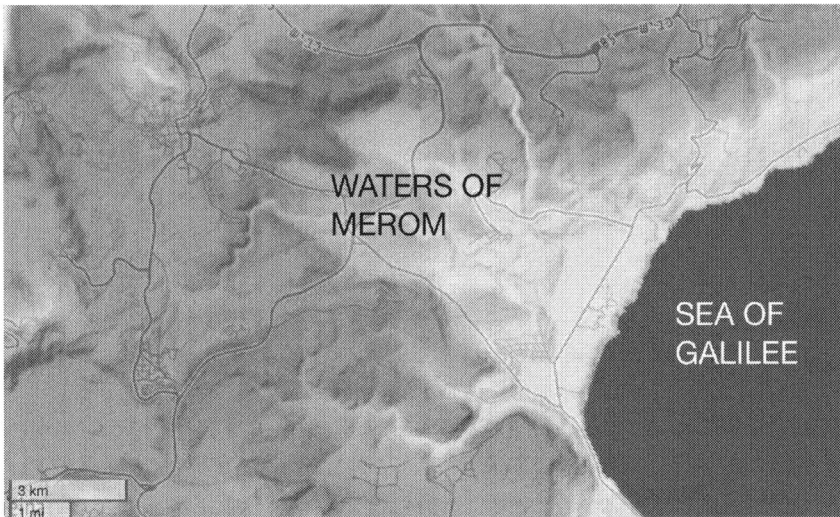

Location of the Waters of Merom

Whatever plan God gave to Joshua, the leader of the Israelites did not hesitate in putting it into action. Joshua and his whole army suddenly attacked the northern army while the enemy was at the Waters of Merom and the Lord provided the victory. (Joshua 11:7) Scripture gives no details of the battle itself: "They defeated them and pursued

213

them all the way to Greater Sidon, to Misrephoth Maim, and to the Valley of Mizpah to the east, until no survivors were left." Greater Sidon is identified as the coastal community of Sidon. It is located on the shore of the Mediterranean Sea about 90 miles from the Waters of Merom by a difficult route. The location of Misrephoth Maim is not known. However, some researchers believe it to be both of Tyre. This would make it about 60 miles from the Waters of Merom. In any event, both of these locations are generally northwest of the Waters of Meron. The Valley of Mizpah is likely the area at the foot of Mount Hermon. This would be about 50 to 60 miles east and then north from the battlefield.

All the reader knows from Scripture is that the Israelites routed the northern army. However, it is likely that the Israelites approached the Waters of Meron from the south under cover of darkness, with only the light of the moon to help with maneuvering through the hilly the terrain. To get his warriors into position in a terrain that was filled with wadis and other irregular features, Joshua would have had to have split his troops into many smaller units. This tactic can sometimes create confusion in an attempt at a coordinated attack. However, there is no doubt from the result that Joshua had formed his plan in great detail and each commander knew his role. Once Joshua gave the signal to attack, every available Israelite stormed into the camp of the northern army. The shock of the initial thrust caught many of the northern warriors off guard. Most of them were asleep and many of them were only awake for moments before they were killed. When those who were not slain in the initial assault broke and ran, the Israelites pursued them. Northern soldiers ran to the west and to the east to escape the Israelites. Based on the routes taken by the fleeing enemy, it appears that the Israelites assaulted the center of the enemy camp and then attacked both east and west. The fact that the enemy fled west and east indicates that Joshua's troops probably blocked the roads to the south. When the battle was over, there were no survivors left of the northern army. They had all been wiped out. The major resistance in the northern part of Canaan vanished in one battle. (Joshua 11:8) Joshua then followed God's command by hamstringing all of the captured horses and burning the enemy's chariots. (Joshua 11:9)

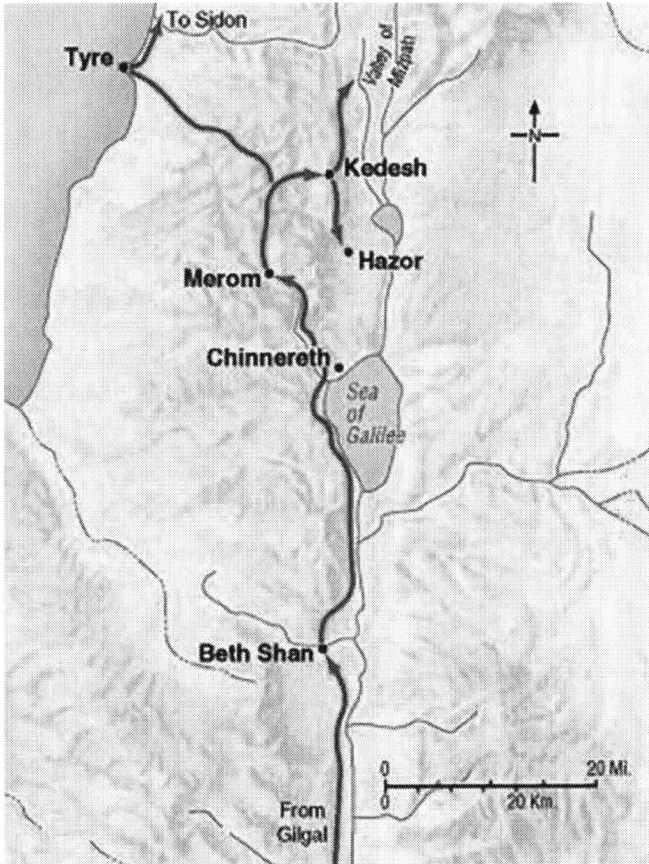

**Routes taken by the defeated northern armies
after being beaten badly by Joshua at the
spot labeled "Chinnereth" on the map.**

Joshua then moved against Jabin and the city of Hazor. It appears that Jabin may not have been at the Waters of Merom at the time of the battle. If he was, then he escaped back to his city. Joshua captured Hazor and killed everyone in the city, including the king. He then burned Hazor to the ground. (Joshua 11:10-11) Joshua then turned his attention to the other cities in the northern region of Canaan. He defeated every city and then put its king and its people to the sword. The soldiers were allowed to carry off all the valuables and all the livestock from each city and to keep the items for themselves. However, Joshua did not burn any of the cities except Hazor. Joshua did everything in his campaign that God had commanded Moses to do and Moses, in turn, commanded Joshua to do. (Joshua 11:12-15)

d. The Aftermath

Canaan was now almost completely conquered. Joshua fought a war against all the kings of Canaan "for a long time." God had hardened the hearts of the kings so they would resist Joshua. In this way, no king attempted to make a peace treaty with the Israelites except for the Gibeonites. Because each king fought a battle against the Israelites, they could be killed without mercy, as God had commanded Moses. The major resistance had been overcome and now only pockets of the original people had to be cleaned up. The land belonged to the Israelites. With a few exceptions, the Israelites were in possession of the Negev in the south, the Arabah (the Jordan River Valley) in the east, the hill country in the east, the foothills (or Shephelah) in the west and the whole region of Goshen (a district in Canaan that was part of the maritime plain of Judah and lay between Gaza and Gibeon). Their territory now extended from Seir in the south to Baal Gad (located in the Valley of Lebanon at the foot of Mount Hermon) in the north. (Joshua 11:16-20)

Some of the people that Joshua killed during the "clean up" war in the south were the Anakites. These were people of exceptional height and strength. Joshua and his loyal followers killed the Anakites who lived in the hill country and especially those in Hebron, Debir, and Anab. As it will be learned later, Caleb and his family participated in the capture of Hebron and Debir. However, not all the Anakites were killed in Hebron. (See Joshua 15:14.) The only Anakites left in Canaan survived in Gaza, Gath, and Ashdod. (Joshua 11:21-22)

The Israelites then had peace. (Joshua 11:23) This statement should not be understood in the wrong way. It was only meant to convey the fact that there was no further organized military resistance to the Israelites from the Canaanites during the leadership of Joshua. It did not mean that all of Canaan had been conquered by the Israelites. There were still many cities that stood against the Israelites in some form of the other. The battle to conquer these cities and their surrounding territories would continue until and into the time of David and Solomon. The reader will learn more about God's view of the matter in Chapter Thirteen.

CHAPTER TWELVE

a. Kings Killed East of the Jordan River

This chapter consists entirely of a list of those kings killed by the Israelites in their conquest of territory both on the east and west sides of the Jordan River.

The kings who were killed and their territories seized by Moses and the Israelites east of the Jordan River were Sihon and Og. Sihon was king of the Amorites. He ruled from this capital at Heshbon. His possessions included all the land from the Arnon Gorge (the border with Moab) in the south to the Jabbok River in the north, with the eastern part of the Jabbok River being the border between Sihon's and that of the Ammonites. This was half of Gilead. Sihon's kingdom continued north of the Jabbok River to the Yarmuk River. The western border of his kingdom was the Jordan River.

Og reigned in the land north of the Yarmuk River called Bashan. It was the upper half of the region called Gilead. He was the last of the Rephaites, a race of extremely tall humans. He reigned in the cities of Ashtaroth and Edrei.

The lands once ruled by Sihon and Og, going from south to north, were allotted to the tribes of Reuben and Gad and the half-tribe of Manasseh. (Joshua 12:1-6)

b. Kings Killed West of the Jordan River

The land conquered by Joshua and the Israelites on the west side of the Jordan River stretched from Baal Gad in the Valley of Lebanon (near Mount Hermon) in the north to

Mount Halak in the south and from the Jordan River in the east to the foothills in the west. The unconquered territories included nations along the Mediterranean Sea. (Joshua 12:7-8) There were 31 kings killed by the Israelites. (Joshua 12:24b)

Here is a list of the cities in southern and central Canaan whose kings were killed as set forth in Joshua 12:9-16. It appears that the list is somewhat in chronological order of the death of the king, with some exceptions. The entries noted in **bold** are mentioned elsewhere in the Book of Joshua as having a king killed or the city captured. The other cities marked with an * are not mentioned outside of this reference. The kings are:

1.   **Jericho** (see Joshua 6:1-25)
2.   **Ai**, near Bethel (see Joshua 8:1-29)
3.   **Jerusalem** (see Joshua 10:22-26)
4.   **Hebron** (see Joshua 10:22-26 and 10:36-37))
5.   **Jarmuth** (see Joshua 10:22-26)
6.   **Lachish** (see Joshua 10:22-26 and 10:31-32)
7.   **Eglon** (see Joshua 10:22-26 and 10:34-35)
8.   **Gezer** (see Joshua 10:33)
9.   **Debir** (see Joshua 10:38-39)
10.   *Geder aka Gedor (between Jerusalem and Hebron)
11.   *Hormah aka Harim (10 miles north of Lachish)
According to Judges 1:17, Hormah was attacked by the men of Judah and Simeon after the death of Joshua. The city was then called Zephath. After it was completely destroyed, its name was changed to Hormah, which means "destruction" in Hebrew.
12.   *Arad (10 miles northeast of Hormah)
13.   **Libnah** (see Joshua 10:29-30)
14.   *Adullam (foothills 10 miles north of Makkedah)
15.   **Makkedah** (foothills, see Joshua 10:28), and

16.   *Bethel (may have been captured after Ai). According to Judges 1:22-25, the tribes of Joseph (Manasseh and Ephraim) attacked Bethel and killed everyone in it except for a man and his whole family. The man and his family were well treated because the man showed the Israelites how to get into the city.

The second half of the listed kings, as found in Joshua 12:17-24, is the most interesting. It include kings from cities in the central and the northern sections of Canaan. However, the vast majority of the kings were from cities in northern Canaan. The entries noted below in **bold** are the only kings mentioned in Scripture that were involved in the battles in northern Canaan. All the rest were either kings who had assembled at the Waters of Merom or were killed when their cities were captured. The entries below which are underlined are located in central Canaan. The kings are:

17.   Tappuah (10 miles south of Shechem)
18.   Hepher (10 miles south of Megiddo)
19.   Aphek (10 miles west of Joppa)
20.   Lasharon (5 miles west of the Sea of Kinnereth/Galilee and 3 miles south of Madon)
21.   **Madon** (2 miles west of the Sea of Kinnereth/Galilee, killed in battle? see Joshua 11:1-8)
22.   **Hazor** (8 miles north of the Sea of Kinnereth/Galilee, see Joshua 11:10-11)
23.   **Shimron Meron** (8 miles north of Megiddo, killed in battle? see Joshua 11:1-8)
24.   **Akshaph/Acshaph** (4 miles southeast of Acco, killed in battle? see Joshua 11:1-8)
25.   Taanach (5 miles southeast of Megiddo)
26.   Megiddo (7 miles northwest of Jezreel)
27.   Kedesh (10 miles north of Hazor)
28.   Jokneam in Carmel (5 miles northwest of Megiddo)

29. Dor (in Naphoth Dor) (12 miles west of Megiddo)
30. Goyim in Gilgal (2 miles east of Shechem?), and
31. Tirzah (5 miles northeast of Shechem).

Tappuah, Goyim in Gilgal, and Tirzah appear to be in central Canaan and far from the battle at the Waters of Merom. It does not seem likely that they were included in the list of kings who were invited to join the coalition to fight the Israelites. What is altogether probable is that these cities were conquered by Joshua as he drove north to fight at the Waters of Merom or while they were on their way back to the Israelite camp at Gilgal. Another possibility is that they were part of a campaign to pacify the central part of Canaan at some later point and that series of battles was not included in the text. It should also be noted that Goyim in Gigal is not the same as the Gilgal where Joshua and the rest of the Israelites were encamped.

The rest of the list were probably cities whose kings joined the coalition at the Waters of Merom or were taken after the battle was won. They are all cities in northern Canaan.

CHAPTER THIRTEEN

a. Land Not Taken

There is no useful time frame between Chapters 11 and 12 and this chapter. Joshua defeated the armies of the northern cities in Chapter 11 and there is a list of the cities that had been conquered in Chapter 12. Most, if not all, of the cities listed in Chapter 12 were captured in the southern and northern campaigns. Joshua was young enough then to have taken an active part in each of the campaigns. The circumstance of Chapter 13 does not give the reader the same impression of Joshua.

God spoke to Joshua after Joshua had grown old. The text gives no age for Joshua when this happened. Joshua died at the age of 110 years and it is believed that he was 85 years old when the invasion of Canaan started. Therefore, it would be safe to conclude that this particular conversation took place when Joshua was 100 years of age or older.

It is difficult to read the conversation and not come away with the idea that God was not pleased with Joshua. God said to Joshua, "You are now very old, and there are still very large areas of land to be taken over." In other words, a significant amount of time has passed since the Israelites had entered the Promised Land and a great deal of the territory had not been conquered. (Joshua 13:1)

In case Joshua was not aware of the Israelites' dereliction in carrying out the conquest of Canaan, God was very specific as to what land remained to be taken (Joshua 13:2-7):

(1)   The regions of the Philistines. This group of people lived in Canaan along the Mediterranean Sea. The major cities were Ashkelon, Ashdod, Ekron, Gath, and Gaza. Their influence in the southern region extended into parts of the Negev and the foothills. This area was part of the inheritance of Judah. According to Judges 1:18, the cities of Ashkelon, Ekron, and Gaza and their territories were captured by the men of Judah after the death of Joshua.

(2)   The regions of the Geshurites. This group of people lived in the desert between Arabia and Philistia (the land of the Philistines). David would later deal with them while he was on the run from Saul. This area was part of the inheritance of Simeon.

(3)   The territory of the Avvites. This group of people dwelled in Hazerim in the southwest corner of the coast of the Mediterranean Sea. Their land would have been southwest of that controlled by the Philistines. This was part of the inheritance of Simeon.

(4)   The land of the Canaanites in the north. This area was defined as being "from Arah of the Sidonians as far as Aphek and the border of the Amorites." In other words, the far north of Canaan. This may be the city of Aphik, a city that was part of the inheritance of Asher. This city most matches the description quoted above.

(5)   The city of Byblos. It was an ancient Phoenician port on the Mediterranean sea. It is now in the country of Lebanon. It is north of Beirut.

(6)   All Lebanon to the east. This region was defined as from Baal Gad at the foot of Mount Hermon to Lebo Hamath. The location of Lebo Hamath was on an elevated mound besides the Orontes river. It was a Hittite city

situated between Carchemish in the north and Kadesh in the south. The city is now called Hamath. The Orontes River has its headwaters in Lebanon. It then flows north into Syria and Turkey. This region was the inheritance of the tribe of Dan and the half-tribe of Manasseh east of the Jordan River.

(7)   The land of the Sidonians. This was defined by God as the mountain regions from Lebanon to Misrephoth Maim. The coastal city of Misrephoth Maim was located south of the city of Sidon. God obviously felt that this would be too trying for the Israelites as he decided that He would drive them out without "help" from the Israelites. God still wanted it included as part of the inheritance of the tribes. It was given to the tribe of Asher as part of its inheritance.

It appears that God named the unconquered territories generally from south to north. Basically, the Israelites conquered most of Canaan. The areas still in control of the original peoples was mostly in the far south and the far north, with the exception of the Philistines, who lived along the southern coastline.

This section ended without any reply from Joshua. At least, not one that was recorded.

What is interesting about the list of unconquered territories God gave to Joshua was the absence of Jerusalem from the list. The absence of Jerusalem can be explained by several theories. One, it is possible that God was giving broad areas where no towns or cities had been captured. If so, then Jerusalem would not be listed because it was within an area that had been conquered by the Israelites and God was not concerned about isolated communities still under the control of their original inhabitants. Two, it is possible, at the time God was speaking with Joshua, Jerusalem had already been conquered. (See Judges 1:8.)

b. Land East of the Jordan River

The second section of this chapter focused on defining the extent of the land east of the Jordan River that was "assigned" by Moses to the tribes of Reuben and Gad and the half-tribe of Manasseh. (Joshua 13:8, 15, 24, 29, 32) The Israelites had defeated the two kings who controlled this vast area. All the Amorite people had been driven out except those in Geshur and Maakah and they continued to live among the Israelites thereafter. (Joshua 13:8-13) Geshur was an independent district that was located between Mount Hermon and the Lake of Tiberias. Later, David married Maakah (Maacah), the daughter of Talmai, who ruled Geshur at the time. It was this daughter who gave birth to Absalom, the son who gave David so much trouble. She may have been called Maakah in honor of the people who lived just to the north of Geshur. Their kingdom was called Maacah or Maacath. It was located in the upper northwest corner of the land inherited by the half-tribe of Manasseh on the the east side of the Jordan River.

The Levites were given no inheritance in this area. Their inheritance were the food offerings made to God. (Joshua 13:14, 33)

The land given to the tribe of Reuben is described. (Joshua 13:15-23) See the map for the exact location.

The land given to the tribe of Gad is described. (Joshua 13:24-28) See the map for the exact location.

The land given to the half-tribe of Manasseh is described. (Joshua 13:29-31) See the map for the exact location.

CHAPTER FOURTEEN

a. Allotments West of the Jordan River

Eleazar, Joshua, and the heads of the tribal clans allotted the land west of the Jordan River to nine tribes and one-half tribe. They also made special allotments to individuals. They did this according to the command that God had made to Moses. The Levites were given no inheritance because Joseph, the son of Jacob, had two sons, Manasseh and Ephraim, who became the heads of tribes. Instead of an inheritance, the descendants of Levi were given towns where they could live and pasturelands for their flocks and herds. (Joshua 14:1-5)

b. Caleb

Caleb approached Joshua while Joshua was at Gilgal. He went to see Joshua because of a promise made to Caleb after Caleb supported the idea of invading Canaan just after the exodus from Egypt. Caleb said he was 40 years old when he explored Canaan at Moses' request and brought back a report that was consistent with what God wanted for the Israelites. Moses then told Caleb, "The land on which your feet have walked will be your inheritance and that of your children forever, because you have followed the Lord my God wholeheartedly." (Joshua 14:6-9 and Deuteronomy 1:36)

Caleb said that God had kept him alive for forty-five years since Moses made his promise to him. He was then 85 years old, but he was still as strong as the day he went into Canaan as a spy. He was still as physically capable as he was 45 years earlier. Caleb then asked Joshua to give him the hill country where the Anakites live and he will drive them out of the large and fortified cities. (Joshua 14:10-12) Joshua then gave Hebron, also called Kiriath Arba, to Caleb as his inheritance. It was named Kiriath Arba after Arba, the greatest man amongst the Anakites. (Joshua 14:13-15) It should be remembered that the Anakites were exceptionally tall and strong people who were considered giants by the Israelites.

This section on Caleb then ends strangely. The author said, "Then the land had rest from war." (Joshua 14:15) If Caleb captured Hebron during the southern campaign to conquer Canaan, then there was no rest from war at that time. Perhaps it meant that Caleb had rest from war. (See Joshua 14:13-19 for a discussion regarding Caleb and his family capturing Hebron and Debir.)

Caleb was 85 years old when he went to Joshua, his fellow spy from years earlier. If Caleb was 85 years, then the Israelites had been in Canaan for five years at that point. If Hebron had not yet been captured, then the battle with the five kings at Gibeon had not yet occurred. It appears that this event involving Caleb asking for land occurred before the southern campaign even started and before Hebron was captured. In short, this section was inserted at this point in the narrative because it had to do with the distribution of land and not because it was after the wars were over.

CHAPTER FIFTEEN

a. Judah's Allotment Generally

Judah was allotted land in the southern part of Canaan. The southern boundary started in the east at the end of the Dead Sea and ended in the west at the Wadi of Egypt as it ran its course to the Mediterranean Sea. The eastern boundary started at the southern end of the Dead Sea and went north to the top of the Dead Sea. The northern boundary started in the east at the top of the Dead Sea and then weaved itself across to the Mediterranean Sea. The Mediterranean Sea was the western boundary. Interestingly, the northern boundary line weaved itself just south of the city of Jerusalem. (Joshua 15:1-12)

It should be noted that the description of the land given to Judah as its inheritance included the land controlled by the Philistines, which had not been conquered at this point.

b. Caleb at War

The text then refers back to the moment when Joshua gave Hebron to Caleb, The story then continued to include what appears to be part of the southern campaign that occurred after Hebron was assigned to Caleb. In the southern campaign, Caleb attacked Hebron and drove out the three Anakites who lived there (and, likely killed the rest of the inhabitants). The three Anakites were Sheshai, Ahiman, and Talmai, all sons of Anak. After securing Hebron, Caleb marched against Debir (formerly called Kiriath Sepher). He then gave a challenge to the men that were with him. He would give his daughter Aksah in marriage to the man who attacked and captured Debir (also known as Kiriath Sepher).

Caleb's nephew Othniel took up the challenge. Othniel was a son of Caleb's brother Kenaz. Not only did Othniel take up the challenge, he accomplished the goal Caleb set for him. Caleb thereafter rewarded him with the hand of his daughter in marriage. (Joshua 15:13-17 and Judges 1:9-13)

c. Caleb at Peace

The author then inserted another story about Caleb, Othniel, and Aksah that appears to have taken place years later when Othniel and Aksah were married and when there truly was peace in the land. One day, Aksah asked Othniel to go to Caleb and ask him to give them a field. Apparently, Othniel did what he was asked, but the author did not include that fact. However, later Aksah went to Caleb on her donkey. Obviously, the circumstance was such that Caleb knew Aksah wanted something. She did. Since her father had given her land in the Negev, she needed water for the land. She asked her father for springs of water and he gave her "the upper and lower springs." Caleb certainly was a generous man. (Joshua 15:18-19 and Judges 1:14-15)

Interestingly, the Book of Judges has the same story about Caleb and the capturing of Hebron and Debir and the giving of springs of water by Caleb to his daughter, but with a little more detail in some areas. And, strangely enough, the author of the Book of Judges has the conquest of Hebron and Debir occurring **after** the death of Joshua! However, considering the Jewish proclivity to ignore chronology for thematic content, the author of Judges may have done just that. (See Judges 1:9-15.)

d. Judah's Inheritance

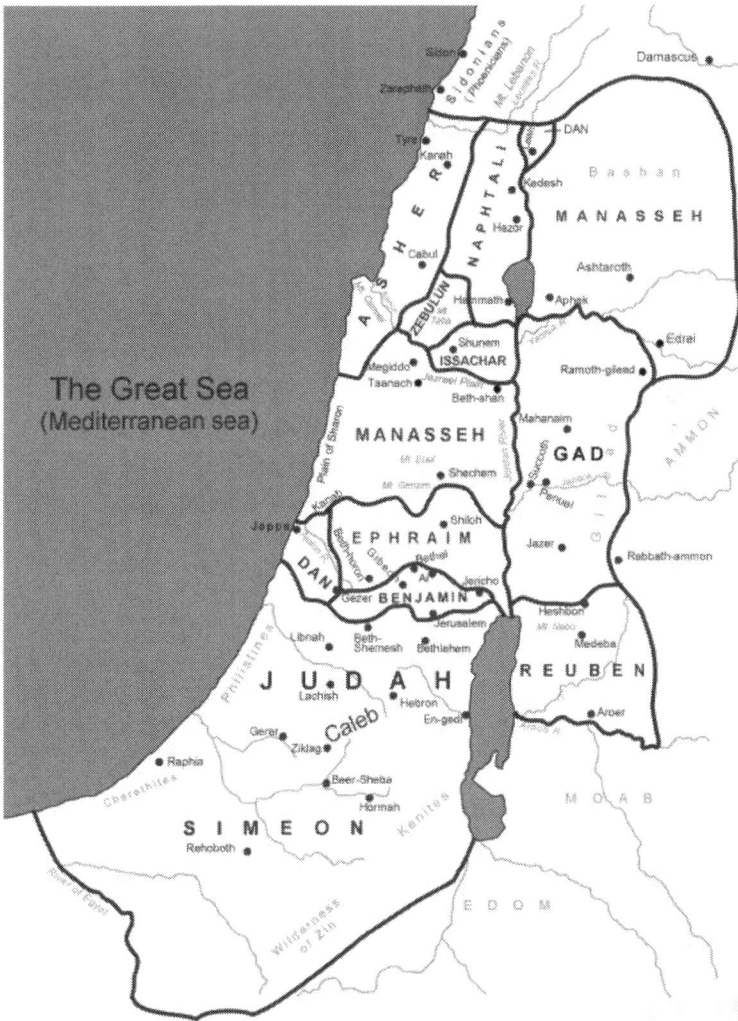

The inheritance for Judah included 29 towns and villages in the Negev toward the boundary with Edom. (Joshua 15:21-32) There were 39 towns and villages in the western foothills. (Joshua 15:33-44) The list of towns and villages in

the western foothills included Ekron, Ashdod, and Gaza. (Joshua 15:45-47) These cities were not listed among those conquered by the Israelites in the Book of Joshua.
However, there is such a claim in the Book of Judges. (See Judges 1:18.)   There were 38 towns and villages in the hill country. And, there were six towns and villages in the wilderness (the area south of the Negev). (Joshua 15:48-62) The total number of towns and villages amounted to 112.

The author ended this section dealing with Judah's inheritance by indicating that Judah did not dislodge the Jebusites living in Jerusalem and had not done so up the time the Book of Joshua was written. (Joshua 15:63) This was an interesting comment to make about Judah as the city of the Jebusites was not included in the land allotted to Judah. It was in the land allotted to Benjamin.

e. Jerusalem

If the tribe of Judah had not captured Jerusalem by the time the Book of Joshua was written, it certainly had been by the time the Book of Judges was started. The tribe of Judah convinced the tribe of Simeon to join with them to fight against the Canaanites. The two tribes then combined to attack the city of Bezek and they killed 10,000 warriors from that city. The author of Judges made it very clear that it was God who provided the victory. The king of Bezek was Adoni-Bezek and he was captured while fleeing from the battlefield. The Israelites cut off the king's thumbs and big toes so he would never again be able to wield a sword or balance himself in battle. Adoni-Bezek then remarked on the irony of what happened to him. He said he had done the same thing to 70 other kings and then made them pick up scraps under his table. He said that God was paying him back for what he had done to the other kings. The Israelites took him to Jerusalem and Adoni-Bezek died there. (See Judges 1:1-7.) The name "Adoni-Bezek" means "lord of the lightening" as Adoni means "lord" and Bezek means "lightening." It was obviously a name that was designed to strike fear into the hearts of his opponents. It obviously worked for awhile, but the king received his just reward. Additionally, the location of the city of Bezek is not known with any certainty today. Some researchers believe it to be the modern town of Bezkah/Bezqah, which is three miles northeast of Gezer, while others dispute that conclusion. A town close to and south of Jerusalem has drawn some support, based on the events described in Judges. Whatever its ancient location, it appears to have been in the territory allotted to Judah.

Whether Bezek was attacked before or after Jerusalem was attacked is not clear from the narrative in Judges. However, the author of Judges was certain that Jerusalem was attacked and the city taken. The people in the city were put to the sword (killed) and the city burned. (See Judges 1:8.)

Despite what was written in Judges at chapter 1, verse 8, there seems to be a contradictory evaluation just verses later. At chapter 1, verse 21, the author of Judges wrote this: "The Benjamites, however, did not drive out the Jebusites, who were living in Jerusalem; to this day the Jebusites live there with the Benjamites." It would appear, at first glance, that verse 8 and verse 21 contradict each other. Since verse 21 was written after verse 8, the logical explanation may be that the tribe of Judah did capture Jerusalem and kill the people. Nonetheless, it would appear that no Israelites then moved into the city. Because the Israelites did not occupy the city, the Jebusites living in the area did. And, once they regained control over Jerusalem, they did not relinquish it until David, a member of the tribe of Judah, conquered it and made it his capital, even though it was still allotted to the tribe of Benjamin. (See Judges 1:21 and 2 Samuel 5:6-10.) Also, it is possible that the city changed hands numerous times over the course of time, in back and forth actions. If so, then it had to be re-taken again and again by the Israelites. Unfortunately, no Biblical author gave us detailed information about Jerusalem.

CHAPTER SIXTEEN

a. Allotment for Ephraim and Manasseh

The next two tribes whose allotments are discussed are
Ephraim and Manasseh. These two tribes descended from

Joseph. Ephraim and Manasseh were his two sons. The author began by giving the dimensions of the entire allotment for both Ephraim and Manasseh. (Joshua 16:1-5)

Once the entire allotment was described, then the author gave the dimensions of the allotment for Ephraim. What was left after subtracting the allotment for Ephraim was the allotment for Manasseh. (Joshua 16:6-9)

b. The Town of Gezer

The town of Gezer was included within Ephraim's inheritance. Unfortunately, the Ephraimites were unable to dislodge the Canaanites from that city. However, the Canaanites of Gezer were forced to do slave labor for the Ephraimites. (Joshua 16:10)

CHAPTER SEVENTEEN

a. Allotment for Manasseh (East Side)

Manasseh was Joseph's first child. Makir was Manasseh's first child. The descendants of Makir were called Makirites.

They were soldiers of renown. Because of their prowess in battle, they received Gilead and Bashan as their allotment. Therefore, Makir became the ancestor of the people called the Gileadites. (Joshua 17:1) Gilead and Bashan are on the east side of the Jordan River.

b. Allotment for Zelophehad's Daughters

The text then focuses on a specific instance to show the sensitivity of Eleazar, son of Aaron, and Joshua to a command of God given to Moses. Zelophehad, a member of the tribe of Manasseh had no sons. Since land was passed down through the male, the daughters of Zelophehad were concerned that they would have no inheritance, directly or indirectly, and the name of their father would disappear. The daughters were Mahlah, Noah, Hoglah, Milkah, and Tirzah. They went to Eleazar and Joshua to ask for an inheritance in the land Manasseh was assigned east of the Jordan River. They claimed that God commanded Moses to provide for them. Joshua then honored that claim by providing them with an inheritance. (Joshua 17:3-6 and Numbers 27:1-11, 36:1-12)

c. Allotment for Manasseh (West Side)

The rest of the tribe of Manasseh received their allotment on the west side of the Jordan River. These were the clans of Abiezer, Helen, Asriel, Shechem, Hepher, and Shemida. They were all descendants of Manasseh through Makir. (Joshua 17:2) The territory allotted to Manasseh west of the Jordan River is described in detail. In essence, it was located north of the tribe of Ephraim, south of the tribe of Asher, and west of the tribe of Issachar. (Joshua 17:7-10) They were even allotted cities within the land allotted to Issachar and Asher. These cities were Beth Shan, Ibleam,

Dor, Endor, Taanach, and Megiddo and their surrounding settlements. However, the people of the tribe of Manasseh were not able to occupy these towns. In other words, these people were too strong for the tribe of Manasseh to drive them out of these cities. Later, when the tribe of Manasseh became stronger, they subjected the Canaanites to forced labor. (Joshua 17:11-3)

Despite the extensive territory allotted to the tribe of Manasseh west of the Jordan River, the members of the tribe were not happy. They went to Joshua and asked for more land. They claimed they were too numerous for what little was given to them. Joshua's response was not positive. He told them to go into the forest and clear the land where the Perizzites and Rephaites reside. The men of Manasseh retorted that they could not clear the forests to create farm land because the Canaanites who lived in the plain had chariots fitted with iron, suggesting that they were no match for them in any conflict. Joshua was not impressed with their arguments. He told them they were "numerous and very powerful" and, even though the Canaanites were strong, the men of Manasseh should be able to drive them out. (Joshua 17:14-18)

d. Cities Not Captured

These verses make one thing very clear: the Canaanites had not been driven out of some of the cities and, in some cases, were still a threat to the Israelites. This sentiment is echoed in the Book of Judges, where the tribe of Manasseh only gained control of the Canaanite residents of Beth Shan, Taanach, Dor, Ibleam, and Megiddo when the tribe of Manasseh became stronger. Then, they did not eliminate the people of these cities, they made them perform forced labor. (Judges 1:27-28) The tribe of Zebulun did the same with the Canaanite people of the cities of Kitron and Nahalol. (Judges 1:30) The tribe of Naphtali did the same with the people of the Beth Shemesh and Beth Anath. (Judges 1:33) The tribes of Manasseh and Ephraim did the same with the Amorite people of Mount Heres, Aijalon, and Shaalbim. (Judges 1:35) On the other hand, the tribe of Ephraim was never able to drive out the Canaanite inhabitants of Gezer, nor make them into slaves. (Judges 1:29) The tribe of Asher was not able to drive out the inhabitants of Akko (Acco), Sidon, Akzib, Helbah, Aphek, or Rehob, nor were they ever strong enough to make these people their slaves. (Judges 1:31-33) The tribe of Dan was never able to extend its control in any way over the plains dominated by the Amorites. (Judges 1:34) In short, the tribes of Manasseh, Ephraim, Zebulun, Asher, and Dan did not carry out God's command in Canaan, even when they became strong enough to do it. Not following God's command to drive out or kill all of the inhabitants of Canaan eventually led to their spiritual downfall.

CHAPTER EIGHTEEN

a. Allotment for the Rest of the Tribes

The tribes of Reuben, Gad, Judah, Manasseh, and Ephraim had already been allotted their land in Canaan. It was time for the rest of the tribes of Israel to receive their inheritance in Canaan.

The Israelites gathered at Shiloh in central Canaan after the Promised Land had been brought primarily under control. Even though Shiloh was in the land allotted to Ephraim, it was probably chosen for three reasons: (1) it was not far from Gilgal, the former encampment of the Israelites, (2) it was a location where all the tribes had a chance to be close to their inheritance, making the move a relatively easy one, and (3) it was a centralized location, making it available to all of the tribes. At this point, the seven tribes had no idea where their allotment would be because each inheritance would be decided by an impartial process that involved determining God's will by lot.

Joshua and the Israelites brought the tent of the meeting with them from Gilgal to Shiloh. The tent of the meeting held the ark of the covenant. Therefore, it appeared that the change of locations was a permanent one. (Joshua 18:1-2) In fact, the ark of the covenant remained at Shiloh until the Israelites brought it to their camp in preparation for a battle with the Philistines. Unfortunately, the ark did not aid the Israelites and they were defeated. The Philistines then took the ark to their cities and kept it for nine months. However, having the ark proved a serious liability and they returned it to the Israelites. The ark was taken to Kiriath Jearmin, where it remained for 20 years. (1 Samuel 4:1-11, 5:1-7:1) David then took the ark to the house of Obed-Edom while en route to Jerusalem. It was left there for three months and then brought to Jerusalem. (2 Samuel 6:1-17)

After the move to Shiloh was made, Joshua addressed the Israelites about the allotting of land to the seven tribes who had not yet received their inheritance. These seven tribes were Asher, Benjamin, Dan, Issachar, Naphtali, Simeon, and Zebulun. Joshua asked how long the tribes would wait until they possessed the land God had for them. However, it was a rhetorical question because Joshua had already determined to parcel out the remaining land in Canaan. He announced that he wanted three men appointed from each tribe. These men would go out to survey the land. When they were done, they would report back to Joshua with their findings, which would be written descriptions of the seven parts of the land. He explained that there would only be seven parts because the Levites would not get a portion because their priestly service to the Lord was their inheritance. (Joshua 18:3-7)

When the 21 men, three men chosen from each tribe, were ready to leave, Joshua addressed them. He told them to map out the land and then write a description of it. Once that was done, they were to return to Joshua at Shiloh. Joshua would then cast lots to determine which parcel of land went to which tribe. (Joshua 18:8)

The men did as they were told and, when they were done, they brought back their surveys on scrolls for Joshua to see. Each town not already allotted was listed on the scrolls. Joshua then cast lots for the tribes at Shiloh. (Joshua 18:9-10) The casting of lots was not considered an exercise in chance. It was a way to determine the will of God. Of course no one has any idea at this time as to how the will of God was fathomed from the throwing of the objects and no one has any idea as to exactly what was thrown. The

242

objects could have been sticks of various lengths, flat stones in the shape of coins, or even some kind of dice. Whatever the objects, it was likely that some meaning had to have been attached to the different objects that was known to everyone assembled. Or, the people depended upon Joshua and/or Eleazar to interpret the results of each throw made by Joshua.

The casting of the lots was done by Eleazar, Joshua, and the heads of the tribal clans. It was done in the presence of God at the entrance to the tent of meeting. (Joshua 19:51) It appears that Joshua threw the the objects, Eleazar interpreted the results, and the heads of the tribal clans monitored the proceedings and accepted the results.

b. Benjamin Is Chosen First

Joshua cast lots before God after the surveys were done and God chose the tribe of Benjamin first. They were allotted territory that lay between that already allotted to the tribe of Judah and the two tribes of Ephraim and Manasseh. Its eastern boundary would be the Jordan River and its western boundary would eventually abut the land allotted to the tribe of Dan. (Joshua 18:11-28)

An issue needs to be discussed at this point. Since some portions of the Book of Joshua were written after Joshua died, perhaps the author took some literary license in how some of the material was presented. According to the command of God, as found in Numbers 26:1-65, the land of Canaan was to be allotted to each tribe based on the percentage of fighting men in each tribe. In other words, each tribe would receive an inheritance that would differ in size from any other tribe. Therefore, it would appear to be impossible for the teams which were sent out to survey

The Great Sea
(Mediterranean sea)

Canaan to come up with tracts that would be allocated to
the tribes and this is especially true if the tribes did not
know ahead of time which piece each tribe was going to
get. It would seem more likely that the land was surveyed
by the different teams so that the total square miles could
be ascertained. In that way, the total amount could be

divided up in any variety of ways, depending on how the lots came out. It appears the author of Joshua wanted to present a coherent picture of what happened at the time the land was allotted to the last seven tribes. In short, the survey of the land may have occurred after the southern, central, and northern campaigns were concluded and before any of the land west of the Jordan River was allotted to any tribe.

CHAPTER NINETEEN

a. The Allotment for Simeon

The second casting of lots was for Simeon. Strangely enough, its inheritance lay within the land originally allotted to Judah. The allotment for Simeon included 13 towns and the villages around them and four other towns and the villages around them as far as Baalath Beer (Ramah in the Negev).

This inheritance was taken from Judah's share because Judah's original inheritance was more than the tribe needed. (Joshua 19:1-9)

b. The Allotment for Zebulun

The third lot was for Zebulun. The allotment was the smallest of all the tribes. The land was located between Lake Kinnereth (Sea of Galilee) and Mount Carmel. (Joshua 19:10-16)

c. The Allotment for Issachar

The fourth lot was for Issachar. There were sixteen towns and their villages. The tribe's eastern boundary was on the Jordan River. It's southern boundary was adjacent to Manasseh, with Zebulun and Naphtali to the north. (Joshua 19:17-23)

The Great Sea
(Mediterranean sea)

Sidon
Zarephath
Tyre
Kanah
DAN
Kedesh
Hazor
Hammath
Cabul
Shunem
Megiddo
Taanach
Beth-shan
Shechem
Shiloh
Bethel
Ai
Jericho
Gezer
Jerusalem
Bethlehem
Beth-Shemesh
Libnah
Lachish
Hebron
En-gedi
Gerar
Ziklag
Raphia
Beer-Sheba
Hormah
Rehoboth

Damascus
Bashan
MANASSEH
Ashtaroth
Aphek
Edrei
Ramoth-gilead
ISSACHAR
Mahanaim
MANASSEH
GAD
Mt. Ebal
Mt. Gerizim
Succoth
Penuel
Jazer
Rabbath-ammon
Heshbon
Mt. Nebo
Medeba
REUBEN
Aroer
MOAB
EDOM

A S H E R
NAPHTALI
ZEBULUN
EPHRAIM
BENJAMIN
DAN
Joppa
JUDAH
Caleb
SIMEON

Philistines
Cherethites
Kenites
Wilderness of Zin
River of Egypt
Jordan River
Plain of Sharon
Sidonians (Phoenicians)
Mt. Lebanon
AMMON

d. The Allotment for Asher

The fifth lot was for Asher. It included 22 towns and their villages. This inheritance ran along the coast of the Mediterranean Sea in the northern part of Canaan. It included land occupied by the Phoenicians. (Joshua 19:24-31)

e. The Allotment for Naphtali

The sixth lot was for Naphtali. It included 19 towns and their villages in the north part of Canaan. This area had the Jordan River and Lake Kinnereth as its eastern border and Asher and Zebulun on its western border. (Joshua 19:32-39)

f. The Allotment for Dan

The seventh and last lot was no surprise. It came out for the tribe of Dan. This area was to the west of the tribe of Benjamin and its western border was the Mediterranean Sea. It also included the Philistine city of Ekron. However, the Danites were never successful in driving out the people in their allotted area which lay between the Mediterranean Sea and the foothills.

Later, when the Danites were displaced, they moved as a tribe to northern Canaan and settled in Leshem after killing all the people in it. They then named the area after their ancestor Dan. (Joshua 19:40-47)

g. The Allotment for Joshua

Once the Land of Canaan was divided up, the Israelites gave Joshua an inheritance, as God had commanded. He asked for the town of Timnath Serah (also known as Timnath Heres) in the hill country of Ephraim. Joshua built up the town and settled there. (Joshua 19:49-50)

CHAPTER TWENTY

a. The Cities of Refuge

In an act of mercy, God told Joshua to designate cites of refuge in the land controlled by the Israelites. The purpose of the cities of refuge was to prevent unnecessary bloodshed of an innocent person. Anyone who accidentally and unintentionally killed another person would be able to flee to one of the the cities of refuge. Once at one of the cities, the refugee would be able to state his case at the entrance to the city gate. If convinced that the death was accidental and unintentional, the city elders would admit the refugee into the city and provide the refugee a place to stay. If the refugee was pursued by a person seeking revenge, the elders were not to surrender the refugee because the elders had already made a determination that there was no probable cause to believe the death was intentional and with malice aforethought. Eventually, the refugee would stand trial before "the assembly." If the assembly found the death to be unintentional and without malice aforethought, then the refugee would still have to stay in the city of refuge until the death of the high priest serving at that time. Only then could the person go back to their own home. (Joshua 20:1-6)

There were six cities of refuge set up. There were three on the west side of the Jordan River and three on the east side of the Jordan River. The three on the west side, going from north to south, were Kedesh in the hill country of Naphtali, Shechem in the hill country of Ephraim, and Hebron in the hill country of Judah. The three on the east side, going from north to south, were Golan in Bashan of Manasseh, Remoth in Gilead of Gad, and Bezer in the wilderness of Reuben. (Joshua 20:7-8)

Any Israelite or foreigner residing in the area controlled by the Israelites could flee to one of the designated cities and be free of the person wanting to avenge a killing that was accidental. Of course, in the end, the assembly would have to find that the death was free of intention and malice aforethought. (Joshua 20:9)

b. Early California Law Based on Old Testament Law

Whenever a defendant is charged with murder in California, the prosecution must prove the homicide was committed with malice aforethought. To find the defendant guilty of murder, the jury must find, among other issues, that the defendant who committed the act that resulted in death possessed a certain state of mind at the time. The jury must find the defendant committed the act with malice aforethought to convict him or her of murder. Malice aforethought can be either expressed malice or implied malice. Expressed malice is when the defendant "unlawfully intended to kill." Implied malice is when the defendant intentionally committed an act, the natural and probable consequences of the act were dangerous to human life, and the defendant knew at the time the act was committed that it was dangerous to human life.   Malice aforethought has also been defined this way: "Such malice may be express or implied. It is express when there is manifest a deliberate intention unlawfully to take away the life of a fellow creature. It is implied, when no considerable provocation appears, or when the circumstances attending the killing show an abandoned and malignant heart." The only escape from sure death under Israelite law was to show that the death was accidental or it was caused by the victim himself or herself.

When California became a state in 1850, a series of laws were enacted to define murder and set the penalty if a defendant was found guilty of murder or pled guilty to a charge of murder. The only penalty for the crime of murder, once there was a conviction, was death. It was automatic and the jury had no discretion. This legislation followed the law of the Old Testament. In 1874, the legislature made changes that distinguished between first and second degree murder. First degree murder was punishable by death or imprisonment for life. Second degree murder was punishable by confinement in the state prison for not less than ten years. There have been a number of changes in the law since 1874, but these amendments were the most significant in California's history. For a full history, see "Death Without Honor: Legal Executions in the History of San Joaquin County, California," by this author.

CHAPTER TWENTY-ONE

a. The Levites Were Given Land

The Levites went to Eleazar, Joshua, and "the heads of the other tribal families of Israel" at Shiloh. They reminded the leaders that God had commanded Moses to set aside towns and pasturelands for them. As a consequence of God's instructions to Moses, the Israelites gave the Levites towns and pasturelands as their inheritance. These lands were taken out of the territories already allotted to the different tribes. (Joshua 21:1-3) Five of the towns assigned to the Levites were cities of refuge.

The three Levite clans of Kohath, Gershon, and Merari asked for the towns and pasturelands. They were all descendants of Aaron.

The Kohathites were allotted 13 towns in the south of Canaan from the tribes of Judah, Simeon, and Benjamin. (Joshua 21:4) The towns from Judah and Simeon were noted later in the text. (Joshua 21:9-6) It was made clear that the city of Hebron and its pasturelands were given to the Kohathites, but the fields and villages around the city belonged to Caleb. Hebron was also a city of refuge. (Joshua 21:11-13) The towns from Benjamin were noted later in the text. (Joshua 21:17)

The Kohathites were also allotted ten towns in central Canaan from the tribes of Ephraim, Dan, and Manasseh. The towns from Manasseh were on the west side of the Jordan River. (Joshua 21:5) The towns from Ephraim, Dan, and Manasseh were noted later in the text. One of the towns was Shechem in Ephraim, a city of refuge. (Joshua 21:20-25)

The Gershonites were given 13 towns in northern Canaan from the tribes of Issachar, Asher, Naphtali, and Manasseh. The towns from Manasseh were on the east side of the Jordan River. (Joshua 21:6) The towns from Issachar, Asher, Naphtali, and Manasseh were noted later in the text. Two of the towns were cities of refuge. They were Golan in Bashan (east of the Jordan River) and Kedesh (north of the Sea of Kinnereth/Galilee). (Joshua 21:27-33)

The Merarites were allowed 12 towns from the tribes of Reuben, Gad, and Zebulun. The towns in Reuben and Gad were on the east side of the Jordan River and the towns in Zebulun were on the west side of the Jordan River. (Joshua 21:7) The towns from Reuben, Gad, and Zebulun were noted later in the text. One of the towns was Ramoth in Gilead, a city of refuge. (Joshua 21: 34-40)

There were 48 towns, along with their pasturelands, which were allowed to the Levite clans. (Joshua 21:41-42)

b. God Gave Israel Rest from War

God gave to the Israelites all the land He promised to the Israelites' ancestors, Abraham, Issac, and Jacob. They had now taken possession of most of it and they had settled there. God then gave them rest, just he had sworn to their ancestors he would do. God had given all of their enemies into their hands and not one enemy had withstood the Israelites. Every one of God's promises had been fulfilled. (Joshua 21:43-45) What these passages mean is that there was no longer any unified resistance from within Canaan. All of the armies gathered against them had been beaten badly. However, these passages do not mean that all of Canaan had been conquered. There were still isolated areas that were still independent of the Israelites and many would not be subdued until the time of David and Solomon.

CHAPTER TWENTY-TWO

a. Eastern Tribes Go Home

The land was now distributed to all of the tribes, the Levites were assigned their towns and pasturelands, and God declared that Israel had peace from war. It was time to summon the warriors of the tribes of Reuben and Gad and the half-tribe of Manasseh, all living east of the Jordan River, and Joshua did just that. He had news for them that they, no doubt, had been wanting to hear for a long time. Joshua told them that they could return to their homes "on the other side of the Jordan." Joshua commended them for doing all that Moses commanded, for obeying Joshua in everything he commanded, for not deserting their fellow Israelites, and for carrying out the mission that their God had given them. (Joshua 22:1-4)

But, Joshua had a warning for them. They needed to be "very careful to keep the commandment and the law that Moses the servant of the Lord gave" them. These included (1) love the Lord, their God, (2) walk in obedience to him, (3) keep his commands, (4) hold fast to him, and (5) serve him with all their heart and with all their soul. (Joshua 22:5)

Joshua's emotions had to have been mixed. He had to have been excited for the men who had served in his army for so long and who were now going home and sad that they were leaving him. He had known them for many years and had served beside them in countless battles. He knew he would never see many of them again. Perhaps they were standing before Joshua in the formations he had seen them in for so long. Perhaps he was reviewing them as a general might, saluting them for their faithfulness and their valor. In the end, he had to let them go. However, he blessed them before they left. He also told them to take with them the great wealth that they had accumulated while fighting side by side with Joshua. Their wealth consisted of large herds of livestock, silver, gold, bronze, iron, and a great quantity of clothing. He also told them to share the plunder from their enemies with the people back home. So the men left Joshua and headed for their homes across the Jordan River. (Joshua 22:6-9)

b. Trouble Developed

Unfortunately, the departing men did something before they crossed the Jordan River that caused a major misunderstanding with the tribes on the west side of the Jordan River. The fighting men from the tribes of Reuben and Gad and the half-tribe of Manasseh must have come up with an idea while en route to the Jordan River as they did not talk to Joshua about it while they were Shiloh. Their idea was to build an altar at Geliloth and they did so. The site was part of the eastern boundary line of Benjamin. It can be found mentioned only in Joshua and only twice. Many commentators believe it is a reference to Gilgal, which certainly seems appropriate. Wherever it was built, when the other tribes heard about it, they were angry. In fact, they were so angry that they wanted to go to war with the men who built the altar. And, they did more than just talk about. They gathered in Shiloh to fight the men who built the altar. (Joshua 22:10-12)

c. Delegation Sent

Fortunately, cooler heads prevailed. The text is quiet as to whose idea it was to send a delegation across the Jordan River to talk about the altar instead of a war party, but it was likely Joshua. The ambassadors consisted of Phinehas, a son of Eleazar, and ten of the chief men, one from each of the nine tribes and the one-half tribe west of the Jordan River. Each of the chief men was head of a family division in his tribe. (Joshua 22:13-14) The delegation went to Gilead and met with representatives of tribes of Reuben and Gad and the half-tribe of Manasseh. (22:15)

Phinehas and the chief men were as one in the accusations they made against the Gileadites (as the people east of the Jordan River were called at this time). In their eyes, the building of the altar would have major consequences. **One**, it was an act that represented a breaking faith with God. **Two**, it was an act that represented a turning away from God. **Three**, it was an act of rebellion. **Four**, it was an act equal to the sin the Israelites committed at Peor that resulted in God sending a plague on the Israelites. **Five**, it was an act that showed they were turning away from God. (Joshua 22:15-18) To Phinehas and the chief men, the altar in Shiloh represented the unity of the Israelites and it represented the presence of God. To build another altar was sacrilege. It represented disunity and the worship of another god.

Phinehas and the chief men were not through with their condemnation of the Gileadites. They now talked about the likely consequences of what the Gileadites had done. They said that if the Gileadites rebelled against God that day, then the Lord will be angry with all the Israelites tomorrow. They reminded them of what happened when Achan was unfaithful regarding the devoted items. Not only did he die, others died also. The did offer one shred of solace. If God defiled the land on which they lived, they were welcome to live with the Israelites on the west side of the Jordan River. This was their way of saying that they were still all one family, one people, one nation. They pleaded with the

Gileadites to not rebel against God or against the Israelites on the west side of the Jordan River by building an altar for themselves, an altar other than the one shared by all Israelites, which was in Shiloh. (Joshua 22:18-20)

What Phinehas and the chief men said must have been a shock to the Gileadites. They immediately answered the accusations and doomsday predictions with an appeal to the Lord himself. They exclaimed, "The Mighty One, God, the Lord! The Mighty One, God, the Lord! He Knows! And let Israel know!" They followed up their appeal to the Lord, with several very excitable hypotheticals: "If this has been in rebellion or disobedience to the Lord, do not spare us today. If we have built our own altar to turn away from the Lord and to offer burnt offerings and grain offerings, or to sacrifice fellowship offerings on it, may the Lord himself call us to account." The hypotheticals were offered to show Phinehas and the chief men that the Gileadites were well aware of the sin of building an alternate altar to the one in Shiloh. It was their way of saying that we know the consequences of committing such a sin against God and they would not do it under any circumstance. (Joshua 22:21-24)

d. A Rational Defense

The Gileadites then told why they had built the altar. They built it to remind the descendants on both sides of the Jordan River that they worship the same God and that the Gileadites will always offer burnt offerings, sacrifices, and fellowship offering only at the Lord's sanctuary, which was then in Shiloh. If any of the tribes on the west side of the Jordan ever make any accusation against the Gileadites, then the Gileadites will point at the altar at Geliloth as a witness that they all worship the same God. They said they would never rebel against the Lord and turn away from the true place to offer sacrifices to the Lord, which is the altar of the Lord that stands before God's tabernacle. (Joshua 22:25-29)

When Phinehas and the chief men heard the spontaneous and eloquent defense presented by the Gileadites, they believed them wholeheartedly. They were "pleased" with what they heard. They said, "Today we know that the Lord is with us, because you have not been unfaithful to the Lord in this matter. Now you have rescued the Israelites from the Lord's hand." (Joshua 22:30-31) Not only was the explanation one that was pleasing to the listeners, it was also pleasing to the Lord. Because the building of the altar was not in rebellion against God, there was no reason for God to bring his wrath down on all the Israelites or even some of them. Of course, Phinehas never mentioned the fact that there was an army in Shiloh ready to invade Gilead if there was any speck of rebellion in what the Gileadites had done. There was no sense in stirring a pot that was only then simmering.

When Phinehas and the chief men returned to Shiloh, they explained to the Israelites what had occurred. Everyone who heard their report was glad that there was good news and they praised God for the outcome. And, there was no more mention of going to war, a war that would have devastated the land where the Gileadites lived and cause the death of countless Israelites from all tribes. (Joshua 22:32-33)

And, true to their word, the Israelites east of the Jordan River gave their altar a name that represented what they had told Phinehas and the chief men: "A Witness Between Us - that the Lord is God." (Joshua 22:34)

CHAPTER TWENTY-THREE

a. The Theme

The theme of this chapter is simple. The Lord has been good to you. Do not turn your back on Him. If you do turn your back on Him, bad things will follow.

b. Joshua's Farewell Address

1. Summary

When Joshua was a "very old man," he summoned all the elders, leaders, judges, and officials. (Joshua 23:1-2) When they had assembled, Joshua gave them some lessons on life. **First**, he gave them a little history. **Second**, he gave them a glimpse into the future. **Third**, he told them the do's and don'ts of life. **Fourth**, he told them what would happen when there were too many don'ts and not enough do's in that land that God had given them.

2. History

First, Joshua reminded them of their recent **history**. He told those gathered before him that they had seen with their own eyes all that God had done for them as they fought the nations who lived in Canaan before the Israelites arrived. Joshua reminded them that "it was the Lord your God who fought for you." (Joshua 23:3) Joshua recalled that God had driven out great and powerful nations and no one has been able to withstand the Israelites because of God. Whenever any of the Israelites had defeated a thousand of the enemy, it was because God had fought with them, just as he had promised. (Joshua 23:9-10) He had given them the land where they then stood. (Joshua 23:11) Joshua also said that those assembled before him knew in their "heart and soul" that every good promise God had given them had come to pass. God had not failed on any promise that He made. (Joshua 23:14)

3. Future

Second, Joshua also brought up the past to talk about the **future**. Joshua said that he had allotted to each of the tribes their inheritance, even at a time when there were remnants of the original nations still in Canaan. (Joshua 23:4) Joshua then moved into the future. He said that it would be God who would rid them of these people "for your sake." When God drove them out, the Israelites will take possession of the land that will be vacated. God will do all of this because it was what He promised. (Joshua 23:5).

4. Do's and Don'ts

Third, Joshua urged them to do **the right things**. He told them (1) to be "very strong," (2) to obey everything that was written in the "Book of the Law" given by God to Moses, (3) to keep on the path that God had given them "without turning aside to the right or to the left" (Joshua 23:6), (4) the Israelites were to cling to God as they had up then (Joshua 23:8), and (5) they were to be careful to love their God. (Joshua 23:11)

Joshua urged them **not to do wrong**. He told them not to associate with the people of the nations that were still in the land they had conquered. They were not to invoke the names of their gods or to swear by them. They were not to serve them or born down before them. (Joshua 23:7) Do not make peace with or have relations with those that remain in the land God had given to the Israelites. Do not intermarry with their women or associate with them in any way. (Joshua 23:12)

5. Consequences

Fourth, Joshua said he was about to go the way of every person who has ever lived on this earth. Therefore, he wanted them to understand the consequences of straying from God's commands and the consequences would ultimately be deadly for the Israelites. One, God would no longer aid them in driving out their enemies. (Joshua 23:13) Two, those nations would become "snares and traps for you, whips on your backs and thorns in your eyes, until you perish from this good land." (Joshua 23:14) Three, God would bring on them all the evil things He said would happen if they strayed from Him. (Joshua 23:15) Four, God's anger will burn against them and, ultimately, they will perish from the land God had given to them.

Just as Moses had warned the Israelites before they entered the Promised Land, so Joshua warned the Israelites now that they had conquered the Promised Land. Both Moses and Joshua had seen how God's people were so easily turned to the right and to the left. Even on the eve of entering the Promised Land, members of the "new generation" had violated God's law and were punished dearly for their transgressions. Joshua feared for the future of his newly-created nation of Israel and he hoped his reminders and his warnings might be a light to a nation embarking on an uncertain future.

CHAPTER TWENTY-FOUR

a. Joshua Assembled The Leaders

After Joshua convened an assembly of the elders, leaders, judges, and officials of Israel at Shechem, God spoke to them through Joshua. (Joshua 24:1)

b. God Reviewed His History

God gave them a history of His people, from Abraham to the present time. God revealed his hand in every important event that occurred during those hundreds of years. God called Abraham to go to a land Abraham had never known and God gave him many descendants. God gave Abraham Isaac and then God gave Isaac Jacob and Esau. God assigned Esau to the hill country of Seir and Jacob went to Egypt. (Joshua 24:2-4)

God sent Moses and Aaron into Egypt and God caused distress to the Egyptians. God brought the Israelites out of Egypt and God saved the Israelites from the pursuing Egyptians by putting darkness between the Israelites and the Egyptians and killing the Egyptians in the Red Sea. The Israelites then lived in the wilderness for a long time. (Joshua 24:5-7)

God brought the Israelites to the land of the Amorites east of the Jordan River. God saved the Israelites when the Amorites attacked them. (Joshua 24:8) God sent his "hornet" ahead of the Amorites to drive them out. (Joshua 24:12) God destroyed the Amorites and God gave the land to the Israelites. God would not listen to Baalam when the king of Moab hired him to put a curse on the Israelites. God delivered the Israelites from Baalam and from the Moabites. (Joshua 24:9-10)

After the Israelites crossed over the Jordan River, God gave the nations in Canaan into the hands of the Israelites. God sent his "hornet" ahead to drive out the enemy. The Israelites did not do it with their own sword and bow. God gave them a land on which they had not toiled, cities in which to live they had not built, and the fruit of vineyards and olive trees they had not planted. (Joshua 24:11-13)

c. Leaders Urged to Follow God

After telling the assembled leaders what God had revealed to him, Joshua then spoke to the leaders. He urged them to "fear" God and to serve him with every ounce of loyalty they could muster. He urged them to throw away any thought of serving the gods their ancestors worshipped beyond the Euphrates River and in Egypt. Joshua then threw out a challenge to them that should have made them think hard about where the Israelites were placing their loyalty. He said that if serving the Lord was not what they wanted, then they should chose the gods of their ancestors (who were worthless) or the gods of their defeated enemies (who were worthless). In contrast to serving the worthless gods they had known, Joshua threw the gauntlet on the table, "But, as for me and my household, we will serve the Lord." (Joshua 24:14-15)

In a spontaneous and united response, the leaders exclaimed, "Far be it from us to forsake the Lord to serve other gods!" They then explained the reason for their obvious choice. God had (1) brought them out of slavery in Egypt, (2) performed great deeds and wonders before their eyes, (3) protected them through the entire journey from

Egypt, through the deserts and wildernesses, and (4) drove out all the nations who possessed the land east and west of the Jordan River. They concluded by saying, "We too will serve the Lord, because he is our God." (Joshua 24:16-18)

Joshua then challenged their response. Sure, they were willing to serve the Lord because of all that he had done for them. However, will they serve him in the future when they are surrounded by the gods of the people God detests? Joshua even went so far as to accuse them of not being able to serve God. Joshua said God is not all-forgiving. "He is a holy God; he is a jealous God. He will not forgive your rebellion and your sins." Joshua warned the Israelites yet again, as had Moses before him, that if the Israelites abandoned God and turned to the gods anathema to God, God will not be their God. He will turn away from them, bring disaster on them, and bring them to a end, even though He had been good to them up to that point. (Joshua 24:19-20) Joshua was doing his best to make the Israelites understand what was before them in the future. Joshua had seen the worst of humanity and he knew there were Israelites, even then, who would be tempted by the loose morality of the nations in and around them. He wanted the Israelite leadership to make a firm commitment that God would be at the center of their lives and that He only would guide their steps. Joshua was forcing them to not only have a head commitment to God, but to also have a heart commitment. In other words, the reverence had to be a full and utter "shalom."

Sensing what Joshua was getting at, the people almost shouted their response, "No! We will serve the Lord." Joshua then judged that they had chosen to serve the Lord and, if they ever tried to back out of the covenant, their words would be used against them and the person who would be accusing them would be God. The people then agreed with Joshua, "Yes, we are witnesses." (Joshua 24:21-22)

Joshua then told them to throw away the very things that would lead them to be indicted by God and those were the foreign gods that were already being used by the Israelites. Joshua followed that acknowledgement of their encroaching moral cancer with an order to immediately yield their hearts (devotion) to their Lord, the God of Israel. The people responded appropriately, "We will serve the Lord our God and obey him." (Joshua 24:23-24)

d. Covenant Renewed

On that very day, Joshua made a covenant between God and the Israelites. Joshua affirmed once again that the Israelites would revere God by serving Him and obeying His law. Joshua recorded the events in the "Book of the Law of God." Joshua concluded the ceremonies by placing a large stone under the oak near the holy place of God. He declared that the stone, which heard every word that was spoken that day, would be a witness against the Israelites if they were ever untrue to God. Joshua then dismissed those who were present to go back to their places of inheritance. (Joshua 24:25-28)

e. Deaths and Burials

Joshua died at the age of 110 years. He was buried at Timnath Serah in the hill country of Ephraim, north of Mount Gaash. (Joshua 24:29-30 and Judges 2:8-9)

Joseph died in Egypt, but his bones were carried by the Israelites into the Promised Land. His remains were buried at Shechem in the tract of land that Jacob had bought from the descendants of Hamor, the father of Shechem. (Joshua 24:32)

Eleazar, the son of Aaron, died and was buried at Gibeah in the hill county of Ephraim. Gibeah had been allotted to Phinehas, the son of Eleazar. (Joshua 24:33)

f. God Was Obeyed after Joshua

Joshua's influence with the Israelites lasted long after he died. The author of the Book of Joshua noted that Israel served the Lord not only through the lifetime of Joshua, but even through the lifetimes of the elders who outlived Joshua and who had seen and heard all that God had done for the nation of Israel. (Joshua 24:31 and Judges 2:7)

APPENDIX

Part One

a. The El Amarna Letters

Almost 400 clay tablets were recovered in Egypt in the 19th century. Thirty-five of the clay tablets that contain references to a conflict that was then-occurring throughout Canaan. The tablets make reference to a group of people who have been identified by some researchers as the Israelites who invaded Canaan under the leadership of Joshua. More research is needed before the connection with Joshua can be made with some certainty. They are referenced here to give the reader an opportunity to make some tentative decisions about the value of the tablets to the study of Joshua.

The El Amarna Letters, as the clay tablets are called, were first discovered in 1887 in the ruins of the ancient city of El-Amarna by local Egyptians, who secretly dug them up and then sold them to collectors. El-Amarna was a city on the east bank of the Nile River located about 190 miles south of modern-day Cairo. This was the site of Akhetaten, the capital of Egypt for a brief period. It was founded by Amenhotep IV, who later changed his name to Akhenaten.

The letters were in the form of cuneiform clay tablets. Later, archeologists searched the same ruins and discovered more letters. The letters were written primarily in one form or another of Babylonian, which was the diplomatic language of the time. There are now 382 El Amarna Letters scattered throughout the world. The vast majority of the letters are housed in museums in Germany and England, with others in museums in Egypt, France, Russia, and the United States. The area were the letters were found in El-Amarna is now called the Bureau of Correspondence of Pharaoh.

El-Amarna tablet number EA161

The letters appear to have been addressed to the pharaohs Amenhotep III and his son Akhenaten (also spelled Akhenaton, Akhnaton, or Ikhnaton and also called Amenhotep IV). A few of the recovered letters appear to be copies of letters sent by the pharaohs to the rulers of other countries. In one letter (EA1), The pharaoh Nibmuarea has been identified as Amenhotep III. Nibmuarea/Nibmuareya was his throne name. In another letter (EA2), he is referred to as Mimmuwareya.

Amenhotep III was the ninth king or pharaoh of the 18th dynasty of Egypt. It is believed that he was born in or about 1398 BC to Tuthmosis IV. His name relates to the god Amun, one of the major gods of Egypt. He was the husband of Queen Tiye, the father of Akhenaten, and the grandfather of Tutankhamun, known to the entire world as King Tut. Amenhotep III began his rule when he was 12 years old. He thereafter married Tiye, who was also only 12 years old. It is believed that Amenhotep III reigned from 1386 to 1353 BC, but these dates can vary by 10 years or more.

Amenhotep III

Amenhotep III was born into great wealth. He was a great hunter and an ardent supporter of the arts and building projects. He was also concerned about the rise in power of the cult of Amun in Egypt. By the beginning of his reign, the priests of Amun owned almost as much land as the pharaoh and, in Egypt and elsewhere, land meant wealth and wealth meant power. Amenhotep III did nothing to interfere with the worship of Amun, but he promoted the worship of the sun god Aten, once a minor god. Amenhotep III believed that Aten had a primary significance to the royal family. Amenhotep III even elevated Aten to the status of the personal god of the pharaoh. Under the leadership of his son Akhenaten, Aten gained even greater stature.

Amenhotep IV aka Akhenaten

Akhenaten, called Amenhotep at birth and given the name Amenhotep IV by Egyptologists, took over the reigns of Egypt in 1353 when his father died. After five years, he had a religious conversion. He then outlawed the ancient worship of Egypt, closed the temples of all other cults, and forbade any other religious practice except for Atenism. He then changed his name to Akhenaten and he created the first state-mandated monotheistic system in the world at that time. It became clear after a time that Akhenaten's primary concern was with his religious reforms and not with foreign affairs. Akhenaten died in 1336 BC after only 17 years as pharaoh. His son, Tutankhamun, took the throne at the age of eight years. He reversed his father's reforms, but he died at the age of 18 years without being able to accomplish all of his goals.

The El-Amarna tablets, according to one source, appear to represent communications between the pharaoh and his vassals between the years 1404 BC and 1340 BC. The exact year of each letter is difficult to ascertain because none of the letters are dated. In fact, it is difficult to determine which pharaoh was the intended recipient of each of the letters. However, a number of the letters are from the rulers of cities within the area defined as Canaan. Many of these letters were requests from the rulers of cities, called mayors, who are being attacked by the Apiru, Habiru, or Hapiru, depending on the translation. Interestingly, the requests were seldom personally answered by any pharaoh. The lack of response is certainly a good indication that Egypt was too weak or too disinterested, or both, in Canaan at this time to render any help to cities that traditionally had been within Egypt's sphere of interest.

The most frequent correspondent to the pharaohs was Rib-Hadda, the king or mayor of Byblos, which is located in modern-day Lebanon. (The leader of each city and its surround towns and other lands appears to be called "king" by his people and "mayor" by the pharaoh.) Rib-Hadda is the author of over 58 letters to the pharaohs, wherein he constantly request aid from the Egyptians to help fight off both the Hittites and the Apiru (Habiru, Hapiru). There were other letters dealing with threats from the Habiru from cities south of Byblos. There are letters from Gaza, Lachish, Ashkelon, and Hebron in southern Canaan; from Jerusalem, Gezer, Aijalon, Joppa, Shiloh, and Shechem in central Canaan; and, from Taanach, Megiddo, Acco, Hazor, Tyre, and Sidon in northern Canaan. None of the requests for aid seem to have been answered in a positive manner.

The Amarna Letters have been numbered based on the geographical origin of the letters, rather than when they were written, starting with the cities in northern Canaan and ending in southern Canaan. The numbering was done by William L. Moran in his book, "The Amarna Letters," published in 1992. Each letter begins with the letters "EA" (an abbreviation of the words El Amarna), followed by a number. There may or may not have been any attempt to put them in any chronological order even within a geographical group.

Many of the El Amarna Letters depict with some clarity the trouble being caused by a people referred to as Hapiru, Habiru, and Apiru. While recognizing that not all scholars will unequivocally identify the people called Hapiru, Habiru, and Apiru with the Israelites, your author has taken the position that they are and that is why the El Amarna Letters have been included in this book. The pharaoh, whether Amenhotep III, Akhenaten, or some other pharaoh, never responded in any effective way to the requests of any of the mayors/kings of Canaan.

It would be of some help to the reader to divide Canaan into three parts: the southern, the central, and the northern. However, this is difficult because the southern and the central regions overlap and the northern and the central regions overlap. Therefore, it might be beneficial to group the letters based on what part of Canaan was first mentioned in the Book of Joshua. Therefore, the letters have been grouped based upon the southern/central campaign and the central/northern campaign.

b. The Southern/Central Campaign

There are five cities that are mentioned in the southern/central campaign by the Habiru. They are **Gezer**, **Hebron**, **Jerusalem**, **Ashkelon**, and **Lachish**. In the map below, **Gezer** is located in the top left, **Hebron** is located in the bottom right, **Jerusalem** is located in the middle right, and both **Ashkelo**n and **Lachish** are located in the bottom left.

1. Gezer

In EA299, **Yapahu**, the king or mayor of Gezer warned the pharaoh about the Israelites. He addressed the pharaoh as "the king, my lord, my god, the Sun, the Sun from the sky." He described himself as "Yapahu, the ruler of Gazru, your servant, the dirt at your feet, the groom of your horses." He continued with his preliminary remarks: "Truly I fall at the feet of the king, my lord, my god, my Sun, the Sun from the sky, 7 times and 7 times, on the stomach and on the back." Once he finished flattering the pharaoh, he got to his point. He described the Apiru as being stronger than his people. He needed help from the pharaoh before the Apiru destroyed them.

In EA298, **Yapahu** once again wrote to the pharaoh. He informed the pharaoh that matters had become even more serious. His younger brother had become Yapahu's enemy by entering Muhhazu (unknown location) and pledging himself to the "Apiru." He added that the pharaoh should be concerned about his land as Tianna was at war with Yapahu.

In EA271, Milkili, the king of Gezer, referred to the pharaoh as "the king, my lord, my god, my Sun." He informed the pharaoh that the war against him and Suwardata was severe. He asked the pharaoh to save the pharaoh's land from the "Apiru" or, as an alternative, send chariots to save Milkili and Suwardata. He told the king to ask Yanhamu, apparently an official of the pharaoh, what was going on in Canaan. Yanhamu is also mentioned elsewhere as Rahmanu.

Gezer was not the only area under attack by the Israelites. In EA366, Shuwardate ("Suwardata"), likely the king of

Hebron, wrote to the pharaoh. He refereed to the pharaoh as "the king, my lord, my Sun, my god." He referred to himself as "your servant, the servant of the king and the dirt at your feet, the ground you tread on. I prostrate myself at the feet of the king, my lord, the Sun from the sky, 7 times and 7 times, both on the stomach and on the back." He wrote to the king that the "Apiru" had risen up and all of his "brothers" had deserted him. Sometimes "brothers" can mean fellow kings. Only he and Abdi-Heba [king of Jerusalem] were at war with the Apiru. However, Surata, the ruler of Akka [Acco], and Endaruta, the ruler of Aksapa [unknown city], have come to his aid. He had requested 50 chariots from them. Of course, it would be helpful if the pharaoh would send Yanhamu (the pharaoh's officer) to restore the pharaoh's lands to him.

2. Hebron

In EA284, Shuwardata ("Suwardata"), the mayor of Hebron, wrote to the pharaoh. He recognized the sovereignty of the pharaoh and his place in the hierarchy: "I fall at the feet of the king, my lord. I fall 7 times and 7 times more, both on the stomach and on the back." He wanted the pharaoh to know that all of the lands of the pharaoh had been taken and he was alone against them. He needed help from the pharaoh and requested the pharaoh to "send forth his powerful hand."

Letter EA215 was written by a person named Bayawa. This person does not identify himself in any way except as "Bayawa, your servant." He obviously knows the standard greeting for the pharaoh as he started the letter this way: "I fall at the feet of the king, my lord, my Sun, my god, 7 times and 7 times, on the stomach and on the back." This is a salutation used by Suwardata, the king of Hebron. Perhaps

Bayawa was connected with Hebron in some way. However, there may never be an answer to that question. In any event, he warned that if Yanhamu, the pharaoh's representative in Canaan, did not come "within this year" all the lands would be lost to the Apiru. "So, give life to the lands."

In EA 280, Suwardata informed the pharaoh that a Lab'ayu who once took Suwardata's town was dead, but another Lab'ayu named Abdi-Heba seized Swardata's town.

3. Jerusalem

After the King of Jerusalem was killed shortly after the Battle of Gibeon, Abdi-Heba became the ruler of Jerusalem. In the Amarna letters, he refers to himself as the "mayor" of Jerusalem and a "servant" to the pharaoh of Egypt, who is addressed as the "king." His letters show great deference to the pharaoh, which clearly indicate that he is subject to the pharaoh. He falls at the feet of "the king, my lord, 7 times and 7 times." However, despite the many pleas from Abdi-Heba, it appears that his letters are not given any consideration by the pharaoh.

In EA289, Abdi-Heba indicated that Milkilu [king of Gezer] was joined with the sons of Labayu and with the sons of Arsawa because they wanted the land of the king for themselves. Abdi-Heba wanted to know why the pharaoh didn't do something about Milkilu. He said that Milkilu and Tagi took Rubutu [a city located between Gezer and Jerusalem].

In EA290, Abdi-Heba complained about the actions of two men called Milkilu [king of Gezer] and Suardatu [also spelled Shuwardata or Suwardata, king of Gath] "against the land of the king." They commanded troops from Gazru [Gezer], Gimtu [unknown city], and Qiltu [Hebron or Keilah]. With the troops, they captured Rubutu [unknown city]. The land of the king deserted to the "Hapiru" (Hebrews). In addition, a town belonging to Jerusalem, called Bit-nin.urta, has gone over to the side of the men of Qiltu. Abdi-Heba asked the pharaoh to send archers to reclaim the lost land. Abdi-Heba believes that if the pharaoh does not send archers, then the land will desert to the "Hapiru." At the end of the letter, Abdi-Heba added the name of Ginti [Gimti, city of Gath] to the men who had taken the land from the pharaoh.

In EA287, **Abdi-Heba** described a dismal state of affair for Jerusalem. He wrote that Milkilu and Tagi brought troops into Qiltu against Abdi-Heba. All the lands around him are at peace, but he is at war. Garzu [Gezer], Asqaluna [Ashkelon], and Lakisi [Lachish] provided the Apiru with food, oil, and other requirements. Abdi-Heba needed archers to fight off the enemy. He asked the pharaoh to think about Jerusalem. Abdi-Heba was not set in power by his father or mother. It was the pharaoh who made him king. Since the pharaoh made him king, the pharaoh should not abandon him. The garrison the pharaoh provided has left and he was almost killed by the Kasites. And, he sent a caravan to the king, but they were captured in the countryside.

4. Askelon

In EA323, **Yidya**, the king or mayor of Ashkelon, wrote to the pharaoh, calling him "the king, my lord, the Sun from the sky." Yidya had probably received a letter from the pharaoh asking him about what Abdi-Heba said about Yidya aiding the Apiru. Yidya said he was guarding the palace of the king in accordance with pharaoh's command. He even sent the pharaoh 30 pieces of glass the pharaoh ordered. He ended his letter by stating, unequivocally, "who is the dog that would not obey the orders of the king."

5. Lachish

Likewise, in EA329, **Zimreddi**, the king or mayor of Lachish, wrote a letter to the pharaoh in response to an envoy the pharaoh sent to Zimreddi. The envoy made demands of Zimreddi, who, in turn, indicated to the pharaoh that he was making preparations in accordance with the order that was made. In EA 330, **Shipti-Balu**, also with the title of king or mayor of Lachish, parroted what Zimreddi had written to the pharaoh. He identified the pharaoh's envoy as Yanhamu. He assured the pharaoh that Lachish was "safe and sound."

Despite the assurances given by Yidya, Zimreddi, and Shipti-Balu, an unknown person by the name of **Paapu** warned the pharaoh about them. It appears that Paapu may have been someone who was in the administration in Lachish. In EA333, Paapu advised the pharaoh that Zimredda [Zimreddi] and Shipti-Balu were acting disloyally together. Paapu overheard Sipti-Balu [Shipti-Balu] and Zimredda [Zimreddi] talking. Sipti-Balu told Zimredda that the town of Yaramu had written to him. They needed 11 bows, 3 daggers, and 3 swords so they could go out against the pharaoh's land.

6. Jerusalem Again

Based on another letter by Abdi-Heba, king of Jerusalem, it appears that Zimreddi may have been a double agent. In EA 288, Abdi-Heba was in the midst of a world turned upside down by the Israelites. Therefore, he approached the pharaoh, who had not heeded any of his advice up to this point in a totally different manner. He wrote, "Behold, the king, my lord, has placed his name at the rising of the sun and at the setting of the sun. It is, therefore, impious what they have done to me. Behold, I am not a mayor; I am a soldier of the king, my lord. Behold, I am a friend of the king and a tribute-bearer of the king. It was neither my father nor my mother, but the strong arm of the king that [p]laced me in the house of [my] fath[er]." In other words, the pharaoh is a god and Abdi-Heba is his servant, almost like a priest. If wrong is done to Abdi-Heba, then it is as if the wrong were done to the pharaoh as god. Interestingly, Abdi-Heba called himself a friend of the pharaoh. This is almost a sacrilege in itself. A friend is someone who is equal to another. No one should ever have made that claim to the pharaoh. Abdi-Heba only had one excuse. He was getting desperate. Every bit of the pharaoh's land was in the hands of others and everyone was at peace except him. He was at war and he could be destroyed at any time. He chided the pharaoh by saying that the Apiru had taken all of the cities that once belonged to the pharaoh and the pharaoh had done nothing to prevent it. He pointed out that even "servants" who were connected with the Apiru had killed Zimredda [Zimreddi] of Lakisu [Lachish] and Yaptih-Hadda was killed in Silu [Shiloh]. Yaptih-Hadda was apparently the king of Shiloh. When this was done, the pharaoh did nothing in response. If the pharaoh refused to respond, especially with archers, then the pharaoh might as well send someone to Jerusalem and take Abdi-Heba and his family to Egypt, where they will die near the pharaoh. Abdi-Heba painted a desperate picture for the pharaoh. He signed the letter: "I am your servant and your son."

It appears that Jerusalem was captured by the Israelites after the death of Joshua. (Judges 1:8) However, they did not prevent the Jebusites from restoring control over Jerusalem. The Jebusites maintained their hold on

Jerusalem until David wrested it from them about 400 years later.

c. The Central/Northern Campaign

The middle of Canaan was likely the next area of Canaan to be conquered by the Israelites. It would have been followed by the conquest of the northern cities and their territories. The major cities along the northern coast of Canaan, going from north to south were Sumur, Area, Byblos, Beirut, Sidon, and Tyre. Hazor was southeast of Tyre and just east of what was later called the Sea of Galilee. Each of these cities was ruled by a king or mayor and they owed their loyalty to the pharaoh. In addition, when there was trouble in the land, their job was to notify the pharaoh of the problem and to request troops to repel any attackers.

The cities that were part of the central/northern campaign were Megiddo (in the Jezreel Valley), Shechem (between Mt. Ebal and Mt. Gerizim), Byblos (north of Sidon on the Mediterranean Sea), Sidon (on the Mediterranean Sea), Tyre (on the Mediterranean Sea south of Sidon), and Kedesh/Kadesh (north of the Sea of Galilee).

1. Megiddo

Megiddo is located in plain of Esdraelon of the Valley of Jezreel. In the El Amarna Letter EA243, Biridija (or Biridiya, as he called himself), the "mayor" of Megiddo warned the pharaoh about the Israelites, called Apiru, in the letter. He addressed the pharaoh in a manner that was common amongst the rulers of the cities. He wrote that "I fall at the feet of the king, my lord and my Sun and my god, 7 times and 7 times. He assured the pharaoh that he was guarding Megidda, as the city was called then, every hour of the day without fail. During the day, Biridija sent out chariots to ward off the Apiru and, during the night, there are sentinels on the walls. He called the warring of Apiru in the land as "severe" and the pharaoh needed to keep a close watch over "his" land. In short, Biridija told the pharaoh that he was doing everything he could to keep the Israelites at bay, but the pressure they were putting on him was serious enough that the pharaoh needed to be very concerned and, eventually, do something about it.

In letter EA246, Biridija, the mayor of Megiddo, went beyond just warning about the Apiru, he let the pharaoh know that there were traitors willing to sell out to the Israelites. He warned the pharaoh that two sons of Lab'ayu [the king of Shechem] had given money to the Apiru and to the Suteans to wage war against Biridija.

2. Shechem

Shechem is in the valley between Mount Ebal and Mount Gerizim. In letter EA254, Labayu, the mayor of Shechem, responded to the charges that his sons had given money to the Israelites to wage war against Megiddo. He addressed the pharaoh respectfully: "Thus Lab'ayu, your servant and the dirt on which you tread. I fall at the feet of the king, my lord and my Sun, 7 times and 7 times." Labayu went on to say that he was a loyal servant of the pharaoh and he had always obeyed the pharaoh in everything. He would certainly not participate in any scheme that would cost the pharaoh any of his land. He went even further. He said he was not a rebel, he had never held back on his payments of tribute, and he had done everything the pharaoh's commissioner had requested. He emphasized that his only act of rebellion was questioning what Milkilu had done for the pharaoh while Labayu was in Gazru (Gezer). Labayu revealed that he knew what Milkilu had done to put Labayu in a bad light before the pharaoh. He denied knowing that his son was aiding the Apiru in any way. To show his good will, Labayu was willing to turn his son over to Addaya, one of the pharaoh's officers. Labayu then used two examples to show what he was willing to do for the pharaoh. If the pharaoh asked for Labayu's wife, Labayu would send her to the pharaoh. And, if the pharaoh asked Labayu to put a bronze dagger through Labayu's heart, Labayu would obey the pharaoh.

3. Megiddo Again

Labayu certainly appeared to be a loyal subject of the pharaoh, but his actions soon showed a different side. In letter EA244, Biridija, the mayor of Megiddo, wrote to the pharaoh about Labayu. Biridija prefaced his comments about Labayu with a reference to the pharaoh's archers being removed from Megiddo. He wrote that the archers returned to Egypt and soon thereafter Labayu attacked Biridija. Because of the attacks, Biridija had been unable to leave the city and harvest the crops. In addition, there was a pestilence in the city that was causing death. Biridija requested 100 men be sent to Megiddo to guard it. Otherwise, the city will fall to Labayu.

4. Byblos

Byblos was and is on the Mediterranean Sea north of modern-day Beirut. Rib-Hadda was the king or mayor of Byblos (also called Gebal and Gubla). In letter EA68, Rib-Hadda informed the pharaoh of the war that was being raged in northern Canaan. He addressed the pharaoh respectfully and he let the pharaoh know that the city of Gubla was undisturbed. However, this did not mean that he did not need the pharaoh's help. He informed the pharaoh that Sumur should not be neglected. If so, it might succumb to the forces of the Apiru. He emphasized that the war against them was "extremely severe" and, therefore, the pharaoh should not neglect them.

The pharaoh apparently did nothing to aid Sumur and it fell to the Apiru. Rib-Hadda wrote letter EA76 to the pharaoh. After the customary courtesies, Rib-Hadda got right to the point: the pharaoh had neglected the northern part of Canaan and Sumur had fallen to the pharaoh's enemies. There was a traitor by the name of Abdi-Asirta, "the dog," who had allied himself with the Apiru and taken the two cities of Sigata and Ampi. In addition, Sumur had joined the Apiru. Rib-Hadda reminded the pharaoh that "for years" archers had come from Egypt to Canaan to make sure the cities remained loyal to the pharaoh ("inspect them"). However, not only had the pharaoh not responded to his letters, the pharaoh had done nothing to recover Sumur. Rib-Hadda literally demanded that the pharaoh send him a garrison of 400 men to help Rib-Hadda. He also urged the pharaoh to send out a large force of archers to drive out the enemy and to reclaim the kings lands. Rib-Hadda ended the letter with his admonition: "You must not neglect this message." (The identity of Abdi-Asirta is unknown. The name "Abdi" is found in the Bible. He was a Levite who was the grandfather of King David's singer Ethan. See 1 Chronicles 6:44. In addition, see the following for a more extended evaluation of this person called Abdi-Asirta: **http://www.whowerethephoenicians.com/wp-content/ uploads/book/phenicos_new%20(2)_p31-p64.pdf**)

Rib-Hadda became desperate. Because the pharaoh had not responded to him, he sent a message to Haya, "the vizier," a commissioner of the pharaoh. He addressed Haya respectfully: "May Man [Amun], the god of the king, your lord, establish your honor in the presence of the king, your lord." Rib-Hadda then accused Haya of being negligent and not speaking to the pharaoh about sending archers to retake Sumur. He referred to Abdi-Asirta has a "servant and dog" and he was only strong because he has the Apira [Apiru] as his auxiliary force. He asked Haya to send him 50 pairs of horses and 200 infantry soldiers to resist Abdi-Asirta in Sigata until the arrival of the archers. Rib-Hadda indicated that only a large military show would prevent Abdi-Asirta and "all the Apiru" from taking Sigata and Ampi.

The anarchy created in northern Canaan continued unabated. Rib-Hadda became desperate in his appeal for aide from the pharaoh. He sent letter EA73 to Amanappa, who he addressed as his father, but was a minister in the court of the pharaoh. He accused Amanappa of not speaking to the pharaoh about the collapse of the pharaoh's control in the area around Byblos. He implied that the land of Amurru has fallen from the grasp of the pharaoh. He argued that the land would revert to the pharaoh if only archers were sent to Canaan. He suggested that the towns and cities were only being allied with Abdi-Asirta because of the absence of the presence of the pharaoh's soldiers, particularly archers. However, Abdi-Asirta has become more audacious. He sent a message to the men of Ammiya, telling them to kill their lord and join up with the Apiru. The rulers of the other cities are afraid that the same thing will happen to them. Rib-Hadda urged Amanappa to speak with the pharaoh and persuade the pharaoh to send an auxiliary force to Rib-Hadd "with all speed."

In letter EA74, Rib-Hadda expressed extreme alarm over the state of matters around Byblos, called Gubla at that time in history, to the pharaoh. His salutation even changed to address the situation [bracket information included by translator]: "Rib-Hadda says to [his] lord, king of all countries, Great King, King of Battle. May [the Lady] of Gubla grant power to the king, my lord. I fall at the feet of my lord, my Sun, 7 times and 7 times. May the king, the lord, know that Gubla, the loyal maidservant of the king since the days of his ancestors, is safe and sound." Rib-Hadda now gave the pharaoh the exalted title of "king of all countries." He added "Great King" and "King of Battle" to make the point that the pharaoh should be engaged in helping Rib-Hadda with the devastation occurring around him. He also wanted the pharaoh to understand that Byblos, known as Gubla, had been loyal to the pharaohs far into the past, just in case the pharaoh was not familiar with that fact. He urged the pharaoh to check the record to find a time when Byblos had not been loyal to the pharaoh. Rib-Hadda also let the pharaoh know that Byblos was safe and sound at that moment, but the situation could change at any moment. He then accused the pharaoh of abandoning Byblos and neglecting his duty to Rib-Hadda, a servant of the pharaoh. He reported of the war that was ongoing with the Apiru and he had sold his sons and daughters to the land of Yarimuta for provisions to keep Byblos alive. He has not been able to harvest anything because the Apiru control the countryside. All of his towns in the mountains and along the sea were then in the hands of the Apiru. All Rib-Hadda controlled was Byblos and two towns. After Abdi-Asirta captured the town of Sigata, he convinced the men of Ammiya to kill their leader and join him: "they are like Apiru." Worse, Abdi-Asirta has called upon all of his troops to assemble to attack Byblos. He has promised them peace forever once the entire country was joined with the Apiru. He even bragged that the pharaoh could do nothing against them once the entire country was united. Rib-Hadda feared what would happen to him once Abdi-Asirta was able to bring all of his troops together. Rib-Hadda wrote that he was like a bird in a cage. He then closed the letter with a plea to the pharaoh todo something. He again accused the pharaoh of neglecting "your country." He asked the pharaoh to speak with Amanappa because Amanappa knew what the situation was like for Byblos. If the pharaoh will not help, he asked that the pharaoh send a man to replace Rib-Hadda so Rib-Hadda could be with the pharaoh. In other words, Rib-Hadda did not want to wait until Byblos was taken by storm and Rib-Hadda was killed.

When the pharaoh did not respond adequately to Rib-Hadda, he sent yet another letter, which is EA121. This letter was short and reflective of the continuing dire situation around Gubla, now known as Byblos. The pharaoh wrote Rib-Hadda and told him to "guard yourself." Rib-Hadda was appalled at the pharaoh's advice. He asked the pharaoh, "What is to guard me?" He said the pharaoh why he had not provided Rib-Hadda with provisions or a garrison. These had been provided in the past, but now they were needed more than ever because Abdi-Asarti told the Apiru and the men who had joined them that Rib-Hadda was defenseless. Rib-Hadda then begged the pharaoh to send archers. He taunted the pharaoh by letting him know that his mayors had been slaughtered like dogs and the pharaoh had done nothing. If the pharaoh was not going to send any archers, then the pharaoh should send for Rib-Hadda himself.

The report Rib-Hadda made in EA88 should have made the pharaoh do something in response. Rib-Hadda wrote that Ardat, Irqat, Ammi, Sigata, Batruna, and one other city whose name was not readable had fallen to Abdi-Asarti, the "servant and dog" and he chided the pharaoh because the pharaoh had done absolutely nothing to prevent it and he had done nothing to recover the cities, all of which had belonged to Gubla (Byblos). Rib-Hadda reminded the pharaoh that he had written a letter each time one of his towns had fallen to the Apiru and the pharaoh had not reacted positively any of the times. Worse, Abdi-Asarti, was now at the gates of Gubla itself. No one can go out into the countryside to plant, tend the crops, and harvest. Rib-Hadda urged the pharaoh to send chariots and troops to guard Gubla. If he did not, then Gubla will be joined with the Apiru and they will control all the lands as far south as Egypt. If the pharaoh does not respond with a ready force of troops and chariots, then the pharaoh should designate a city where Rib-Hadda could go to stay alive. Rib-Hadda reminded the pharaoh of the loyalty of Gubla to the pharaoh, more loyal, in fact, that the king of Akka (Acco), whose messenger was furnished with one horse by the pharaoh. Rib-Hadda requested that his messenger be given two horses, obviously as a show of respect for Rib-Hadda.

In EA77, Rib-Hadda responded to Amanappa, who Rib-Hadda called his father. Amanappa apparently requested copper and something called "sinnu of copper" from Rib-Hadda. It appears that Amanappa was attempting to take advantage of Rib-Hadda's desperate situation by soliciting a bribe from Rib-Hadda. The letter Rib-Hadda sent to Amanappa in return was not solicitous in the least. He denied having any copper or sinnu of copper. He had given it to the king of Tyre for provisions. He accused Amanappa of knowing how badly the war was going for him and Amanappa was doing absolutely nothing. Rib-Hadda wrote that if Amanappa did not come to rescue him with archers, all the land would belong to the Apiru. If the city could not be rescued, then Amanappa should send a ship to bring all the men and gods of Gubla to Egypt. Rib-Hadda expressed the fear for the first time that the peasantry would strike him down.

When Rib-Hadda sent letter EA90 to the pharaoh, reminding him that Gubla was in desperate straits. The sons and daughters and all of the furnishings of the houses had been sold in the land of Yarimuta to provide Gubla with provisions. The fields could not be cultivated to provide food for Gubla. Every town belonging to Gubla had been taken by Abdi-Asirta, who was then in Mittana. However, Abdi-Asirta still had his eye on Gubla. Rib-Hadda reminded the king that Rib-Hadda had written a letter while in Sigata, but the pharaoh failed to respond and Sigata was taken. The same story applied to Batruna. Despite, Rib-Hadda's pleas, they fell on deaf ears. The pharaoh knew of his needs, but the pharaoh had been negligent in providing the proper military response. Because of the pharaoh's negligence, the Apiru had taken all of the cities. Gubla was void of grain and Rib-Hadda could only turn to the pharaoh for help. He pleaded for men and horses to be used to guard the city as Rib-Hadda was afraid for his own life.

When Rib-Hadda sent letter EA118, matters had worsen beyond what even Rib-Hadda had feared. It appeared that both Sidon and Beirut had gone into league with the Apiru. Their kings no longer wrote to the pharaoh. Rib-Hadda needed for the pharaoh to provide for the peasantry and send archers to protect the city. If the peasantry left the city, there would be no one to guard Gubla from the Apiru. The only cities left to the pharaoh were Gubla and Yanhamu.

Letter EA82 went to Amanappa, a member of the pharaoh's court. Rib-Hadda reviewed all the letters that had gone back and forth between the two men. Rib-Hadda told Amanappa again and again that the Apiru are on the side of Abdi-Asirta and all of the leaders of the other cities tell him everything they learn. Amanappa responded by telling Rib-Hadda to send a man to Amanappa at the palace and Amanappa would send out an auxiliary force, followed by archers. Rib-Hadda responded by saying he could not send a man because Abdi-Asirta would hear about it and attack

Gulpa. When he finally did send a man to the palace, that man gave orders to another man who attacked Rib-Hadda with a knife and stabbed him nine times. Rib-Hadda warned Amanappa that in two months he would abandon Gulpa if archers are not sent. Rib-Hadda also mentioned that the land of Amurru also needed to be rescued.

Letter EA101, contains a surprise. The pharaoh was notified by an unidentified writer, thought to be Rib-Hadda, that Abdi-Asirta was killed by men of Amurru. Apparently, Abdi-Asirta was sent by the pharaoh himself to rule over the land of Amurru. However, when Abdi-Asirta did not bring garments of lapis lazuli or other precious stones as tribute to Mittana, the men of Amurru killed him. Therefore, the pharaoh should punish the land of Amurru by boycotting it. In addition, the pharaoh should seize all of the ships that belong to the men of Arwada.

5. Sidon

Letter EA144 was from Zimreddi (also known as Zimredda), the ruler or mayor of Sidon. This Zimreddi is different than the Zimreddi who ruled Lachish. His address to the pharaoh, which is indirect, went like this: "Say to the king, my lord, my god, my Sun, the breath of my life: Thus Zimreddi, the mayor of Sidon. I fall at the feet of my lord, god, Sun, breath of my life, at the feet of my lord, my god, my Sun, the breath of my life 7 times and 7 times. May the king, my lord, know that Sidon, the maidservant of the king, my lord, which he put in my charge, is safe and sound. And when I heard the words of the king, my lord, when he wrote to his servant, then my heart rejoiced, and my head went [h]igh, and my eyes shone, at hearing the words of the king, my lord. " This took up about one-half of the letter. The rest of the letter dealt with the preparations that were being made by Zimreddi to anticipate the arrival of the pharaoh's archers. Zimreddi indicated that the archers will help retake all of the cities lost by Zimreddi to the Apiru.

Despite Zimreddi's assurances to the pharaoh, it appears that he protested a little too much about his loyalty. In letter EA147, Abi-Milku, the ruler or mayor of Tyre, gave the pharaoh information about Zimreddi. However, before he did, he opened his letter with a salutation that took up eighty percent of the letter! Once he got down to business, Abi-Milki told the pharaoh that Zimredda, the king of Sidon, tells Aziru, the son of Abdi-Asratu [Abdi-Asirta], everything that he learns from Egypt. (See below for the full text of the letter).

6. Tyre

Abi-Milki, the ruler or mayor Tyre, wrote to the pharaoh again in Letter EA148. He complained to the pharaoh that all he could send to the pharaoh was 100 units in weight of glass. However, the real troubling news had to do with both Sidon and Hasura (Hazon). He wrote that the king of Sidon is the one who raids the land of the king and the king of Hasura (Hazon) has aligned himself with the Apiru and taken over the land for them. He suggested that the pharaoh be concerned about "the palace attendants," as they are treacherous fellows.

7. Kadesh or Kedesh

There was one bright spot for the Pharaoh in all the El Amarna letters and it appears to have come from the city of Kadesh aka Kedesh. Kadesh/Kedesh was the southern capital of the Hittites. Kedesh was located just west of the Jordan River above the city of Hazor. Etakkama, mayor of

Qadesh (Kadesh), informed the pharaoh in letter EA 189 that he had defeated Biryawaza, mayor of Damascus, who had allied himself with the Habiru in his treachery, and had recovered all the land that had been lost. In addition, Etakkama had beaten the Habiru and "disbanded" them.

Part Two

d. Some El Amarna Letters in Full Text

There are 35 tablets recovered at El Amarna in upper Egypt that contain references to the conflict in Canaan, pitting the Israelites against cities in that region. The Israelites were referred to as Hibaru, Hiparu, and Apiru. Below are some samplings of the letters.

The full text translation of each Amarna tablet below was done by W. L. Moran and published in 1992 in his book "The Amarna letters." The site where the tablets can be viewed is this: **http://www.bible.ca/archeology/bible-archeology-maps-conquest-amarna-tablets-letters-akhenaten-habiru-abiru-hebrews-1404-1340bc.htm**

This is the key to the free on-line translation of the Amarna Letters:

- [ ] restored text
- […] missing text
- … obscure or greatly damaged text
- ‹ › omission by scribe
- « » sign(s) repeated by error
- ( ) word(s) supplied by editor to clarify text
- boldface numbers: line numbers
- italics: translation doubtful

- centered colon: indication of a gloss (the gloss is translated only if it has a different meaning from the word glossed; glosses in Akkadian are not indicated)

In the text below, the references to Habiru, Hapiru, or Apiru have been highlighted in **bold** by the author of this book. It has been done to bring the reader's attention to that part of the letter where these people are mentioned specifically.

Full text translation of Tablet EA74:
(From Rib-Hadda, mayor of Gubla (Byblos), to the Pharaoh about the Apiru)

"Rib-Hadda says to [his] lord, king of all countries, Great King, King of Battle:[2] May [the Lady] of Gubla grant power to the king, my lord. I fall at the feet of my lord, my Sun, 7 times and 7 times. **5–10** May the king, the lord, know that Gubla, the loyal maidservant of the king since the days of his ancestors, is safe and sound. The king, however, has now withdrawn his support of his loyal city. **10–12** May the king inspect the tablets of his father's house (for the time) when the ruler in Gubla was not a loyal servant. **13–19** Do not be negligent of your servant. Behold, the war of the ‹**Apiru** against ‹me› is severe and, as the gods of y[our] land [are ali]ve, our sons and daughters (as well as we ourselves) are gone since they have been sold in the land of Yarimuta for provisions to keep us alive. "For lack of a cultivator, my field is like a woman without a husband."[6] **19–22** All my villages that are in the mountains: ḫa-ar-ri or along the sea have been joined to the ‹**Apiru**. Left to me are Gubla and two towns. **23–30** After taking Šigata for himself, ‹Abdi-Aširta said to the men of Ammiya, "Kill your leader and then you will be like us and at peace."They were won over, following his message, and they are like ‹**Apiru**.[8] **30–38** So now ʿAbdi-Aširta has written to the troops: "Assemble in the temple of NINURTA,[10] and then let us fall upon Gubla. Look, there is no one that will save it from u[s]. Then let us drive out the mayors from the country that the entire country be joined to the ʿ**Apiru**, … to the entire country. Then will (our) sons and daughters be at peace forever. **39–45** Should even so the king come out, the entire country will be against him and what will he do to us?"Accordingly, they have made an alliance among themselves and, accordingly, I am very, very afraid, since [in] fact there is no one who will save me from them. **45–50** Like a bird in a trap: *ki-lu-bi* (cage), so am I in Gubla. Why have you neglected your country? I have written like this to the palace, but you do not heed my words. **51–57** Look, Amanappa is with you. Ask him. He is the one that knows and has experienced the stra[its] I am in. May the king heed the words of his servant. May he grant provisions for his servant and keep his servant alive so I may guard his [lo]yal [city], *along with our L[ad]y* (and) our gods, *f[or you]*. **57–62** May [*the king*] vis[*it*] his [land] and [*his servant*]. [May he] give thought to his land. *Pac[ify yo]ur [land]*! May it seem go[od] in the sight of the k[ing], my [lo]rd. May he send a [*ma*]n of his to stay this time so I may arri[ve] in the presence of the king, my lord. **62–65** It is good for me to be with you. What can I do by [my]self? This is what I long for day and night." (The Amarna letters, W. L. Moran, introduction, 1992 AD, EA 74)

Full text translation of Tablet EA144:
(From Zimreddi, mayor of Sidon,
to the Pharaoh about the Apiru)

"Say to the king, my lord, my god, my Sun, the breath of my life: Thus Zimreddi, the mayor of Sidon. **6–12** I fall at the feet of my lord, god, Sun, breath of my life, «at the feet of my lord, my god, my Sun, the breath of my life» 7 times and 7 times. May the king, my lord, know that Sidon, the maidservant of the king, my lord, which he put in my charge, is safe and sound. **13–21** And when I heard the words of the king, my lord, when he wrote to his servant, then my heart rejoiced, and my head went [h]igh, and my eyes shone, at hearing the words of the king, my lord. May the king know that I have made preparations before the arrival of the archers of the king, my lord. I have prepared everything in accordance with the command of the king, my lord. **22–30** May the king, my lord, know that the war against me is very severe. All the cit[i]es that the king put in [m]y ch[ar]ge, have been joined to the ʿAp[ir]u. May the king put me in the charge of a man that will lead the archers of the king to call to account the cities that have been joined to the ʿApiru, so you can restore3 them to my charge that I may be able to serve the king, my lord, as our ancestors (did) before." (The Amarna letters, W. L. Moran, introduction, 1992 AD, EA 144)

Full text translation of Tablet EA287:
(From Abdi-Heba, mayor of Jerusalem, to the pharaoh)

"[Say to the kin]g, m[y] lord: [Message of ʿAb]di-Ḥeba, yo[ur] servant. [I fall at the feet] of my lord 7 t[imes and 7 times. **4–9** *Consider*] *the* ent‹ire› *affair.* [*Milkilu and Tagi* brou]ght [*troop*]s into [*Qiltu*] *against me.* [Consider] the deed that they did [*to your servant*]. Arrow(s)4 […] … **10–19** […] they brought into [*Qilt*]*u*. May the [kin]g know (that) all the lands are [at] peace (with one another), but I am at war. May the king provide for his land. Consider the lands of Gazru, Ašqaluna, and *L*[*akis*]*i*. They have given them food, oil, and any other requirement. So may the king provide for archers and6 send the archers against men that commit crimes against the king, my lord. **20–24** If this year there are archers, then the lands and the mayors will belong to the king, my lord. But if there are no archers, then the ki[ng] will

296

have neither lands nor mayors. **25–32** Consider Jerusalem! This neither my father nor m[y] mother gave to me. The [str]ong hand: *zu-ru-uḫ* (arm) [of the king] gave it to me.) Consider the deed! This is the deed of Milkilu and the deed of the sons of Lab‹ayu, who have given the land of the king ‹to› the ‹**Apiru**. Consider, O king, my lord! *I am in the right*! **33–42** With regard to the Kašites, may the king make inquiry of the commissioners. Though the house is well fortified, they attempted a very serious crime. They [t]ook their tools, and *I had to seek shelter by a support* for the roof: *ga-ag-gi*. A[nd so i̇]f he is going to send [troop]s into [Jerusalem], let them come with [a garrison for] (regular) *service*. May the king provide for them; [all] of the land *might be in dire straits* on their account. **43–52** May the king inquire about the[m. Let there be] much food, much oil, much clothing, until Pauru, the commissioner of the king, comes up to Jerusalem. Gone[13] is Addaya together with the garrison of soldiers [that] the king [provided. May the king know (that) Addaya [sa]id to me, "[Beh]old, he has dismissed me."Do not abandon it, [and] send this [year] a garrison, and send right here[15] the commissioner of the king. **53–59** I sent [as gift]s to the king, my lord, [x] prisoners, 5000 ... [...],[17] [and] *8 porters* for the caravans of the k[ing, my lord], but they have been taken in the countryside: *ša-de₄-e* of Ayyaluna. May the king, my lord, know (that) I am unable to send a caravan to the king, my lord. For your information! **60–63** As the king has placed his name in Jerusalem forever, he cannot abandon it—the land of Jerusalem.

64–70 Say to the scribe of the king, my lord: Message of ‹Abdi-Ḫeba, your servant. I fall at (your) feet. I am your servant. Present eloquent words to the king, my lord: I am a soldier of the king. *I am always yours*. **71–78** And please make the Kasites responsible for the evil deed. I was almost killed by the Kašites [i]n my own house. May the king [make an inquiry] in the[ir] regard. [May the kin]g, my lord, [provide] for th[em. 7 t]imes and 7 times may the king, my lord, [*provide*] for me." (The Amarna letters, W. L. Moran, introduction, 1992 AD, EA 287)

Full text translation of Tablet EA288:
(From Abdi-Heba, mayor of Jerusalem, warns about the Habiru, who killed Zimredda [Zimreddi] of Lachish and Yaptih-Hadda of Shiloh - Silu)

"Say [t]o the king, my lord, [my Su]n: [M]essage of ʿAbdi-Ḫeba, your servant. I fall at the feet of the king, my lord, 7 times and 7 times. **5–10** Behold, the king, my lord, has placed his name at the rising of the sun and at the setting of the sun. It is, therefore, impious what they have done to me. Behold, I am not a mayor; I am a soldier of the king, my lord. **11–15** Behold, I am a *friend* of the king and a tribute-bearer of the king. It was neither my father nor my mother, but the strong arm of the king that [p]laced me in the house of [my] fath[er].³ **16–22** [… c]ame to me. … […]. I gave over [to *his* char]ge 10 slaves. Šuta, the commissioner of the king, ca[me t]o me; I gave over to Šutaʾs charge 21 girls, [8]0 prisoners, as a gift for the king, my lord. **23–28** May the king give thought to his land; the land of the king is lost. *All of it has attacked me.* I am at war as far as the land of Šeru and as far as Ginti-kirmil [Gath]. All the mayors are at peace, but I am at war. **29–33** I am treated like an ʿ**Apiru**, and I do not visit the king, my lord, since I am at war. I am situated like a ship⁷ in the midst of the sea. **34–40** The strong hand (arm) of the king took the land of Naḫrima and the land of *Kasi*, but now the ʿApiru have taken the very cities of the king. Not a single mayor remains to the king, my lord; all are lost. **41–47** Behold, Turbazu was slain in the city gate of Silu [Shiloh]. The king did nothing. Behold, servants who were joined to the ʿ**Api[r]u** *smote* Zimredda of Lakisu [Lachish], and Yaptiḫ-Hadda was slain in the city gate of Silu [Shiloh]. The king did

nothing. [*Wh*]*y* has he not called them to account? **48–53**
May the king [pro]vide for [his land] and may he [se]e to it
tha[t] archers [come ou]t to h[is] land. If there are no archers
this year, all the lands of the king, my lord, are lost. **54–61**
They have not reported to the king that the lands of the
king, my lord, are lost and all the mayors lost. If there are no
archers this year, may the king send a commissioner to
fetch me, me along with my brothers, and then we will die
near the king, our lord. **62–66** [To] the scribe of the king, my
lord: [Message] of ꜥAbdi-Ḫeba, (your) servant. [I fa]ll a[t (your)
feet]. Present [the words that I hav]e offered to [the king, my
lord]: I am your servant [and] your [s]on." (The Amarna
letters, W. L. Moran, introduction, 1992 AD, EA 288)

Full text translation of Tablet EA289:

(Abdi-Heba, mayor of Jerusalem, is concerned about
Shechem - Sakmu)

"[Say t]o the king, my lord: Message of ꜥAbdi-Ḫeba, your
servant. I f[all] at the feet of my lord, the k[ing], 7 times and 7
times. **5–10** Milkilu does not break away from the sons of
Labꜥayu and from the sons of Arsawa, as they desire the
land of the king for themselves. As for a mayor who does
such a deed, why does the king not ‹c›all him to account?
11–17 .Such was the deed that Milkilu and Tagi did: they
took Rubutu. And now as for Jerusalem, if this land belongs
to the king, why is it ‹not› *of concern* to the king like
Ḫazzatu? **18–24** Gintikirmil belongs to Tagi, and men of
Gintu are the garrison in Bitsanu. Are we to act like Labꜥayu
when he was giving the land of Šakmu to the **Ḫapiru**? **25–
36** Milkilu has written to Tagi and the sons ‹*of Lab*ꜥ*ayu*›, "Be
the both of you a protection. Grant all their demands to the
men of Qiltu, and let us isolate Jerusalem."[4] Addaya has
taken the garrison that you sent in the charge of Haya, the
son of Miyare; he has stationed it in his own house in

299

Ḫazzatu and has sent 20 men to Egypt. May the king, my lord, know (that) no garrison of the king is with me. **37–44** Accordingly, as truly as the king lives, his *irpi*-official, Puʾuru, has left me and is in Ḫazzatu. (May the king *call* (*this*) *to mind when he arrives.*) And so may the king send 50 men as a garrison to protect the land. The entire land of the king has deser[ted]. **45–51** Send Ye«eh»enḫamu that he may know about the land of the king, [my lord]. To the scribe of the king, [my lord: M]essage of ʿAbdi-Ḫeba, [your] servant. Offer eloq[uent] words to the king: *I am always, utterly yours.* I am your servant." (The Amarna letters, W. L. Moran, introduction, 1992 AD, EA 289)

Full text translation of Tablet EA290:
(From Abdi-Heba, mayor of Jerusalem, about the Hapiru)

"Sa]y [t]o the king, my lord: Message of [ʿAbdi]-Ḫeba, your servant. I fall at the feet [of the kin]g, my lord, 7 times and 7 times. **5–13** Here is the deed *against the land* that Milkilu and Šuardatu did: against the land of the king, my lord, they *ordered* troops from Gazru, troops from Gimtu, and troops from Qiltu. They seized Rubutu. The land of the king deserted to the **Ḫapiru**. **14–21** And now, besides this, a town belonging to Jerusalem, Bit-dNIN.URTA by name, a city of the king, has gone over to the side of the men of Qiltu. May the king give heed to ʿAbdi-Ḫeba, your servant, and send archers to restore the land of the king to the king. **22–30** If there are no archers, the land of the king will desert to the **Ḫapiru**. This deed *against the land* was [a]t the order of Milki[lu and a]t the order[4] of [Suard]atu, [*together w*]*ith* Gint[i]. So may the king provide for [his] land." (The Amarna letters, W. L. Moran, introduction, 1992 AD, EA 290)

Full text translation of Tablet EA323:
(From Yidya, the mayor of Ashkelon, lying to the pharaoh)

"To the king, my lord, my god, my Sun, the Sun from the sky: Message of Yidya, your servant, the dirt at your feet, the groom of your horses. **6–13** I indeed prostrate myself, on the back and on the stomach, at the feet of the king, my lord, 7 times and 7 times. I am indeed guarding the [pl]ace of the king, my lord, and the city of the king, in accordance with the command of the king, my lord, the Sun from the sky. **13–16** As to the king, my lord's, having ordered some glass, I [her]ewith send to the k[ing], my [l]ord, 30 (*pieces*) of glass. **17–23** Moreover, who is the dog that would not obey the orders of the king, my lord, the Sun fr[o]m the sky, the son of the Sun, [wh]om the Sun loves?" (The Amarna letters, W. L. Moran, introduction, 1992 AD, EA 323)

Full text translation of Tablet EA329:
(From Zimreddi, the ruler of Lachish, lying to the Pharaoh)

"To the king, my lord, my god, my Sun, the Sun from the sky: Message of Zimreddi, the ruler of Lakiša, your servant, the dirt at your feet. I prostrate myself at the feet of the king, my lord, the Sun from the sky, 7 times and 7 times. **13–20** As to the messenger of the king, my lord, whom he sent to me, I have listened to his orders very carefully, and I am indeed making preparations in accordance with his order." (The Amarna letters, W. L. Moran, introduction, 1992 AD, EA 329)

Made in the USA
Monee, IL
02 December 2019